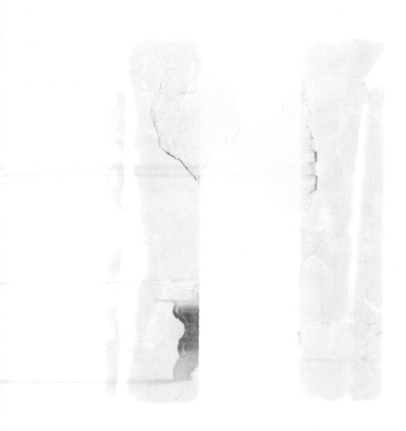

Melancholics in Love

Melancholics in Love

Representing Women's Depression and Domestic Abuse

Frances L. Restuccia

ROWMAN & LITTLEFIELD PUBLISHERS, INC.
Lanham • Boulder • New York • Oxford

This book is dedicated to Judith Feher Gurewich

ROWMAN & LITTLEFIELD PUBLISHERS, INC.

Published in the United States of America
by Rowman & Littlefield Publishers, Inc.
4720 Boston Way, Lanham, Maryland 20706
http://www.rowmanlittlefield.com

12 Hid's Copse Road
Cumnor Hill, Oxford OX2 9JJ, England

British Library Cataloguing in Publication Information Available

Library of Congress Cataloging-in-Publication Data

Restuccia, Frances L., 1951–
    Melancholics in love : representing women's depression and domestic abuse /
Frances L. Restuccia.
        p.   cm.
    Includes bibliographical references and index.
ISBN 0-8476-9828-9   (alk. paper)—ISBN 0-8476-9829-7 (pbk. : alk. paper)
    1. English fiction—Women authors—History and criticism.   2. Abused women
in literature.   3. American prose literature—Women authors—History and
criticism.   4. Man–woman relationships in literature.   5. Depression, Mental,
in literature.   6. Psychoanalysis and literature.   7. Melancholy in literature.
8. Violence in literature.   9. Women in literature.   10. Love in literature.
I. Title.
PR830.A27 R47   2000
823.009′352042—dc21   99-045718

Printed in the United States of America

♾ ™ The paper used in this publication meets the minimum requirements of
American National Standard for Information Sciences—Permanence of Paper for
Printed Library Materials, ANSI Z39.48-1992.

Ideas come to us as the successors of grief.

—Marcel Proust, *Remembrance of Things Past*

Contents

Acknowledgments

I must heartily thank first of all Jean Wyatt and John Limon for their painstaking, long-term attention to this project. Both are admirably scrupulous, intelligent, close readers on conceptual and technical levels. Jean has informed this project with her vast knowledge of, and insight into, the women's texts as well as the theory I invoke. John has brought to bear on my work his absolutely unrivaled logical powers as well as his tact and taste for subtlety. Second, I must thank a triumvirate of brilliant Lacanians—Judith Feher Gurewich, Kalpana Seshadri-Crooks, and Charlie Shepherdson—who, whether they knew it or not, provided me with the necessary stimulation to think and write, who produced for and with me a vibrant, intimate intellectual community that I had been seeking all my life and had nearly given up believing could ever materialize. For several years during the course of my writing *Melancholics in Love,* Judith's Lacan Workshop at Harvard University's Center for Literary and Cultural Studies (for which I am still grateful to Marjorie Garber, as I wrote on the acknowledgments page of my first book in 1989) has been an unbelievably rich source of ideas. Chapter 3, "Mortification: Beyond the Persuasion Principle," was inspired by a seminar in which Judith spoke of a case of a woman/daughter whose mother committed suicide and whose desire was clearly curtailed in relation to that tragedy; hearing the case enabled me to grasp meaning buried in a classic literary text.

I am grateful as well to Kelly Oliver and Ewa Ziarek for shrewd suggestions that resulted, for one thing, in the production of my afterword. I am extremely honored to have had them as my readers; I cannot think of preferable ones. And Rebecca Hoogs has been a dream editor: efficient, reasonable, friendly, smart. I never had a moment of discomfort dealing with her.

Other readers and supporters of the project whom I thank are Alan Richardson, who takes a distinctively different approach to Austen's *Persuasion* but is intellectually big enough never to let it interfere with appreciating and improving mine; Chris Wilson, whose nuanced, precise, and sensitive reading of Chapter 5 on Tina Turner and *Defending Our Lives* resulted in some vital changes; Rosemarie Bodenheimer, Andrew Von Hendy, and Judith Wilt, who gave a few of my chapters generous, helpful readings; and Anne

Fleche, who interacted with one of my chapters uncannily, since she made the same analysis I did prior to reading it, which confirmed my sense that I was intuitively correct, since intuitive correctness is one of Anne's many fine talents.

As for journals and editors who showed enthusiasm for my work along the way: I heartily thank Martin Gliserman, whose support of my ideas lasted through two publications (" 'A Black Morning': Kristevan Melancholia in Jane Austen's *Emma*," *American Imago*, vol. 51, no. 4 [Winter 1994], pp. 447–69; "Tales of Beauty: Aestheticizing Female Melancholia," *American Imago*, vol. 53, no. 4 [Winter 1996], pp. 353–83); James Barron at *Gender and Psychoanalysis*, whose interest in my reading of *Story of O* was gratifying ("Conjurings: Mourning and Abjection in *Story of O* and *Return to the Château*," *Gender and Psychoanalysis*, vol. 3, no. 2 [April 1998], pp. 123–53); and the editors at *Genders*, Thomas Foster and Carol Siegel, who raised the sophistication level of the article that became chapter 6 ("Literary Representations of Battered Women: Spectacular Domestic Punishment," *Genders*, vol. 23 [Spring 1996], pp. 42–71). Much thanks, too, to the American Association of University Women for offering me their Founders Fellowship, which enabled me to launch the project during a quiet sabbatical at Williams College.

Finally, I thank my daughter, Emma, for being born and offering me nothing but pure joy while simultaneously thrusting me into an entirely new state—one of vulnerability and sensitivity to women's and children's pain. Perhaps it all started, I realize just now, with the twelve hours of labor pains that led illogically to a C-section. Soon thereafter, I spent one and a half years, in Bennington, Vermont, counseling battered women, helping them to fill out affidavits at the Bennington Police Department, and driving them (often along with their children and late) on black, snowy nights to Safe Houses. I am still haunted by scenes of horrific violence actually seen and others told to me firsthand of, for example, children tossed through glass windows, a hundred terrified women. Although I am aware that my project is far removed from their lives, in writing it over the past eight years, I hoped that it would serve as at least a thread reaching from the academic world to their depressing domestic prisons.

Introduction

M ost broadly, *Melancholics in Love* attempts to join psychoanalytic theories of melancholia and mourning (mainly in the spirit of Julia Kristeva) with cultural studies and its attention to power relations in cultural practice (in the spirit of Michel Foucault). The first four and a half chapters present and illustrate my thesis, produced in reaction to Kristeva's *Black Sun: Depression and Melancholia,* that a melancholic woman, a woman abandoned by her mother, is predisposed to cathect an abusive erotic object, a partner who knows well how to seize on her inclination. A later emphasis in the book on a Foucauldian reading of domestic woman abuse complements that idea with the view that culture at large, and not just individual batterers, is working simultaneously to produce battered women, and is therefore also eager to take advantage of any vulnerability to such a position. *Melancholics in Love* gradually moves, then, from a psychoanalytic explanation of the formation of women melancholics, whose troubled relation to the maternal object renders appealing a certain *jouissance* of abusive men, to the cultural coconstruction of battered women.

Melancholia, I am hypothesizing, opens up a woman to abuse; culture facilitates that process and at the same time surely works from the opposite direction as well, producing battered women independently. An act of mourning—the quilting point of this study—needs to be performed in either case. Women artists, as I show throughout the book, enact mourning by aesthetically signifying the traumas, whatever their origins, of domestic woman abuse. The myriad representations of abandonment and woman abuse discussed in *Melancholics in Love* are meant to demonstrate Kristeva's idea that symbolic activity itself may activate mourning by transforming absence and loss into new signification. And while an actual lost or abusive mother is not apparently behind each case of domestic woman abuse treated in this study, the very idea that melancholia leads to woman abuse helps us to realize that to the extent that women have abusive partners (whether or not they have pre-encrypted a maternal object/Thing blocking their entry into the symbolic), they are barred from language or representation. Elaine Scarry's work in *The Body in Pain* undergirds this point in stressing the capacity of pain to wipe out language. The pain of battering therefore may be seen as an obstruction of the battered woman's passage beyond a nonverbal register or as powerful enough to thrust her back into asymbolia.

In other words, battered women are coerced into the conditions of melancholia and abjection insofar as they lose access to the symbolic and are rendered silent as well as boundless. What Kristeva regards as the first step in subject formation, the process of committing "matricide," is in a sense reversed as a woman's language as well as her autonomy is stolen from her, at the same time as her wounded and torn body literally produces an indistinction of interior and exterior. Subjectivity is undone. The woman is forced back into a relation with abjection, the Thing, even death. And so, while it is not always possible to know whether a particular battered woman was actually maternally abandoned (in one form or another), it is possible to see her nevertheless as located in a depressed or even abject state, and thus in dire need of the mourning afforded by representation.

In this conception, battering compels the unpredisposed battered woman to revert to a nondesiring state of inertness and, paradoxically, to a state of plenitude, of lack of lack, where her only hope is to hang onto an abstract maternal Thing now that the symbolic has been rendered inaccessible. Finding themselves in the same condition of depression and perhaps even abjection as the melancholic and abject woman, such battered women are in equal need of mourning through aesthetic representation to resubjectify themselves. Melancholic battered women are doubly damaged and silenced, doubly in need of representation.

My final chapter and a half, in which the literal mother, or loss thereof, is not featured but where severe domestic violence and torture come to the fore, serves as the culmination of this study insofar as the representations of domestic woman abuse that they put forward constitute a substantial part of a recent cultural outburst that grants signification to the pain and losses endured by battered women in general. After centuries of such abuse and close to total silence in response to it, the current emergence of novels, stories, autobiographies, documentaries, films, and various types of artistic displays focused on battered women plays a necessary cultural role not just in mourning the losses of a specific author or individual woman but in participating in a collective mourning by providing resignification for all.

For whatever reasons, women figured in all of the texts of this study, from Jane Austen's *Emma* to Alice Walker's *The Third Life of Grange Copeland*, wind up with partners who, to varying degrees, mistreat them; symbolic representations of such mistreatment allow a nonviolent, homeopathic engagement with domestic woman abuse for the sake of achieving release from a sadomasochistic or sadomelancholic social dynamic. Upon being transferred from their original contexts to artistic representation, the traumas (whether single or double) described in the following pages are loosened, unmoored from their origins, as they are set in motion in signifying chains, necessarily constituted by gaps that mediate desire for women whose access to it was barred.

Melancholics in Love commences with Julia Kristeva's hypothesis that matricide precedes subjectivity: one must "kill" the mother to become individuated. In *Black Sun*, Kristeva writes that "For man and for woman the loss of the mother is a biological and psychic necessity, the first step on the way to becoming autonomous" (Kristeva, 1989, 27). Daughters, however, are especially prone to forestall this murderous act by enclosing within themselves, by consuming "the lost object" or in Kristeva's lexicon "the mother-Thing," the "maternal Thing," which is then not entirely lost. Kristeva theorizes that "language starts with a *negation* (*Verneinung*) of loss. . . . 'I have lost an essential object that happens to be, in the final analysis, my mother,' is what the speaking being seems to be saying. . . . Depressed persons . . . *disavow the negation:* they cancel it out, suspend it, and nostalgically fall back on the real object (the Thing) of their loss, which is just what they do not manage to lose, to which they remain painfully riveted" (Kristeva, 1989, 44).

Chapter 1, " 'A Black Morning' in Jane Austen's *Emma*," reads Austen's novel as an exemplar of the Kristevan paradigm: the represented syndrome is Kristevan, as is, I try to show, the representational "therapy." Melancholia surfaces in *Emma*—where the death of the mother is presented on page one—on both the level of the story and the level of textual dynamics. By way of an analysis of D. A. Miller's psychoanalytic work on *Emma,* I make the argument that Miller denies: that Austen's 1816 novel grapples with an unspeakable loss by hanging on to it and yet refusing engulfment by it.

Austen's response to the problem of overattachment is expressed in what becomes a refrain throughout *Melancholics in Love:* "Where the wound had been given, there must the cure be found, if anywhere" (Austen, 1972, 97). By remaining at the site of the trauma of loss at the same time as it fends off implosion, the novel functions as the sort of therapy Kristeva locates in "aesthetic and particularly literary creation." Kristeva has discovered that literary representation "set[s] forth a device whose prosodic economy, interaction of characters, and implicit symbolism constitute a very faithful semiological representation of the subject's battle with symbolic collapse" and thus can aid the subject in coming closer to catharsis (Kristeva, 1989, 24). (She urges psychoanalysts to employ such "subliminatory solutions" as counterdepressants.) *Emma* refuses to relinquish the maternal object/Thing even as it refuses to accede to matriarchal cannibalism, and hence tells a tale of resilient mourning, a tale of beauty, "the depressive's other realm." Considering the power of beauty to enthrall us, Kristeva wonders whether "the beautiful object" might not "appear as the absolute and indestructible restorer of the deserting object" (Kristeva, 1989, 98–99). Aesthetically, the maternal object, or Thing, is transcended, though not abandoned; for in order to be transcended, it must be engaged, just as the analysand must relive traumatic events through transference for the sake of overcoming symptoms.

My specific argument about the workings of *Emma*'s plot is that because of Mr. Knightley's critical resemblance to Emma's mother—in whose death Emma lost the only person, until Knightley, capable of coping with her—marrying him turns out to be a guarantee of, rather than a threat to, Emma's melancholic state. Because Knightley is a disciplinarian from the outset, he can fill her dead mother's shoes. Upon incorporating the maternal object, the melancholic Emma puts herself to death (as an alternative to matricide), and Knightley facilitates the affective suicide. Kristeva recommends that a melancholic woman locate a partner who can lead her to cathect "her auto-eroticism in a jouissance of the other (separate, symbolic, phallic)" (Kristeva, 1989, 78). But instead of offering Emma a version of Kristeva's "other jouissance" as a bridge to the symbolic order, Knightley sucks her back into the masochistic/melancholic jouissance of surrogate maternal subjection.

Austen's classic novel of manners therefore serves as a curious recipe for woman abuse. Looked at from a certain feminist angle, one can observe in *Emma* expression of the caveat that a woman who loses her mother (through death, abandonment, other forms of neglect, or abuse) may be susceptible to overinvesting an abusive erotic object—a notion that extends in this study from Austen through Anita Brookner (*Look at Me*), Margaret Atwood (*Lady Oracle*), Margaret Drabble (*Jerusalem the Golden*), and "Pauline Réage" (*Story of O* and its sequel), all the way to Tina Turner (*I, Tina*). Austen implies that the allure of the power of a man is apt to be that of the power of a mother in disguise: attraction to the lost, subjugating mother becomes an attraction to the distant, punishing husband. Neither catharsis nor cure comes to Emma's rescue, which is in a sense why *Emma* must provide therapeutic sublimation. In compensating for the disciplinary husband replacing the lost mother as well as for the lost mother, *Emma* serves as a counterdepressant. The novel translates the double trauma into language and in this way gazes back at the patriarchal subjugation enacted and in turn represented in the text by Knightley, subjugation facilitated by passionate attachment to the lost maternal object.

Chapter 2, "Mortification: Beyond the Persuasion Principle," revisits Jane Austen, pushing further in the direction of crisis, for *Persuasion* (Austen's last novel) demonstrates the seductiveness of mortification, of a death-driven jouissance. Again we pursue melancholia in an Austen text, but here Kristeva is supplemented with concepts from André Green's "The Dead Mother" as well as Lacanian theory. Still, the mother, the maternal object, the maternal Thing remains central. And probably that is because, as Judith Feher Gurewich simply states: "Our unconscious finds its roots in the discourse of the first Other of our existence: the mother" (Gurewich, 1996, 9). Just as in *Emma*, the mOther in *Persuasion* has written the unconscious script, here in part because she is identified herself as depressed. As a result we need to look at Anne Elliot's love of loss as well as, rather than the object of her desire, *from where she "desires."* Since the origin of her "desire" turns out to lack the lack of desire (Lady Elliot is barely not indifferent to life), I alter the usual terms of Lacan's axiom that desire is the desire of the Other. Anne, too, becomes fascinated with a deadly Thing. The depressed daughter's jouissance is the jouissance of the mOther.

Though Lacan and Kristeva are by no means always compatible, and in fact Kristeva overlaps mainly with early rather than late Lacan, it is the case here that Lacan's concepts of desire, jouissance, and *objet a* may be used to translate Kristeva's notion that depressives "cannot endure Eros, [that] they prefer to be with the Thing up to the limit of negative narcissism leading them to Thanatos" (Kristeva, 1989, 20). This idea, of the melancholic's refusal of desire and embrace of jouissance, emerges through my reading of Anne Elliot's various restagings of the loss of her dead mother: first, by not allowing herself to be persuaded to marry; and second, by transferring the maternal object onto Captain Wentworth and thereby rendering him psychically attractive. Too closely identified in Anne's mind with Anne's mOther, now he becomes a dangerous objet a: the "reminder or remainder of the [lost] hypothetical mother-child unity, to which the subject clings in fantasy to achieve a sense of wholeness," to use Bruce Fink's definition in *The Lacanian Subject* (Fink, 1995, 83). In the end Anne can live thankfully in "the dread of a future War" as "all that could dim her Sunshine" (Austen, 1995, 177)—that is, she can continue to live under the deadly rays of a black sun. In displacing in this way the violence of her matricidal drive, Anne clinches the bond with Lady Elliot by suffering *as Lady Elliot did*. André Green's "dead mother complex" helps out here considerably—leading to the question of whether all mothers of melancholics are depressed. They certainly are in Marguerite Duras's *The Lover* and Marilynne Robinson's *Housekeeping* as well as in Atwood's *Lady Oracle* and Drabble's *Jerusalem the Golden* (the last two novels to be discussed), all of which together with *Persuasion* suggest a compelling paradigm.

Chapter 2 also turns to writing, here in direct response to the Lacanian proposition that fantasies that entail a craving for a dangerous jouissance may be traversed. The proposal I elaborate depends on my idea that narratives that appear as mirror images to readers in mourning and suffering from melancholia (as well as possibly to writers in such states) may actually serve as altering encounters with an Other's desire. For language necessarily submits to splitting and barring. Here then is the crux: writing transferentially preserves at the same time as it masters, thus attenuating, if not eradicating, melancholia and setting mourning in motion. A dominant notion of *Melancholics in Love* is that writing has the potential to assist in mourning because it simultaneously preserves the lost object and demonstrates desirousness. This conception of writing converges with Freud's late meditations on mourning in *The Ego and the Id,* where he posits that instead of surpassing or disposing of loss, the ego reconfigures itself in relation to its losses. Freud writes paradoxically that through melancholic introjection—by which he means the "setting up of the object inside the ego"—"the ego makes it easier for the object to be given up or renders that process possible. . . ." Hence the ego is "a precipitate of abandoned object-cathexes," containing their history (Freud, 1923, 24). New landscapes of ego are fertilized by the corpses of old object-cathexes.

Chapter 3, "Tales of Beauty: Brookner's, Atwood's, and Drabble's 'Feminine Symbolic,' " begins by challenging Juliana Schiesari's contention in *The Gendering of Melancholia* that the discourse of melancholia "encodes male eros and male subjectivity" (Schiesari, 1992, 81). I supplement my analysis of melancholia in Austen with an examination of three contemporary women writers who also achieve the symbolic status that Schiesari attributes to male melancholic artists. In *New Maladies of the Soul,* Kristeva notes that the unnamable and deadly object unseparated from depressed subjects is "embedded in the 'form' as well as the 'content' of depressive discourse" (Kristeva, 1995, 41)—which is what in effect I am taking the contemporary novels of this chapter paradoxically to be.

Yet, even as they mark progress by aestheticizing, and thereby politicizing, a recognizably pathological melancholia, expressing women's losses through literary technique, Brookner, Atwood, and Drabble underscore the liability of Kristeva's theory that I touch on in chapters 1 and 2: Austen's caveat. They too diagnose a propensity on the part of a melancholic woman to favor a domineering man, whom she psychically identifies with her lost and at least in this way neglectful, if not abusive, mother. If the cure for melancholia requires a kind of transferential duplication of the lost, neglectful, or abusive mother—which is, let me point out, just what such a propensity for a domineering man itself suggests—the means of therapeutic duplication needs to be unprone to cruelty.

Brookner, Atwood, and Drabble in a sense surpass Kristeva not only by taking into account the propensity of the male Other (with whom the Kristevan melancholic unites ideally to enter the symbolic order) to act in accord with his acculturation, that is, to dominate or, worse, abuse, but also by inquiring into the cultural sources of melancholia. Why is the mother herself depressed and/or angry, neglectful, abusive? In *Lady Oracle* and *Jerusalem the Golden*, socioeconomic factors do not cancel but rather reinforce psychoanalytic explanations of the daughter's melancholic addiction to the mother. Causation is ultimately overdetermined: neither the cultural construction of the family or of maternity nor a psychoanalytic etiology is isolated, or ought to be, as the sole cause of melancholic womanly woe. Atwood and Drabble especially inject the social into the psychic and thereby signal a primary concern of *Melancholics in Love* as a whole: to balance psychoanalytic interpretation with cultural critique.

The contemporary women writers taken up in chapter 3, again like Austen, represent melancholia homeopathically, by holding on to the maternal Thing in writing, while at the same time, by virtue of the fact that writing is their medium, providing a passageway into the symbolic order. Enhancing the social dimension of their analysis, Atwood and Drabble in particular also consider that when social constraints contribute to the production of psychic pain, they may exacerbate it by barring its aesthetic expression, making mourning even more remote for working-class girls and mothers who, like Deleuzean postmodernists, *Jerusalem the Golden* implies, cannot get by without it.

With chapter 4, "Conjurings: Mourning and Abjection in *Story of O* and *Return to the Château*," *Melancholics in Love* takes a plunge from melancholia to masochism in the form of a severe case of abjection. This fourth chapter treats what has myopically been considered to be merely pornographic discourse—discourse that produces a woman through the intricate exercise of power—as a literary paradigm of female masochism, a *Venus in Furs* for women. I take my cue that *Story of O* and its sequel may serve as testaments to the therapeutic value of masochistic writing in part from the collection *Coming to Power: Writings and Graphics on Lesbian S/M*, where it is demonstrated that consensual S/M fulfills various psychic needs, if not provides a form of psychoanalytic transference.

In addition to asking how phallic meaning defines O (Kaja Silverman's thesis), we need to ask what psychic forces propel O's masochism, in order to comprehend how O *becomes* a product of pornographic discourse. Following the lead of Jessica Benjamin, who in *The Bonds of Love* urges her reader to comprehend submission as the "*desire* of the dominated" (Benjamin, 1988, 52), I pose the question of what motivates O's craving for recognition through the power of the Other to the point that she is driven to submit to the repeated torture of her body. *Powers of Horror* logically follows. For Kristeva ties abjection to masochism, in part since abjection is signaled by a crossing of borders normally left intact for the sake of stabilizing the subject, enabling a free passing of pleasure and pain over the boundary between interior and exterior. Extending an implication of the earlier chapters on melancholia, my analysis of O leads to the view that the masochism of abjection originates in incest, where the most fundamental border of all is transgressed, especially in the incestuous longing of the daughter for the mother, a daughter who may have "swallowed up maternal hatred." My thesis is that O and its sequel are textual embodiments of a masochistic consumption of a mOther—a possession previous to the advent of subjectivity. At the same time, these novels too confront the maternal entity and through this confrontation begin the process of mourning.

But while Kristeva's depressed woman achieves a certain unhealthy balance in reattaching to her lost, neglectful, or abusive mother by submitting to discipline or even abuse from a male partner, O exemplifies Kristeva's "deject," the woman whose abjection pulls on her so forcefully that she literally opens her bodily borders. Needing maternal inhabitation to avoid the alternative of rejection and loss, as well as to alleviate the guilt of the original abandonment, the dejected daughter acquiesces to cruel men who liquefy her self so that she may melt together with the "bad object" instead of retaliating against it. O "uses" sadistic men to assist her in punishing herself so as not to lose the maternal object/abject, whose love she seeks, and all aggression toward whom she hopes to cover over. The experience of other jouissance with an abusive male, at least at the level of the abused woman's unconscious, nonthreateningly sustains the bond to the abject.

Story of O and its sequel collapse the crumbling wall between the dejected daughter and the abjected mother (a role played in these novels by the wicked Anne-Marie), give the abject free reign and then sublimate the collapse. The originally intimidating maternal abject is embraced; the absent maternal figure is made amorphously present, re-presented. But finally the newfound "object" is not the mother, or her representatives; it is symbolic activity itself.

The opening section of chapter 5, "Redirecting Spectacles of Woman Abuse in *I, Tina* and *Defending Our Lives*," also draws from *Black Sun* to probe what conditioned, if not produced, Tina Turner's vulnerability to Ike Turner's abuse as it is represented in her autobiography. *I, Tina* fits the pattern we have been tracing of the maternally abandoned daughter/woman cathecting an abusive erotic object. Ike's violence enables Tina to continue the self-punishment necessary to cover her hatred for her encrypted mother—displacing it onto herself—and thus to sustain the punishing maternal relation. It is because one of the psychic benefits of the production of "Tina Turner" is the preservation, through Ike, of Anna Mae's bonds of love with Zelma that Ike is able to induce in Tina battered women's syndrome.

Picking up on the cultural issues broached in chapter 3, I psychoanalyze in chapter 5 within a Foucauldian framework of social power to call attention to the terrible mutuality of a psychology within a social system that institutionalizes domestic woman abuse, that is dedicated in many ways to the production of "the battered woman." While the psychology feeds into the social system, the social system exploits the psychology. In chapter 5, I show how Ike played an invisible role in a Foucauldian disciplinary structure as well as how he reigned quite visibly in the manner of Foucault's prenineteenth century sovereign—as the King of the Kings of Rhythm. In his obsessive psychological manipulation of Tina, Ike was keenly aware of the power of the mind; he simultaneously used physical violence to ground and substantiate his retrograde notions.

And yet such a reversal of Foucault's historical arrow (Foucault of course fails to take into account gender dynamics in the domestic sphere), so that husbands and lovers unsatisfied with discipline can always revert to punishment, is both a particular horror and a feminist blessing in disguise. Given the unmoored quality of spectacle that, as Foucault illustrates in *Discipline and Punish,* gave rise to a two-sided discourse that enabled the crowd to wrest for the criminal glory that the sovereign intended to wrest for himself, this analogy between Foucault's premodern, spectacular punishment and domestic violence is meant to bring out the strategy of resistance through counterspectacle and counterrepresentation in the various artifacts considered in *Melancholics in Love.* And since the purpose of such a strategy is to signify women's pain, such appropriation simultaneously constitutes a long overdue process of mourning through resignification.

I expand this idea, of resistance through counterspectacle and counterspectacle as an art of mourning, based on a homology between spectacular domestic violence and the specular forms that artwork meant to combat such violence tends to assume, through a reading of the 1994 documentary *Defending Our Lives.* It is as if the specular/spectacular aspect of such art were necessary to tap into domestic woman abuse for the sake of transmutation, to recover the pain generated by such violence. Again using strategic homeopathy in aesthetic acts of mourning, artists of domestic woman abuse sabotage male spectacularizing of the woman's exposed body and the resulting power, as well as pleasure in that power. Whether the source of woe is originally a maternal inadequacy of some sort or, at least as it appears on the surface in *Defending Our Lives,* "merely" a violent male partner, mourning entails symbolic activity that returns to and incorporates the wound, if not the wounder. The homeopathic aspect of the aesthetic strategy effects a transference, from the source of disturbance to discourse. It is because *Defending Our Lives* is isomorphic with the batterer's, as well as the system's, violence that the film can serve, in the spirit of bell hooks, as a "talking back" that in turn serves as a talking cure, a talking cure that operates as a talking as well as a gazing back.

Especially given that the power of battering is spectacular, such power is susceptible to a mournful takeover. For it is instability, as Judith Butler has pointed out so hopefully, that enables resignification: bodies are not always compliant with the norms that attempt to govern their materialization. Spectacular gazing back at the world in reflection of the insidious ways in which the social, especially the legal, system colludes with individual batterers might, as I've suggested, be seen as the commencement of a process of widespread public mourning, which will eventually complete itself by opening up the realm of signs to the sites of women's pain as well as the sites of women's pain to the realm of signs.

My sixth and final chapter, "Literary Representations of Battered Women: Spectacular Domestic Punishment," analyzes mainly contemporary novels by women to demonstrate this double embrace. Whereas approximately the first four and a half chapters of the book delve into melancholic and masochistic (psychic) "uses" of male violence, here I explore the cultural production of victims. I expand the cultural component of the psychoanalytic/cultural coproduction mentioned earlier, only this time with the spotlight on representations of severely battered women. Although a psychoanalytic etiology of melancholia and abjection may not be visible or even operative in the texts of this last chapter, here the conditions of these pathologies are certainly achieved, so that the mourning of loss, the move from asymbolia to the symbolic, is as critical as ever.

In my final chapter, I therefore find it theoretically and politically vital to take issue with Nancy Armstrong and Leonard Tennenhouse's view that the violence of representation is on par with "empirical violence" (violence on the street), and that feminist discourse is necessarily colonizing. I extend in chapter 6 my argument, reinforcement of which can be found in Foucault himself, that there are narrative strategies by which certain artists—positioned in ways that enable them to counter the dominant ideology—evade, often to attack and undermine, the dominant power systems that may at the same time furnish them with their basic weapons. Hurston's "Sweat," Drabble's *The Needle's Eye,* Cisneros's "Woman Hollering Creek," Naylor's *Linden Hills,* and Walker's *The Third Life of Grange Copeland* expose both subtle, modern disciplinary power—in the form of noncorporeal systemic battering—as well as the grosser, premodern spectacular power—in the form of literal encryptment and physical torture of the female body—to which the former mode of violent domestic power inevitably relapses. But it is not merely a matter of the coexistence of the two Foucauldian forms of power. While there may no longer be a supreme sovereign publicly marking bodies and thereby sanctioning corporeal punishment, faceless systemic "battering" encourages and protects physical brutality on the part of "sovereigns" whose castles are their embattled homes.

Modern or disciplinary power camouflages premodern or spectacular power, but premodern power heavily tips the power balance against women. Especially because two forms of power still operate at the domestic level, all discourse in this arena is not the same, as Armstrong and Tennenhouse would argue. Discourse backed by the power to mark bodies is not the same as discourse on behalf of those bodies. The expression of woman's nondiscursiveness (for example, intermittent madness and maternal love in Drabble, triumphant dehumanized howling in Cisneros, extravagant masochistic acts in Naylor) does not join forces with conventional modern power so long as the energy of the nondiscursiveness itself is harnessed in the production of a subliminary solution—a talking cure—as well as a counterhegemony—a talking/gazing back. Those scraps of the Real that can be regarded as traumatic, for both political and psychoanalytic reasons, need symbolization, the symbolic being exactly the register in which women's desire may emerge. I end with the political *and* therapeutic value of aesthetics because, as Homi Bhabha in *The Location of Culture* passionately contends, "Forms of popular rebellion and mobilizations are often most subversive and transgressive when they are created through oppositional cultural practices" (Bhabha, 1994, 20) and because mourning remains incomplete until losses discover their signifiers.

1

~~~~~

"A Black Morning" in Jane Austen's *Emma*

What two letters—express perfection? . . . M and A. Emma. Do you understand?

—*Emma*, Jane Austen

I.

In *Narrative and Its Discontents*, D. A. Miller perceives a clash in Austen's *Emma* (1816) between the narratable—"various incitements to narrative, as well as the dynamic ensuing from such incitements"—and the nonnarratable—the "state of quiescence assumed by a novel before the beginning and supposedly recovered by it at the end" (Miller, 1981, ix). Miller's Austen unleashes drifting signs and wandering desire on which her official values in the end clamp down, so that it might be said (and here I extrapolate) that her writing is in sadomasochistic conflict with itself. To Miller, Austen's writing arises out of "disequilibrium, suspense, and general insufficiency" only to be whipped into a "state of absolute propriety"—that is, only to be suppressed, beaten into social shape (Miller, 1981, ix–x). At times it seems that the abuse—of the novel's production by the ideology of representation (requiring closure), or of the polyvalent by the univocal—is a purely technical matter, as if narrative exigencies alone were at war. Yet Miller gestures too in the direction of the author: Austen suffered from "ideological ambivalence toward narrative itself" (Miller, 1981, 50). He contends that Austen finally repudiates the sinful frivolity of narrating—for the sake of being exculpated of an act she enjoyed, as she had "fascinated delight [in] unsettled states of deferral and ambiguity" (Miller 1981, 66).

Austen's fascination with deferral, to Miller, is manifested in *Emma* through her heroine's indecisiveness in finding a satisfying erotic object/husband. "Until her reformation, Emma is unable to 'fix' her 'affections' on 'the proper object,' much as, *mutatis mutandis,* a Freudian narcissist cannot 'cathect' his 'libido' onto an external 'object choice' " (Miller, 1981, 13). Emma's narcissism generates what Miller calls a "structure of narratability" (Miller, 1981, 14): the "enterprise of relocating a blocked narcissism in the outside world . . . threatens to produce an interminable narrative"; "[i]f uncorrected, the narrative of Emma's desire would turn the text into what might be called a radical picaresque: an endless flirtation with a potentially infinite parade of possibilities" (Miller, 1981, 15). Thus Emma, the narrative she engenders, and that naughty part of Austen that secretly takes illicit pleasure in sinful narrative frivolity—all do battle with, but finally submit to being crushed by, a proper moral ending that contains the transgressing. All must be "cured." Emma cathects her libido onto Mr. Knightley, just as the narratable is "cathected onto the final configuration of event and meaning" (Miller, 1981, 19). Austen's "rigorous ideal of a wholly and properly intelligent world" (Miller, 1981, 53) is preserved, although of course the closural system to which Austen resorts fails to accommodate fully the signifiers set in motion by the text. The narratable is subsumed, or at least that is the illusion: "Closure can *never* include . . . the narratable in its essential dimension: all suspense and indecision" (Miller, 1981, 98). Still, Miller's idea of the narrative dynamic in *Emma* accords with what Eve Sedgwick, in "Jane Austen and the Masturbating Girl," describes as "the punishing, girl-centered moral pedagogy and erotics of Austen's novels" in general. Endorsing the psychologically sensational terms with which I may have seemed to begin, Sedgwick characterizes Austen criticism in terms of its "unresting exaction of the spectacle of a Girl Being Taught a Lesson" and "the vengefulness it vents on the heroines whom it purports to love, and whom, perhaps, it does" (Sedgwick, 1991, 17:833).

Miller defines the nonnarratable as elements of a text, such as Emma's marriage, that are simply incapable of spawning a narrative, but instead correct an insufficiency or fill a void. This would not include mere omissions, such as the Napoleonic Wars, characters' sex lives, or labor issues. Nor, writes Miller, is the nonnarratable synonymous with "the unspeakable" (Miller, 1981, 5): it is not (again, as Miller states it) that the text fails ultimately to plumb certain depths.

However, *Emma* seems to me to be grappling throughout with an unspeakable loss—simultaneously resisting engulfment by it and trying to hang onto it—to which some of Miller's own remarks attest. It is striking that Miller should invoke the "unspeakable" at all; one would not be tempted to confuse the "nonnarratable," as Miller defines it, with whatever the "unspeakable" might mean, since the nonnarratable cannot generate an action precisely because it is so easy (in ordinary, boring, conventional life) to speak it. In imitation of Miller's assessment that Austen's hatred of "perversely aimless narrative" cloaks an affinity for it (Miller, 1981, 64), his sense of her "strategy of negation," one might therefore be apt to infer from Miller's emphasis that the nonnarratable in Austen is not an effort to speak the unspeakable, that that is just what it is. (It is appropriate to the unspeakable that this would be how Miller chooses to speak it.) Perhaps he even unveils the identity of the unspeakable in *Emma* in using the following patient-analyst exchange, from *Beyond the Pleasure Principle,* to substantiate his point that, although she denies it, Austen is aware of the mutual dependency of the narratable and her ideology of closure: " 'It was *not* my mother,' says the patient, from which the analyst infers, 'So it *was* his mother' " (Miller, 1981, 65). A second analogy may clinch the point: Miller compares the child's game of *fort/da,* which "takes place in the context of an original loss of [the] mother," to Austen's "symbolic staging of the disappearance and retrieval of 'the reality of reason and truth' " that occurs "within a certain anxiety about whether the full meanings of her ideology can ever be established once for all" (Miller, 1981, 65–66). It begins to sound as if the nonnarratable is the unspeakable (mother) after all.

Invoking the mother again through the analysand, Miller shifts her status to the unmentionable negatively inscribed: "Negation allows the patient at least to thematize his mother in the analytical discourse. Similarly, Jane Austen's moral negation permits her to bring into language what otherwise, according to a strict construction of her ideology, could never properly be mentioned" (Miller, 1981, 66). Whether or not the mother's positions within these analogues can be reconciled (she stands for Austen's repressed awareness of the mutual dependency of the narratable and her ideology of closure; for "the reality of reason and truth"; and for the illicit that negation allows her to insert into language), Miller's parallels between Austen and psychoanalysis persistently suggest that Austen's preoccupation, as well as his conception of Austen's preoccupation, is buried and is maternal. Do we not have more than analogies here? After characterizing Miss Bates's language as "An ill-sorted clutter of names and half-sentences" (Miller, 1981, 37) that never rise to a point (a semiotic discourse?), Miller reminds us that Roland Barthes calls the "undetermined language of chatter" " 'an unweaned language' . . . whose motions are those of 'an objectless sucking' and 'an undifferentiated orality' " (Miller, 1981, 39). Miller further identifies Miss Bates's language with the maternal in proposing that Austen can acknowledge kinship with Miss Bates "only when the traces of family resemblance have been practically effaced. The daughter's language needn't fear the mother tongue" (Miller, 1981, 40).

Later in Miller's work, the mother tongue expands to include not only Miss Bates's chatter but Austen's entire corpus, or just about. In a *Raritan* essay, "The Late Jane Austen," Miller shamelessly describes himself (in bed with a cold or flu) being nursed on Jane Austen novels (just as "Miss Taylor nursed little Emma") "as effectively as [his] own mother—who first invited [him] to read them and who of course was no longer appropriate to expect in attendance on [his] sickbed—might have done" (Miller, 1990, 10:55). Miller associates a guarantee of health with Austen. Her novels (except *Sanditon*) offer maternal assurances—Miller's "Janeism" boils down to "the notion that while you may sometimes fall sick, you can always get better"—for which, he explains, he is now in mourning. Not for an "historical period (the so-called quiet England about to disappear in the noisy business of the Industrial Revolution) or a cultural ideal (a community whose leisure bore fruit in an ethics of civility and an esthetics of elegance)," but for "an even more patently utopian fantasy about the body in a morbid state" (Miller, 1990, 10:55–56). Miller's mourning curiously seems a reflection of the incomplete mourning (which he overlooks) that *Emma* embodies.

Contradicting the exuberance that Miller attributes to the novel's heroine (a sign of the mania that alternates, Kristeva states, "more often than not" with melancholia [Kristeva, 1989, 9]), Emma is at the end of the book, although poised to marry her knight, silenced, deflated, effaced in a sense *because* (I will argue) of "the perfect happiness of the union" (Austen, 1972, 335). Emma's marriage to Knightley is acceptable insofar as it *fails* to offer a cure. Whereas Miller sees a text full of wandering (narratable) desire that battles it out with, but ultimately submits to, official (nonnarratable) values that cleanse that desire, the novel's wandering "desire" seems to me symptomatic of a melancholic/masochistic attachment to the mother whom Miller himself, in his analysis of *Emma*, invokes periodically as its unspeakable or nearly unspeakable theme. Austen's *Emma* can be read, on the model of Kristeva's *Black Sun*, as a melancholic/masochistic text, whose addiction to the "maternal Thing" operates at the level of the plot and gets worked through at the level of the text itself.

II.

In a way it is remarkable that *Emma* exists at all, since the novel seems so predicated on loss and so potentially implosive. Austen's novel struggles to hoist itself up out of despondency over a series of losses, almost every one involving a mother. Needless to say these are barely speakable losses—references to which fill the interstices of a seemingly lighthearted, carefree world, as the first line indicates. Emma Woodhouse is famously presented as living "twenty-one years in the world with very little to distress or vex her" (Austen, 1972, 1). Yet her mother has died (we are invited to calculate that it was when she was five); and her substitute mother governess, and friend, of sixteen years, Miss Taylor, has just been married. "It was Miss Taylor's loss which first brought grief"; on page one Emma sits in "mournful thought"; she meditates on "what she had lost" (Austen, 1972, 1). The novel registers its laborious effort in getting started by continuing to refer to Mrs. Weston as Miss Taylor, as if doing its utmost to keep Emma's substitute mother available to her, as if not wishing to progress but longing to lapse back. But by page 1, "Miss Taylor" is merely a linguistic chimera, itself substituting for the real thing. The novel commences with a double maternal loss—the latter so traumatic, effecting "a melancholy change" (Austen, 1972, 3), because founded on the former. Kristeva writes that she can "discover antecedents to [her] current breakdown in a loss, death, or grief over someone or something that [she] once loved" (Kristeva, 1989, 5); the erasure of that essential being is lived as a wound that new separation or losses cause to fester. *Emma* begins by offering a glimpse of the abyss—sustained throughout the novel by the accumulation of lost, dead, and dying mothers, in excess even of the typical high number of maternal deaths in nineteenth-century fiction—for which it attempts to provide compensation.

Their bodies pile up as the novel unfolds. Frank Churchill's mother, the first Mrs. Weston, dies when he is only two of an illness that eventually ceased to linger. Miss Hawkins is an orphan, raised by an uncle. Jane Fairfax is also an orphan, her mother having died (when Jane was three) of consumption and grief over her husband's dying in action, their dazzling marriage now a "melancholy remembrance" (Austen, 1972, 108). Harriet's illegitimate parentage is unveiled: she proves to be "the daughter of a tradesman" (Austen, 1972, 333), as though no mother's body ever bore her. And, toward the end of the novel, as if to allow for a general expression of resentment and revenge over maternal death, Mrs. Churchill—clearly an evil, manipulating hypochondriacal (substitute) mother—dies a death that mainly inspires relief and quiet rejoicing. (Kristeva writes that her "grief is but the deferment of the hatred or desire for ascendency that [she] nurture[s] with respect to the one who betrayed or abandoned [her]" [Kristeva 1989, 5].) Even the narrator interjects a surprising snide reference against Mrs. Churchill: "Goldsmith tells us, that when lovely woman stoops to folly, she has nothing to do but to die; and when she stoops to be disagreeable, it is equally to be recommended as a clearer of ill-fame" (Austen, 1972, 266). Still, before Jane and Frank can marry, there "must be three months, at least, of deep mourning" (Austen, 1972, 317). Despite its apparently ebullient beginning and the hale body of its primary figure, *Emma* is bloated with mourning and the incomplete mourning known as melancholia. Kristeva's black sun shines from the day of Miss Taylor's wedding, which brings "a black morning's work" for Emma (Austen, 1972, 2).

Emma's "work" is of course the active-passive job of matchmaking, which enables her vicariously to pursue an "Other" who, ideally, can liquefy the mother inhabiting her or in other words vicariously to experience Kristeva's "other jouissance." Thus access to symbolic life is gained: according to Kristeva, as we know, this "other" or "vaginal jouissance" depends on "a relation to the Other" that ensures the "*outward* displacement" of the incorporated mother. The "language of the female body," through other jouissance, wins a victory over depression, to which anyone "abandoned, neglected, or misunderstood by the mother" is especially prone (Kristeva, 1989, 79). But Emma's matchmaking also conveniently exempts her from participating in desiring bonds that would threaten her primary allegiance: "Depressive persons cannot endure Eros" (Kristeva, 1989, 20). Kristeva emphasizes the effort required for a woman to be attracted erotically to the opposite sex: the process of "shifting to the symbolic order *at the same time* as to a sexual object of a sex other than that of the primary maternal object represents a gigantic elaboration in which a woman cathexes a psychic potential greater than what is demanded of the male sex" (Kristeva, 1989, 30). In her role as matchmaker, Emma (an "imaginist") puts her imagination in the service of recruiting Others for others in love, and in each case her scheme fails to materialize, so that she is doubly removed from, even as she toys with, actual lovematches. She keeps up a metonymy of virtual desire to fend off the indefatigably metaphorical maternal Thing threatening to engulf her, erecting (like Kristeva's manic person who sheathes depression) "variegated arrays of substitutive erotic objects" (Kristeva, 1989, 50). Yet that "desire" is distant enough to pose no ultimate threat to the mother whose loss she refuses to negate. Emma tells her father of her compulsion to make matches, promising not to make one for herself. In D. A. Miller's words, she is "an equivocal mediatrix. With so little sense of her own desires, she points Harriet's in unproductive, potentially disastrous directions, almost as though by unwittingly frustrating Harriet's love life she meant to mirror the intrinsically blocked nature of her own" (Miller, 1981, 9–10).

Emma fails to release herself from the mother's clutches through either of the two dominant methods Kristeva prescribes, being unable to gain liberation from her loss by means of an Other or by means of art. Addressing the topic of the "Death-Bearing Woman," Kristeva claims that "Matricide is our vital necessity, the sine-qua-non condition of our individuation, provided that it takes place under optimal circumstances and can be eroticized—whether the lost object is . . . transposed by means of an unbelievable symbolic effort . . . which eroticizes the *other* . . . or transforms cultural constructs into a 'sublime' erotic object (one thinks of the cathexes, by men and women, in social bonds, intellectual and aesthetic productions, etc.)" (Kristeva, 1989, 27–28). Not only is Emma's matchmaking displaced desire, but it also fails at displacing desire, just as in the role of artist she fails to complete her portraits. Steadiness in her reading, playing music, and singing is also deficient. Testifying to Kristeva's sense of the challenge for women of psychically detaching from the primary maternal object in an effort to attach to a heterosexual partner, Emma seems more than content in her state of ostensible incompletion. She confides in Harriet that were she to marry she would probably regret it, developing a self-protective theory that "old maids" are contemptible chiefly for economic reasons.

The novel itself inherits its morphology from the masochism of Emma's matchmaking, as it is built on the painful pattern of her errors of imagination. The book divides into three phases, all dedicated to Emma's foolish plans that inevitably founder. She pumps up Harriet's expectations about Mr. Elton, missing his about herself, and (after everything is disentangled) experiences pain, humiliation, and self-blame. She resolves subsequently to suppress her imagination; yet again it inflates, beginning volume 2, this time over Jane and Mr. Dixon. She misses Jane's romance with Frank and believes erroneously that Frank loves her and that she loves him in return. By volume three, however, she imagines Harriet marrying Frank, oblivious to Harriet's blossoming love for Mr. Knightley. Emma (on the level of the plot) invites a real pounding, which culminates after Box Hill in her breakdown into tears, self-reproach, and depression: "She had never been so depressed" (Austen, 1972, 258). The narrative is equally self-thwarting: after each of Emma's matchmaking fiascos, as well as after her misbehavior on Box Hill, *Emma* deflates, needing a new narrative push—away from mortification and shame that could easily serve as channels back to the silence of the all-absorbing mother surrounding the text. Barely resisting symbolic abdication—through especially delayed narrative movement—*Emma* simultaneously preserves death, in particular maternal loss, through flirtation with its own collapse.

Even more threatening to narrative progress than its carefully calibrated delays is the novel's wanderlust. D. A. Miller stresses the resistance of the narratable to containment at the end of *Emma* on theoretical grounds: the narratable necessarily bursts beyond closural attempts to bind it, since it "inherently lacks finality," whether "in its erotic or semiotic dimension" (Miller, 1981, xi). But I would underscore in Miller's analysis of narrative exorbitancy the interminable quality of "desires" and discourses in *Emma* in particular, especially Harriet's and Emma's "desires" and Miss Bates's and Mrs. Elton's discourses. At certain ostensibly interminable moments in the text, narrative collapse ironically seems imminent: students at these points—where there is, as Miss Bates herself sputters, "Nothing to signify" (Austen, 1972, 218)—are often at risk of a boredom that jeopardizes their ability to continue. The novel meanders to the extent of producing the lurking danger of Peter Brooks's narrative short-circuiting. Emma is determinedly reluctant to marry, a significant threat to the marriage plot's necessity of putting in place an ultimate object of desire toward whom the narrative is driven, and through whom it can consummate itself. The novel can simultaneously seem endlessly self-perpetuating (evading an end) and therefore, paradoxically, on the verge of premature breakdown.

But while the narrative—insofar as it repeatedly hesitates to make progress—is the formal correlative of Emma's urge for proximity to the mother, it simultaneously serves—insofar as it manages to fend off caving in—as the sort of therapy Kristeva locates in art and especially literature. Considering the power of beauty, "the depressive's other realm" (Kristeva, 1989, 25), to enthrall us, Kristeva wonders whether the beautiful object might not have the capacity to restore the abandoning object as part of its effort to contain it.

It goes without saying that *Emma* is an aesthetic creation that puts the highest premium on elegance, as do its central characters: "Jane Fairfax was very elegant, remarkably elegant; and [Emma] had herself the highest value for elegance" (Austen, 1972, 111). The renowned elegance of *Emma* (R.W. Chapman articulates the consensus in praising "the matchless symmetry of its design" [Austen, 1972, vii]), like "feminine finery concealing stubborn depressions, . . . emerges as the admirable face of loss, transforming it in order to make it live" (Kristeva, 1989, 99). As a signifying system, a particularly satisfying one aesthetically, *Emma* inscribes the loss it is founded on, preventing total immersion as well as total emergence, which as Freud suggests may enhance the process of mourning. Austen's playing out of a marriage phobia (Mr. Woodhouse's obsession) doubly serves the interest of the melancholy subject seeking to remain true to, without being swallowed up by, the lost object as it constitutes the novel's elegant, dilatory symmetrical structure.

The cultivation of novelistic elegance relies too on a more concealed phobia. *Emma* seems obsessed (not only through Mr. Woodhouse) with the stamping out of "contamination," which would spoil the design of the text as well as disturb the maintenance of intimacy with the melancholy object. Although one hardly thinks of any section of Austen's " 'little bit (two Inches wide) of Ivory' " as befouled by crime, the distance between Randalls and Hartfield is described as if such a threat exists. It is said to be an "easy" distance, "so convenient for even solitary female walking" (Austen, 1972, 10), ironically as if (since solitude would seem to have little relevance to convenience) a female strolling alone might be at risk. Females accompanied in carriages are, at any rate, in jeopardy. Although toward the end of the Christmas party at Randalls alarm is raised over an innocuous snowfall, in retrospect the weather worries seem like displaced anxiety over the "violent love" that Mr. Elton makes to Emma in their carriage (Austen, 1972, 88). She feels compelled to "restrain him" (Austen, 1972, 88); he accuses her of "encouragement" (Austen, 1972, 90). Modern discourse of date rape infects the scene, contributing to the novel's expression of fear of insemination. Sustaining such a fear, Mrs. Elton comments to Mr. Weston that she had adopted her sister Selina's "nicety" of bringing her own sheets to sleep on when she stays at inns, "an excellent precaution" (Austen, 1972, 209).

Nancy Armstrong, in *Desire and Domestic Fiction*, misses at least some of the novel's phobias, as well as the threats they are based on, in asserting that, unlike *Pamela*, Austen's novels "bring to culmination a tradition of ladies fiction that concentrated on the finer points of conduct necessary to secure a good marriage . . . rather than on the will and cunning it took to preserve one's chastity from impending rape" (Armstrong, 1987, 134). Most dramatically, the well-known gypsy scene focuses this fear. Miss Smith and Miss Bickerton take the "apparently public enough for safety" Richmond road (Austen, 1972, 226). A child approaching to beg provokes "a great scream" from Miss Bickerton who, "excessively frightened," flees. Harriet is in turn "assailed by half a dozen children, headed by a stout woman and a great boy," offers them a shilling, and is surrounded by "the whole gang, demanding more" (Austen, 1972, 226–27). Harriet is terrified, which may also seem excessive unless one realizes that at some level she, and the text, are worried about the "great boy" turning *her* into "a stout woman." This event—which captures the text's anxiety over children and everything pertaining to their production (sex, pregnancy)—is then tied to Mr. Woodhouse's nervousness, by Emma's resolution to keep him ignorant of what occurred. It has a special fascination for Emma: "in her imagination it maintained its ground" (Austen, 1972, 229). As if to gain mastery over the event through repetition, she recites the story repeatedly to her nephews. Emma's compulsion is to master the threat to the bond with the mother rather than, more typically (as in the fort/da game), to negotiate her loss.

By means of these phobias, *Emma* expresses at least temporary resistance to Kristeva's other jouissance. The marriage phobia sabotages the possibility of union with a partner capable of dissolving the incarcerated mother, who himself would preclude the trials and errors of the narrative, and therefore the narrative. The contamination/insemination phobia sabotages the possibility of the outward displacement of the maternal object by, what that partner might have offered—"the major gift [the mother] was never able to offer: a new life" (Kristeva, 1989, 78)—which likewise would put a halt to the text's melancholic waywardness. Contentedly imagining herself as an "old maid," Emma tells Harriet that "as for objects of interest, objects for the affections, . . . I shall be very well off, with all the children of a sister I love so much, to care about. There will be enough of them . . . to supply every sort of sensation that declining life can need. There will be enough for every hope and every fear; and though my attachment to none can equal that of a parent, it suits my ideas of comfort" (Austen, 1972, 58–59). Paradoxically, however, the melancholia at the level of the plot enables the work of mourning finally to be accomplished at the level of the text. That is, insofar as Emma's melancholia is inscribed, the novel may slowly unfold, generating the very form necessary in the end to mourn. And considering the turn Emma eventually takes, that mourning becomes doubly crucial.

III.

It might seem likely, given the novel's fear of consummation/contamination, that marriage would be avoided at all costs. Yet Mr. Woodhouse condones Emma's marriage to Mr. Knightley on the grounds that it is a prophylactic. The robbery of Mrs. Weston's poultry-house, "of all her turkies—evidently by the ingenuity of man," as well as other poultry-houses in the neighborhood, provokes Mr. Woodhouse to consent, even cheerfully. "Pilfering was *house-breaking* to Mr. Woodhouse's fears" (Austen, 1972, 334); and the metonymy invites us to ask, what is house-breaking? Contrary to general expectation, Mr. Woodhouse in the end does not regard Mr. Knightley as possessing his daughter. (In Margaret Drabble's *The Waterfall*, Jane has a compatible reaction to their union: "What can it have been like, in bed with Mr. Knightley? *Sorrow* awaited that woman" [Drabble, 1969, 66; my emphasis].) Knightley is not whisking her away geographically either, since this ménage à trois will live happily ever after at Hartfield. Emma refuses to leave home; so Knightley—of "true gentility, *untainted* in blood and understanding" (Austen, 1972, 245; my emphasis)—devises the unconventional plan of moving in. Obviously, marriage to Mr. Knightley *ends* the plot; but the nuptial arrangement is presented in ways that indicate preservation of the central ailment, precluding the kind of therapeutic closure that D. A. Miller takes for granted.

That Mr. Knightley, Emma's senior by sixteen years, of an age that would allow him to be her parent and fond of using epithets ("a spoiled child," "little Emma" [Austen, 1972, 67]) that italicize his attraction to the idea of being her parent, will live at Hartfield in a protective role (with Emma and her father, and thus in a position to complete the family triangle) is suggestive but insufficient proof that he becomes Emma's new, and presumably last, mother surrogate. The nature of his appeal must be taken into account. The prospect of marrying Mr. Knightley does not fully occur to Emma until Harriet seems on the verge of securing him; only then does Emma become "acquainted with her own heart." Her epiphany is put in terms of a masochistic metaphor: "It darted through her, with the speed of an arrow, that Mr. Knightley must marry no one but herself!" (Austen, 1972, 280). Just as the loss of Miss Taylor revives Emma's sadness over the loss of her mother, the potential loss of Mr. Knightley seems instantaneously to trigger panic that is a function of Emma's history of loss. As if speaking for Emma at this juncture, Kristeva laments, "My depression points to my not knowing how to lose—I have perhaps been unable to find a valid compensation for the loss? It follows that any loss entails the loss of my being—and of Being it-self" (Kristeva, 1989, 5). Not only would it be devastating for Emma to incur another loss by not bonding with Mr. Knightley, but such a bond has a great deal to recommend it as a mode of fending off loss in the abstract. Because of his critical resemblance to Emma's mother—in whose death, we are told, Emma lost the only person, until Knightley, able to handle her—marrying Mr. Knightley turns out not to be a disruption of Emma's melan-cholic state (wedding her to her mother), but rather a reinforcement of it. Preparing to inform her father of Mr. Knightley's proposal, Emma advises herself that she must not use "a melancholy tone" (Austen, 1972, 321).

On Mrs. Woodhouse (an uncanny name that fails to surface in the text) and Mr. Knightley, Armstrong and I tend to agree (although she takes the point in an entirely different direction): "Emma's problem, as the narra-tor notes in the second statement of the novel, originates in her absent mother. . . . it is the self-regulatory function missing along with the mother that is significant, and it is this which Emma acquires in learning that she loves Mr. Knightley" (Armstrong, 1987, 154). A disciplinarian from the outset—"Mr. Knightley, in fact, was one of the few people who could see faults in Emma Woodhouse, and the only one who ever told her of them" (Austen, 1972, 5)—Knightley walks into the vacuum of Emma's double ma-ternal loss and immediately criticizes her. He challenges Emma's sense of success in matching up the Westons, while accusing her of "interference" (Austen, 1972, 7); he labels Emma's intimacy with Harriet "a bad thing" (Austen, 1972, 22). He denigrates Emma before Mrs. Weston, asserting that she "will never submit to any thing requiring industry and patience, and a subjection of the fancy to the understanding" (Austen, 1972, 23). He com-prehends all too well, since it accords him an advantage over other suitors, that Emma "must have been under subjection" to her mother (Austen, 1972, 23). When Knightley's insights are coupled with his conception of marriage (he jokes with Mrs. Weston that her work as Emma's governess was excellent training for marriage, since it required submitting to another's will and "doing as [Mrs. Weston was] bid" [Austen, 1972, 24]), not to men-tion his unyielding attempts at correction of Emma's behavior, it seems as if *he* envisions *himself* as a substitute for Mrs. Woodhouse, his objective being to put Emma, and her fancy, under subjection to him, and his famous under-standing.

A feisty Emma in fact capitulates eventually to Knightley's seductive disci-pline and punishment. After a strenuous argument with him, over Mr. Mar-tin's proposal to Harriet, in which Emma shrewdly exposes male objectifi-cation of women, and he blasts her with "Nonsense, errant nonsense, as ever was talked," Emma does not regret her influence over Harriet, finding herself "a better judge of such a point of female right and refinement than he could be." Yet, terribly split, she cannot overcome her "habitual respect for his judgment in general" (Austen, 1972, 43). At the Crown ball, Emma yields to a dance with Knightley only after admitting to her error regarding Mr. Elton; Knightley agrees not to "scold" her. Their banter over not being "so much brother and sister as to make [dancing] improper" (Austen, 1972, 225) intimates the incestuous nature of their mutual attraction. Mr. Knightley melts Emma further through his condemnation of her obnoxious behavior on Box Hill: afterwards she wants to run into him to display her "penitence, so justly and truly hers" (Austen, 1972, 259).

Emma's disciplinary schooling culminates in the threat of the loss of Mr. Knightley. The idea of Knightley's "confidence towards Harriet" gives Emma "severe pain" (Austen, 1972, 282): "Till now that she was threatened with its loss, Emma had never known how much of her happiness depended on being *first* with Mr. Knightley[;] . . . only in the dread of being supplanted" does she discover "how inexpressibly important it had been" (Austen, 1972, 285). Emma of course has no interest in relieving herself of the pain of losing Knightley, for her wish is not to move on. And pain draws her. Yet, desperately craving her disciplinarian, she does not seek the pain of loss either but rather the pain of retention. Given what Mr. Knightley (who at the Crown ball looks "grave," and later leaving for London looks "graver than usual") represents, given his disciplinarian bent, marrying him (it is easy for Emma to apprehend) is a way of preserving desirable pain. Emma had taken for granted his loving and watching "over her from a girl, with an endeavour to improve her, and an anxiety for her doing right" (Austen, 1972, 285); she had even thought that such solicitude earned him a claim on her. Now she will secure this "care."

It may be tempting to ignore Knightley's linkage with Emma's mother and to conceive of him (despite the paternal redundancy this would produce, although Mr. Woodhouse might be shifted to the mother's place) as Emma's access to the symbolic arena (the "third party—father, form, schema" that Kristeva points to as "what makes . . . triumph over sadness possible" [Kristeva, 1989, 23]), the narrative correlative of which would be the victorious close of the story—all threads tied, everyone neatly and happily coupled, all traces of the mother wiped out. A major stumbling block, however, is that Emma's signifying ability is in steady decline. The diagnosis comes from Kristeva: "The *denial (Verleugnung) of negation* would thus be the exercise of an impossible mourning, the setting up of . . . an artificial, unbelievable language, cut out of the painful background that is not accessible to any signifier" (Kristeva, 1989, 44). In the last chapters, we find Emma parroting Mr. Knightley's views (especially on Harriet) and failing to speak, as if in rehearsal for what promises to be a silencing marriage celebrated at the very end. The Emma we knew, sparkling with wit, is reduced to insipid remarks of gratitude to Knightley: "But I had the assistance of all your endeavours to counteract the indulgence of other people. I doubt whether my own sense would have corrected me without it" (Austen, 1972, 318).

Kristeva writes that "Our gift of speech, of situating ourselves in time for an other, could exist nowhere except beyond an abyss. Speaking beings, from their ability to endure in time up to their enthusiastic, learned, or simply amusing constructions, demand a break, a renunciation, an unease at their foundations" (Kristeva, 1989, 42). Renouncing nothing—except her subjectivity, since "the maternal object having been introjected, the depressive or melancholic putting to death of the self is what follows, instead of matricide" (Kristeva, 1989, 28)—no longer split, as she is during the exfoliation of the story, and sounding like a precursor of Pauline Réage's O, Emma makes selfhood into a form of echolalia: "I can hardly imagine that any thing which pleases or amuses you," she says to Knightley, "should not please and amuse me too" (Austen, 1972, 324). On the verge of marriage, Emma fits Kristeva's description of melancholy persons for whom "meaning . . . seems secondary, frozen, somewhat removed from the head and body of the person who is speaking . . . 'one' speaks without believing in it" (Kristeva, 1989, 43). Rather than sanctioning social prescriptions by rendering them romantically appealing, as Miller argues in his essay, Austen introduces "malfunction" (Miller's term) in the marriage plot, *"withdraws affect,"* well before *Sanditon* (Miller, 1990, 10:78). "[I]nstead of bonding the affect caused by loss," writes Kristeva, "the depressed sign disowns the affect as well as the signifier, thus admitting that the depressed subject has remained prisoner of the nonlost object (the Thing)" (Kristeva, 1989, 47).

The novel ends as a result of Emma's contractual union with a mother surrogate who is this time extremely powerful. Hence the narrative that has been keeping such a surrender in abeyance can now relax. This incorporation of the mother in *Emma* prohibits further narrative progress at the same time as, ironically, the narrative progress to this endpoint serves to cancel the disavowal of the negation of the loss of the mother with which the novel began. Having worked through loss by re-presenting it in felicitous prose, the text itself enables the negation of that loss. Unredeemed by Knightley, Emma's melancholia is assuaged by the aesthetic pleasure of the text, which in a sense comes to her rescue not regardless of the novel's politically disturbing conclusion but in part because of it. While there may be no cause for celebration, Austen, especially given her historical context, articulates well the melancholic woman's vulnerability and the inadequacy of her seeking other jouissance.

IV.

Like Peter Brooks in "Freud's Masterplot," I have been examining the motions of "plot and its motor force in human desire, its peculiar relation to beginnings and ends, its apparent claim to rescue meaning," although not from "temporal flux," as he proposes, but from an abyss/the Thing. I have relied on Kristeva (who in turn relies on Freud) for her "inquiry into the dynamics of the psychic life" (Brooks, 1985, 90); and following "Freud's Masterplot," I have tried to extend that inquiry into the dynamics of a text. Brooks describes textual energy as being bound in "usable 'bundles,' " which delay or postpone "the discharge of energy," and which therefore are "painful." He writes that "The most effective or, at the least, the most challenging texts may be those that are most delayed, most highly bound, most painful" (Brooks, 1985, 101–102). So there is a degree of masochism intrinsic to Brooks's own model, which should not surprise us given the model's roots in *Beyond the Pleasure Principle*. This severely delayed, painful text seems akin to the sort of melancholic/masochistic narrative I have been tracing in *Emma*. The pain of lengthy delay is eventually purged in Brooks's main paradigm; and likewise in Austen's novel, a therapeutic, although at times tedious if not tortuous, prolongation of narrative, often barely "circuiting" at all, manages to eventuate in purgation.

Yet especially for political reasons pertaining to the subtle, insidious form of woman abuse touched on in this novel, the *novel's* capacity to mourn must be carefully distinguished from that of the heroine. The ideal end of a love match of Emma's own that would offer her autonomy from maternal bonds, access to language, and some sort of agency is forever delayed. Finally, an incestuous "mistaken erotic object choice," a too perfect annihilatory husband (Brooks speaks of the "too perfect and hence annihilatory bride," for example, "of the 'Belle Dame sans merci' variety" [Brooks, 1985, 109]) blocks Emma's curative process. Despite the appearance of diegetic stability, the ending fails to offer at least Emma, or women—it is a different story for Mr. Knightley—"a *solid implication* in the symbolic and imaginary code" (Kristeva, 1989, 36), a "proper" close. Instead, there is "a downfall . . . into the invisible and unnameable" (Kristeva, 1989, 15), a "sinking into the blankness of asymbolia" (Kristeva, 1989, 33), as the heroine is sucked back into the masochistic jouissance of surrogate maternal subjection.

The current version of the standard reading of *Emma* regards Mr. Knightley as the "proper" erotic object choice that supplies the "proper" ending: Knightley, officer of the law, brings promiscuous desire into line. But it is dangerous to promote the idea of Mr. Knightley as a proper erotic object choice, given the sadomasochistic terms of his conventionally gendered relationship with Emma. In spite of his irony, Miller's stress on Austen's triumphant "official values"—"settlement, moral insight, and judgment" (Miller, 1981, xiv), "knowledge," "serious revelations" (Miller, 1981, 44), "meaning and truth" (Miller, 1981, 46)—allows the sadistic nature of the ending to slip by. Something more horrific than the imposition of humanist values brings *Emma* to a close. The choice Miller offers the reader between univocality and plurivocality, between stability and instability is simple enough: and surely not every interpretive community will find it obvious that settlement, moral insight, and knowledge are regrettable eventualities. But the end of *Emma* is not the termination of a free-floating, genderless desire; it is the subjection—the containment through an insidious disciplinary process—of a woman, whose desire remains inchoate.

Miller glosses over the subjugating nature of the values that close *Emma*, as he assigns them names that in other times and places would carry considerable prestige. Although a sadomasochistic tension can be inferred from his account of narrative plurivocality being forced into univocal narrative submission, Miller accepts that tension, insufficiently bringing out the police work that is operating or its underlying misogyny. I am trying both to pathologize and politicize it. Knightley's discipline, punishment, and final control of Emma are as sadistic as Emma's and the text's "wandering desire" is melancholic/masochistic, insofar as that "desire" is regressive, seeking absorption in a prelinguistic maternal realm. Miller overlooks whose desire or, more accurately, whose jouissance—a woman's—is wandering and whither it wanders—back to her mother. Emma does not make a suitable erotic object choice but enters an "incestuous" union facilitated by: her compliance with Mr. Knightley's values and wishes; his turning her to property ("She was his own Emma, by hand and word" [Austen, 1972, 298]); and the cultural construction of ladyhood (to Knightley's proposal, she says "Just what she ought, of course. A lady always does" [Austen, 1972, 297]). That melancholia primes a woman to be constituted by Foucauldian discipline is apparent already in Austen.

Kristeva recommends that a melancholic woman locate a partner who can lead her to cathect "her autoeroticism in a jouissance of the other (separate, symbolic, phallic)" (Kristeva, 1989, 78). While she underscores "the tremendous psychic, intellectual, and affective effort a woman must make in order to find the other sex as erotic object" (Kristeva, 1989, 30), she defends this therapeutic attachment. (Ostensibly Emma joins with such a partner.) Kristeva believes that "verbal or desiring bonds with others" are necessary to keep the melancholy woman from being "abandoned within herself," "[m]odest, silent," from wasting "away by striking moral and physic [sic] blows against herself, which . . . do not give her sufficient pleasures. Until the fatal blow—the definitive nuptials of the Dead Woman with the Same, whom she did not kill" (Kristeva, 1989, 30). Yet it is by virtue of following Kristeva's therapeutic program that Emma manages to receive "the fatal blow": she is ensnared by disciplinary bonds with an Other so that her nuptials end up being in effect with the Dead Woman "whom she did not kill."

Knightley's double empowerment is finally achieved by the ease with which, for Emma, he fills her mother's shoes. What Austen, in *Emma*, con-

tributes proleptically to Kristeva's analysis is the caveat that a woman abandoned by her mother, especially if that mother neglected or subjected her
(making her subjectivity a function of her attachment to the mother), may
be seduced by an abusive erotic object choice: having consumed her mother,
the daughter thus plays out the usual matricide against herself. A surprising
number of works by contemporary women writers—for instance, Anita
Brookner, Marguerite Duras, Margaret Drabble, Margaret Atwood, even
Tina Turner—extend Austen's expression of this grave liability, within patriarchy, of being addicted to the easily co-opted maternal Thing, as the following pages will elaborate. It turns out that a chief danger and source of
seductiveness of a patriarchy is that it is founded on the matriarchy with
which all life begins.

In publishing this idea while preserving the dead mother in especially elegant artistic form, and in thereby compensating for both the maternal ob-
ject/Thing and the disciplinarian lover that Emma's unconscious overattachment to the maternal object/Thing renders seductively and therefore
dangerously appealing, *Emma* serves as a powerful counterdepressant. The
novel translates the losses it is founded on into representation that serves
the purpose of mourning what otherwise would have been engulfing. It represents traumas that in the course of that transference to discourse get re-
configured and as a result loosened. Again, the novel effects this reconfigu-
ration without reabandoning the lost mother, by keeping her alive in the
myriad diegetic and stylistic ways that I have discussed, as well as shrewdly
through a quiet feminist analysis of the potential liabilities of a woman's
addiction to the maternal Thing.

NOTE

This chapter is a reprint of Frances L. Restuccia, "A Black Morning: Kristevan Melancholia in Jane Austen's *Emma*," *American Imago*, vol. 51, no. 4 (Winter 1994),
pp. 447–69. © 1994 The Johns Hopkins University Press.

2

Mortification: Beyond the
Persuasion Principle

I.

*The disappearance of that essential being continues to deprive me of
what is most worthwhile in me; I live it as a wound or deprivation. . . .
My depression points to my not knowing how to lose—I have perhaps
been unable to find a valid compensation for the loss?*

—Julia Kristeva, *Black Sun*

It is well known that *Persuasion* is Jane Austen's autumnal novel. The
novel itself seems to know, for the heroine, Anne Elliot, takes pleasure in
a walk in part by "repeating to herself some few of the thousand poetical
descriptions extant of autumn, . . . that season which has drawn from every
poet, worthy of being read, some attempt at description, or some lines of
feeling" (Austen, 1995, 56). In 1862, in "The Language of Feeling," Julia
Kavanagh wrote that even the happy close of *Persuasion* fails to efface "the
sorrowful tone of the tale." To Kavanagh, "This melancholy cast . . . distinguishes *Persuasion* from Miss Austen's other tales. . . . this is sad" (Austen,
1995, 209). More recently, Tony Tanner has pointed out the novel's "un-
characteristically lyrical passages about the sea," which give *Persuasion* its
"markedly different atmosphere" (Austen, 1995, 248–49). Cheryl Ann
Weissman notes the novel's "narrative ambivalence"; taking up this topic,
Anita Sokolsky has written "The Melancholy Persuasion," which traces an
ambivalent struggle in the novel between tendencies melancholic and melio-
rist, although Sokolsky's concluding observation—that Anne's "exquisite
sensibility . . . makes her, finally, melancholy at the loss of melancholy" (Sokolsky, 1994, 141)—supports a paradox that sets in motion a melancholic

17

mise-en-abyme. It turns out, as Sokolsky also suggests, that Anne Elliot is more in love with loss than with Captain Frederick Wentworth, her rebuffed lover, which is perhaps one reason why she allows herself to be persuaded to reject him, in the first place. Why Anne is in love with loss, however, can stand a fuller explanation—one that, I am hopeful, may be generated through considering not the object of Anne's desires but from where Anne desires.

Sokolsky toys with the idea that reading *Persuasion* might be therapeutic. And if *Persuasion* ameliorates melancholia, it is persuasion that is meliatory. While mortification, which Anne finds alluring, "becomes a privileged effect of melancholy," persuasion is the name of "a system of melioration" (Sokolsky, 1994, 133). Sokolsky sees Anne's first opportunity "to escape her melancholy fatalism," to act on "the enterprising notion that one makes one's fate" as the catastrophe of Louisa's fall. Sokolsky writes (initially) that Anne lives up to this crisis, by recouping her losses through the removal of this rival, and interpreting Louisa's fall as "a consequence of her obstinate temperament" (Sokolsky, 1994, 134), as opposed to Anne's persuadability. But Sokolsky's subsequent formulation—that Anne "lives it up in" a crisis—seems more acute.

Why *is* Louisa's fall, which results in what appears to be lifelessness—"her face was like death"; "'She is dead! she is dead!' screamed Mary" (Austen, 1995, 74)—the pivotal point in the book? Wouldn't a melancholic woman be more apt to identify with such a "dead" female body, or at least to be overcome by it, rather than be spurred on by it to enterprising notions of taking one's fate into one's own hands? "Faced [already] with a rupture to her personal narrative, a rupture signified by her mother's premature death and restaged in her lover's loss" (Sokolsky, 1994, 132), as Sokolsky writes, Anne would seem to risk a relapse of melancholia through confrontation with a "poor corpse-like figure" (Austen, 1995, 74). "Where does this black sun come from?" asks Kristeva in *Black Sun*; and she answers: "A betrayal, a fatal illness, some *accident* or handicap that abruptly wrests me away from what seemed to me the normal category of normal people" (Kristeva, 1889, 3–4, my emphasis). Rather than help Anne to vanquish melancholia, Louisa's corpse-like figure would seem to be an eruption in the form of a traumatic return of the Lacanian Real. To Lacan, "trauma is *real*—it is a hard core resisting symbolization" (Zizek, 1989, 162).

In *Looking Awry*, Slavoj Zizek sees myriad corpses as epitomizing "the void that gapes in the very heart of the symbolic" (Zizek, 1991, 33); he regards the corpse, moreover, as an object that binds people together (Zizek, 1991, 59). Repeatedly, Zizek focuses on the corpse as a "remainder of the real that 'sticks out'" (93), as in Hitchcock's *The Birds* where the camera's tracking movement quickly, for anamorphotic effect, shows a corpse's head. Oddly, that Louisa-as-corpse bears such meaning, renders a jouissance beyond the pleasure, or persuasion, principle (pleasure, Lacan writes, "sets the limits on *jouissance*" [Lacan, 1977, 319]) is hinted at in a strange passage on the enjoyment that men working about the Cobb will take in this sight of "a dead young lady" (Austen, 1995, 75). "[T]he report of the accident had spread among the workmen and boatmen . . . , and many were collected near them, to be useful if wanted, at any rate, to enjoy the sight of a dead young lady, nay [since Henrietta "lost her senses too" (74)] two dead young ladies" (Austen, 1995, 75).

It is not at all, at this point, that Anne's mortifications "have become a form of charm" (who is charmed?) or that her rare disposition and sensibility have become more visible, countering her earlier melancholic invisibility. Sokolsky writes that mortification had been for Anne a device by which her "obscurity became a displaced mark of the melancholic's disavowal of an introjected loss" (Sokolsky, 1994, 134), whereas now Anne deploys melancholy, makes her melancholy visible, as a form of seduction. But, to begin with the latter point first, a seductive deployment of melancholia by no means indicates a necessary escape from melancholia, as Sokolsky at one point in her own ambivalent argument ambiguously implies ("By the end of the novel Anne appears to have shed melancholy" [Sokolsky, 1994, 135]). Second, rather than disavowing her introjected loss, Anne has disavowed the negation of her loss and thus incorporated it, and thereby sustains it. As Kristeva clarifies: "Depressed persons . . . *disavow the negation*: they cancel it out, suspend it, and nostalgically fall back on the real object (the Thing) of their loss, which is just what they do not manage to lose, to which they remain painfully riveted. The *denial (Verleugnung) of negation* would thus be the exercise of an impossible mourning, the setting up of a fundamental sadness . . . " (Kristeva, 1989, 43–44). Consumed with the loss that inhabits her, Anne mourns melancholically. After her borderline experience with Louisa's near death, Anne clings even more faithfully to loss. With no hesitation—in danger, it would appear, even of masochism—she agrees to nurse the "poor corpse-like figure," the ostensible object of desire of her ostensibly lost lover, and laments that she is replaced by Mary. His command, that she care for her rival, is Anne's abject wish: "she would have attended on Louisa with a zeal above the common claims of regard, for his sake" (Austen, 1995, 78).

Prior to this point, Anne shows myriad signs of clinging to her object-loss, i.e., signs that reflect Freud's "distinguishing mental features of melancholia" (Freud, 1917, 244). She has scant interest in the outside world: "Anne had been too little from home, too little seen. Her spirits were not high. A larger society would improve them" (Austen, 1995, 11). She shows a "disturbance of self-regard": she allows her father and both sisters to denigrate, manipulate, and use her. And she in a sense reveals an "expectation of punishment" (Freud, 1917, 244), especially if we understand Anne's acquiescence to Lady Russell's advice not to accept Wentworth's marriage proposal as, at some level, unnecessary and unwanted compliance. Freud specifies that it is usually on moral grounds that the melancholic is dissatisfied; the conscience in melancholia can become "diseased" (Freud, 1917, 247). Early on in *Persuasion,* it is established that Anne's conscience has prompted a "severe degree of self-denial," that her usual fate (therefore?) is to have "something very opposite from her inclination fixed on": e.g., "She disliked Bath, and did not think it agreed with her—and Bath was to be her home" (Austen, 1995, 10).

Anne's persuadability in the case of Captain Wentworth's first proposal is connected to self-denial in odd and complicated ways. Curiously, Anne believes that the *engagement* is unworthy, incapable of "success, and not deserving it." She is "self-denying," moreover, for Wentworth's own good, "principally for *his* advantage," in the oppositional face of his feeling "totally unconvinced and unbending," "ill-used by so forced a relinquishment" (Austen, 1995, 19). Yet, fitting Freud's description of the melancholic's torn psyche (the libido battling the critical agency of a strict conscience), Anne can simultaneously identify with Wentworth's position. She is cognizant of having sacrificed, knowing that "she should yet have been a happier woman in maintaining the engagement, than she had been in the sacrifice of it" (Austen, 1995, 20). She should/would have been a happier woman, that is, *had* she not been melancholic, had she not psychically required/desired the preservation of loss, i.e., reinforcement of her encryptment of it, and therefore a redoubling of her melancholic mourning.

Eight years later, however, marriage to Frederick becomes a possibility—this *is* a turning point—not because there has been a break in Anne's melancholia (on the contrary, I am arguing that Anne's melancholia intensifies at this point) but because, through his brush with death, Frederick has been sucked in, smeared with the enjoyment/jouissance of Louisa's "poor corpselike figure." No longer persuadable, well beyond the persuasion principle, Anne pitches toward sadness, now pulling Wentworth with her. To be persuaded (by Lady Russell) is *not* to marry, not to become rigid (like Louisa/death). To resist persuasion, to head toward marriage, to marry, is to become rigid (like Louisa/death), especially when one's spouse-to-be is Captain Wentworth. For Wentworth is himself shocked and fully absorbed by Louisa's near-death (he looks on Louisa "with a face as pallid as her own" [Austen, 1995, 74]), as well as Captain of the sea (mer/mère), and a successful warrior in a war that has continued fourteen years—the very length of time during Anne's life that her mother, Lady Elliot, lived. Before becoming firm (corpse-like), Louisa had given a speech, to Wentworth and overheard by Anne, championing hardness as the desirable antithesis to being persuaded. Wentworth takes it up, using a nut jokingly to illustrate his allegiance to firmness:

"let those who would be happy be firm.—Here is a nut . . . —a beautiful glossy nut, which, blessed with original strength, has outlived all the storms of autumn. Not a puncture, not a weak spot any where.—This nut," he continued, with playful solemnity, . . . "is still in possession of all the happiness that a hazel-nut can be supposed capable of." Then, returning to his former earnest tone: "My first wish for all, whom I am interested in, is that they should be firm" (Austen, 1995, 59).

Wentworth's and Anne's melancholic seduction is actually mutual (as perhaps all seductions must be). Wanting Wentworth to be "interested in" her, Anne (following Louisa) becomes firm; realizing Wentworth's allegiance to inertness, to the Lacanian Real, "usually conceived as a hard kernel resisting symbolization" (Zizek, 1989, 161), Anne gravitates in his direction. Unwittingly, Zizek further explains the nature of her trajectory and destination: "this object, this traumatic kernel, is the dimension . . . of a 'death drive', of a traumatic imbalance, a rooting out. Man as such is 'nature sick unto death', derailed, run off the rails through a fascination with a lethal Thing" (Zizek, 1989, 181).

Captain Wentworth is smeared with death not only in the ways I have mentioned—in particular by virtue of his participation in Louisa's fall—but also by virtue of Mrs. Musgrove's identification of him with her son, Richard, who died at sea, and who, just prior to his death, was under the Captain's authority. This connection to Wentworth throws Mrs. Musgrove "into greater grief for [Richard] than she had known on first hearing of his death" (Austen, 1995, 35); it appears to enable Mrs. Musgrove to initiate belatedly her own process of mourning. The grieving mother makes the strange, hyperbolic assumption that had heaven spared her son he would have been another Captain Wentworth. And this talk apparently sets off Wentworth, who then spins navy tales that draw attention to the thin line between the dead Richard and the now alive Captain. He recalls the precarious Asp, a worn out and broken up ship he commanded, "Hardly fit for service then" (Austen, 1995, 43): "I knew that we should either go to the bottom together, or that she would be the making of me" (Austen, 1995, 44). It is only good fortune that by the time Captain Wentworth finally encountered a storm, "which would have done for poor old Asp," he had changed vessels. Anne shudders as she listens to Wentworth describe the obscurity to which his memory would have been relegated: "I should only have been a gallant Captain Wentworth, in a small paragraph at one corner of the newspapers; and being lost in only a sloop, nobody would have thought about me" (Austen, 1995, 44).

Wentworth's naval pal Harville regards Wentworth as the only appropriate messenger to Benwick of the news of the death of Fanny Harville. And we can finally be assured that Wentworth's rapport with death is a large part of Anne's later attraction to him by the fact that the novel culminates with alarm over it. Perhaps critics (such as Kavanagh) have trouble perceiving the happiness of the happy ending because its instability is stressed. Sokolsky too, by the end of her article, is no longer grinning. (She *had* confessed to finding a grin on her face because the conclusion of the novel gratifies fantasy "in a way rarely indulged except in one's most exalted reveries" [Sokolsky, 1994, 135].) But Sokolsky finally concedes that when Anne . . . allows her happiness to become apparent in the last phase of the novel she appears most "attenuated" and "elusive." Anne's tenderness "suggests that she too has been bruised into an even greater delicacy. . . . Anne appears to have been granted a precarious extension so as to be whittled away by apprehensions as to the fragility of her happiness" (Sokolsky, 1994, 142).

The last line of *Persuasion* is that Anne "gloried in being a sailor's wife, but she must pay the tax of quick alarm for belonging to that profession . . ." (Austen, 1995, 168). For all Anne knows—or is this what she knows?—Wentworth may be remobilized. Marry a navy captain at this time (1814), and you are apt to lose him to the sea, to war, even to death. In fact, in just a few months from this point in Austen's fiction, in historical reality, England returns to war. There are one hundred days to go of the Napoleonic Wars, Napoleon's "abortive return, concluded by the battle of Waterloo in 1815" (Austen, 1995, 234). Anne's fascination with Wentworth very well might be part of the magnetism of the abyss. *Persuasion,* whose first page contains three references to the dead (two to Lady Elliot and one to her still-born son), seems so bogged down with characters who have been wounded (Harville), damaged severely by traumatic falls (little Charles, Louisa), and thrust into mourning (e.g., Mr. Elliot, Mrs. Smith, Benwick, Harville, the Musgroves) over dead loved ones that the novel seems to career toward death, to be so weighed down that only the fragility of persuasion/*Persuasion* barely props it up.

II.

Object (a) is the leftover of that process of constituting an object, that scrap that evades the grasp of symbolization. *It is a reminder that there is something else, something perhaps lost, perhaps yet to be found . . . it is the rem(a)inder of the lost hypothetical mother-child unity.*

—Bruce Fink, *The Lacanian Subject*

By endowing Wentworth with evident flaws (he glances contemptuously at Mary and misjudges the extent of Benwick's devotion to his dead fiancée; he flirts with two sisters at once and seems to let resentment toward Anne bar him for many years from renewing his marriage proposal) and by making him paper thin, Austen shows us Anne's oblivion to Wentworth in all his particularity and therefore hints that Wentworth serves as merely a blank slate on which Anne can project her desires. He serves, in other words, as "the place where the truth of the subject is articulated." What transpires between Anne and Frederick is aptly described by Zizek's account of love in Hitchcock's films: "it is a kind of 'miracle' that explodes 'out of nothing'" (Zizek, 1991, 76), a by-product, that which occurs as a result of "what we *are* and not on account of what we *do*" (Zizek, 1991, 77). Lacan calls this " 'by-product' of our activity"

> *objet petit a,* the hidden treasure, that which is "in us more than ourselves," that elusive, unattainable X that confers upon all our deeds an aura of magic, although it cannot be pinned down to any of our positive qualities. It is through the *objet a* that we can grasp the workings of the ultimate "by-product" state, the matrix of all the others: the *transference.* The subject can never fully dominate and manipulate the way he provokes transference in others. . . . All of a sudden, one appears to possess an unspecified X, something that colors all one's actions, submits them to a kind of transubstantiation (Zizek, 1991, 77).

The transference does not go into effect right away for Anne. In fact, Wentworth was, at the time of his first proposal, undesirable to Anne paradoxically because he would have fulfilled her desire. For we recall that depressives must circumvent Eros; they prefer to remain attached to the Thing drawing them to Thanatos. Marriage the first time around would have been a betrayal of Lady Elliot for two reasons: 1) Anne's encrypted mother would then have been ousted by Wentworth, and 2) Lady Elliot herself apparently died with unfulfilled marital desire, so to remain identified with her, Anne needed to stay romantically and sexually unfulfilled. (As for Anne's identification with Lady Elliot: Anne plays the maternal role in caring for Mary's children, even briefly for Louisa and Mrs. Smith; Lady Russell tells Anne, "You are your mother's self in countenance and disposition," and Anne's imagination and heart are "bewitched" by Lady Russell's words [Austen, 1995, 106].) Although *Persuasion* hardly mentions Lady Elliot, it does establish that she scarcely had enough interest in life to hang onto life: she was "not the very happiest being in the world herself"; only her "duties, her friends, and her children . . . attach[ed] her to life, and [made] it no matter of indifference to her when she was called on to quit them" (Austen, 1995, 4). Hence Anne, at nineteen, clings to loss, by restaging the loss of her mother so that she can reencrypt that lost object, by allowing herself not to consummate her desire in marriage, by stifling her desire. As a result she enables herself to retain her maternal identification. "[F]or such a person," as Kristeva explains, "no erotic object could replace the irreplaceable perception of a . . . preobject confining the libido or severing the bonds of desire." The depressed person "retreats, disconsolate and aphasic, alone with the unnamed Thing": "the real that does not lend itself to signification" (Kristeva, 1989, 13).

It is not until Anne projects onto Wentworth the maternal Thing, through a gradual transference that occurs somewhere between Anne's nineteenth and twenty-seventh years, and Wentworth becomes coterminus with Lady Eliot/death/the Real (in the various ways I have described), that he attains a certain desirability. Wentworth is appealing now not as himself but as objet a—as "the rem(a)inder of the lost hypothetical mother-child unity" (Fink, 1995, 94). Wentworth is to Anne much more than himself; he exceeds himself, due to his position in the structure of Anne's psyche, or fundamental fantasy. That Wentworth is to Anne more than himself is dramatized in *Persuasion* in the scene in which Anne is "perfectly conscious of Lady Russell's eyes being turned exactly in the direction for [Wentworth], of her being in short intently observing him." Anne thinks she can "thoroughly comprehend the sort of fascination [Wentworth] must possess over Lady Russell's mind, the difficulty it must be for her to withdraw her eyes, the astonishment she must be feeling that eight or nine years should have passed over him, and in foreign climes and in active service too, without robbing him of one personal grace!" But the fascination turns out to be Anne's alone, Anne's delusion. All Lady Russell claims to have had her eyes fixed upon are "some window-curtains" (Austen, 1995, 119).

This scene not only must be looked at awry for us to grasp its depiction of Wentworth as objet a, but it is also *about* looking awry. While Lady Russell straightforwardly seeks out drawing-room window curtains, Anne imagines Lady Russell staring at Anne's obscure, phantasmatic cause of desire. And perhaps, for the sake of avoiding premature mortification, it is critical here that Anne is imagining her object of fascination indirectly through Lady Russell's eyes. Had that object gazed directly at Anne, textual movement would have been frozen. For "[t]he gaze in itself not only terminates the movement, it freezes it" (Lacan, 1973, 117). "At the moment the subject stops . . . , he is mortified. The antilife, antimovement function of this terminal point is the *fascinum,* and it is precisely one of the dimensions in which the power of the gaze is exercised directly" (Lacan, 1973, 118). Or, in Zizek's formulation: "The sublime object is an object which cannot be approached too closely: if we get too near it, it loses its sublime features and becomes an ordinary vulgar object—it can persist only in an interspace, in an intermediate state, viewed from a certain perspective, half-seen. If we want to see it in the light of day, it changes into an everyday object, it dissipates itself, precisely because in itself it is nothing at all" (Zizek, 1989, 170).

Anne, having been so focused on Lady Russell, laments losing her chance to see whether Wentworth saw them. Perhaps it is even doubtful that Wentworth was ever there, in the streets of Bath, in the first place: Anne distinguishes him at "a distance," amid "many other men" and "groups walking the same way" (Austen, 1995, 118). For the object of desire, writes Lacan in *The Four Fundamental Concepts*, "is either a phantasy that is in reality the *support* of desire, or a lure" (Lacan, 1973, 186).

Anne will have Wentworth now, for these psychic reasons, despite everyone's disapproval—not that, in the end, they all staunchly disapprove. Yet it is not simply that social and familial disapproval has diminished, that Wentworth's cachet has improved. Wentworth states toward the very end that he "had no reason to believe [Lady Russell was] of less authority now" (Austen, 1995, 163). Anne will have him at this point because like a mother he has protected her: by securing a place for her, when she is weary, in the Croft carriage; by lifting Mary's younger son, Walter, off her back. Anne will have him now because like *her* mother he is "very fond of music" (Austen, 1995, 119): "*excepting one short period of her life*, she had never, since the age of fourteen, never since the loss of her dear mother, known the happiness of being listened to, or encouraged by any just appreciation or real taste" (Austen, 1995, 32, my emphasis).

The idea that Lady Elliot is transferred onto Wentworth is reinforced toward the novel's end by Judith Butler's Freudian point in *Bodies That Matter* about the relationship of love and illness: that "narcissism must give way to objects, and that one must finally love in order not to fall ill" (Butler, 1993, 63). Butler reasons that if "one must either love or fall ill," "then perhaps the sexuality that appears as illness is the insidious effect of . . . such a censoring of love." Perhaps the "very production of the *morphe* can be read as an allegory of prohibited love, the *incorporation* of loss" (Butler, 1993, 65). Upon reading Wentworth's impassioned love letter—that is, upon *devouring* Wentworth's words with her eyes—Anne needs to recover. Her happiness is mixed with "agitation." She is desubjectified: "The absolute necessity of seeming like herself produced then an immediate struggle." "[O]bliged to plead indisposition," Anne "looked very ill," in need of "cure" (Austen, 1995, 158). The narrator confirms the idea that upon absorbing Wentworth's love Anne falls ill (instead of in love) by commenting that Mrs. Musgrove, who thinks Anne needs a doctor, "thought only of one sort of illness" (Austen, 1995, 159). Other types of illness (besides physical illness) exist, in other words—one of which seems to have struck Anne down. She, we are told, "is rather done for this morning [mourning?], and must not go so far without help"; and for *this reason*, because she needs to refuel her mourning, Anne is "more exquisitely happy, perhaps, in their reunion" (Austen, 1995, 160).

"Re-union"? This term is peculiar here. It helps us to realize that Anne is by no means completing mourning by marrying Wentworth, since Anne had not earlier been united with him. In a sense the entire novel hinges on their earlier lack of union, the breach between them. Union with Wentworth, however, may serve, as I am suggesting, to *re*unite Anne with her earliest lost love object, and all that she stands for. Uncannily, in the end Anne "was at home again." Having redoubled, and therefore reinvigorated, her encryptment, Anne can now subside into its comforts: the "painful part[s] of the morning [mourning?]" have been dissipated by conversation. Approaching Louisa's "poor corpse-like figure," Anne had grown "steadfast and fearless in the thankfulness of her enjoyment" (Austen, 1995, 163). Now Anne can live thankfully in "the dread of a future war" as "all that could dim her sunshine" (Austen, 1995, 168). She can indulge anxiously in the constant anticipation of war and death, and therefore in the light of a dimmed sun, in proximity to the Thing, "a light without representation: . . . an imagined sun, bright and black at the same time" (Kristeva, 1989, 13).

In a way Austen's *Persuasion* intimates that melancholic desire is the desire of the Other—just as Lacan states over and over that desire is the desire of the Other—since Anne's "desire" is, like her mother's, to fuse with death. By uniting with Wentworth, I have argued, Anne reunites with Lady Elliot, *and* she also achieves the "desire" of Lady Elliot, insofar as Lady Elliot's life drive was weak, and so it might be said that she desired death. In fact, because Anne seems to have been in a state of melancholic mourning for Wentworth for approximately the past eight years, it is as if *he* returns as a living corpse, with whom Anne then unites. In this connection—of Wentworth to a corpse and in turn to Lady Elliot, who is now of course herself a corpse—it is intriguing that after Anne's eyes devour the words of Wentworth's letter and she seems ill (Mrs. Musgrove says, "She must not walk" [Austen, 1995, 159]), Mrs. Musgrove invokes elliptically Louisa's "poor corpse-like figure" by having to be assured that "there had been no fall in the case; that Anne had not, at any time lately, slipped down, and got a blow on her head" (Austen, 1995, 159). But we know that limited Mrs. Musgrove only thinks in physical, and not psychoanalytic, terms and that we are not to follow in her footsteps, all of which implies that perhaps a fall like Louisa's, only on a psychic level, *has* occurred, making Anne too, psychically, a kind of "poor corpse-like figure."

Persuasion is powered by a drive more forceful than persuasion, a drive beyond the persuasion/*Persuasion* principle. Even as it manages to continue to unfold (about the narrative style, Weissman writes: "Patterns of doubleness and refrain have taken the place of progressive momentum, creating a cadence exquisitely suited to this heroine's step" [Austen, 1995, 312]), the novel heads toward death/the Real. (This in a way should come as no surprise, given that Austen, suffering from Addison's disease as she writes, is herself about to metamorphose into a corpse.)

My argument, then, is that Anne is in love with loss to be with her mother, to be like her, to be her. Being in love with loss leads Anne to exchange the usual urge to commit matricide for the urge to "put herself to death." For when matricide is hindered, the "violence of matricidal drive," as we know, inverts on the self. And in displacing in this manner the violence of her matricidal drive, Anne further sustains—clinches—the bond with Lady Elliot by suffering *as Lady Elliot did.*

Throughout *Persuasion,* Anne responds to events that ought to have been pleasurable with pleasure and pain, as if some form of pain must accompany her pleasure as a function of her need to deprive herself. "Modest, silent, without verbal or desiring bonds with others," writes Kristeva, the melancholic "wastes away by striking moral and physic blows against herself, which, nevertheless, do not give her sufficient pleasures" (Kristeva, 1989, 30). When Mary relates to Anne that Captain Wentworth found her "so altered he should not have known [her] again," Anne is initially mortified—she "fully submitted, in silent, deep mortification." Soon, however, Anne begins "to rejoice that she had heard" these words (Austen, 1995, 41). Immediately after Captain Wentworth peels Walter off Anne's back and neck, Anne is "perfectly speechless," and so unable to thank him. She imagines that he wishes to avoid her thanks and any conversation, which establishes a silence between them. Through this incident Anne has been given reason to hope; yet she is suffused with "painful agitation, as she could not recover from." On top of this, she feels shame for "being so nervous, so overcome by such a trifle" (Austen, 1995, 54). Likewise, when Wentworth arranges for a place for Anne in the Croft carriage, she minimizes the significance of his caring gesture, which enables her again to feel "emotions so compounded of pleasure and pain, that she knew not which prevailed" (Austen, 1995, 61). Later, when Anne runs into Wentworth in Bath, now knowing that he is not to be engaged to Louisa, and *he* is nonplussed—she realizes for the first time since their renewed acquaintance that she is "betraying the least sensibility of the two," so that "[s]he had the advantage of him"—still she experiences "agitation, pain, pleasure, a something between delight and misery" (Austen, 1995, 116).

Anne is seriously, self-destructively split, and even seems to know it: she advises herself that "one half of her should not be always so much wiser than the other half, or always suspecting the other of being worse than it was" (Austen, 1995, 116). When Anne and Captain Wentworth meet before the concert and speak about Lyme, Anne tells him, "The last few hours were certainly very painful." Then she waxes masochistic: "but when pain is over, the remembrance of it often becomes a pleasure. One does not love a place the less for having suffered in it . . ." (Austen, 1995, 122). Might not all Anne's misery in happiness and happiness in misery reflect her depressive state of ambivalence? As Kristeva elaborates:

According to classic psychoanalytic theory (Abraham, Freud, and Melanie Klein), depression, like mourning, conceals an aggressiveness toward the lost object, thus revealing the ambivalence of the depressed person with respect to the object of mourning. "I love that object," is what that person seems to say about the lost object, "but even more so I hate it; because I love it, and in order not to lose it, I imbed it in myself; but because I hate it, that other within myself is a bad self, I am bad, I am non-existent, I shall kill myself." The complaint against oneself would therefore be a complaint against another, and putting oneself to death but a tragic disguise for massacring an other. . . . the aggregate of these activities being based on the mechanism of *identification* (Kristeva, 1989, 11).

Anne punishes herself (for these psychic reasons) to keep the maternal object intact and protected, to guarantee maternal identification. In doing so, in fact, she doubles her identification with the (formerly unhappy) mother she possesses.

III.

This mirror-identification is almost obligatory, after reactions of complementarity (artificial gaiety, agitation, etc.) have failed. This reactive symmetry is the only means by which to establish a reunion with the mother—perhaps by way of sympathy. In fact there is no real reparation, but a mimicry, with the aim of continuing to possess the object (who one can no longer have) by becoming, not like it but, the object itself. This identification, which is the condition of the renouncement to the object and at the same time its conservation in a cannibalistic manner, is unconscious from the start.

—André Green, "The Dead Mother"

Kristeva's theory of melancholia takes us far in comprehending Anne Elliot's initial withdrawal from Wentworth and society as well as her later commitment to marriage, both of which preserve her maternal encryptment. Using André Green's "The Dead Mother," we can tighten the relation of theory to text, since he also explores the mother's psyche and discovers *her* depression. Green's "dead mother complex" is essentially about the preservation of an object loss in the form of a psychically dead mother who herself was or is *"absorbed by a bereavement.* The mother, for one reason or another, is depressed" (Green, 1983, 149), "psychically dead in the eyes of the young child in her care" (Green, 1983, 142).

Green moreover enhances our sense of the damage to Anne Elliot of having such a mother by writing that "The consequence of the real death of the [psychically dead] mother—especially when this is due to suicide—is extremely harmful to the child whom she leaves behind" (Green, 1983, 142). While Lady Elliot does not technically commit suicide, she appears to let herself lapse: only her "duties, her friends, and her children . . . attach[ed] her to life, and made it no matter of indifference to her when she was called on to quit them" (Austen, 1995, 4). The way the narrator puts Lady Elliot's modicum of desire to cling to life, as a matter of indifference, leaves the reader with a sense of Lady Elliot's verging on indifference. We know that she was, after a foolish infatuation, disappointed in love.

Green enumerates possible "precipitating factors" of the mother's depression. "[A]mong the principal causes of this kind of maternal depression, one finds the loss of a person dear to her: child, parent, close friend, or any other object strongly cathected by the mother. But it may also be a depression triggered off by a deception which inflicts a narcissistic wound: a change of fortune in the nuclear family or the family of origin, a liaison of the father who neglects the mother, humiliation, etc." (Green, 1983, 149). Hence we are provoked to wonder: When did the Elliot family finances begin to dwindle, to seem inadequate? When did the womanizing Sir Walter begin to express his attraction to other women, such as the lower-class, freckled, and therefore perhaps syphilis-carrying Mrs. Clay, who appears, toward the novel's end, to be Mr. Elliot's mistress?[1] Did Lady Elliot experience more than her share of humiliation, just as Anne does as a result of her father's crass treatment? Green adds to his list of what might trigger the dead mother's depression that "the most serious instance is the death of a child at an early age"; he mentions miscarriage. One of the first things we are told about Lady Elliot is that she had a still-born son, a fact that is featured on page one of *Persuasion*. Is this Lady Elliot's "secret" that needed to be "reconstructed by . . . analysis from minute indications" (Green, 1983, 149)?

The dead mother complex usually develops within an unstable triangulation: although the child may look to the father for salvation, "in reality, the father more often than not does not respond to the child's distress. The subject is thus caught between a dead mother and an inaccessible father" (Green, 1983, 150). Sir Elliot fits this paradigm snugly: he is more than inaccessible to Anne. She repels him; he is cruel to her. Moving from etiology to diagnosis: other features of the complex as well are specifically manifested in Anne's case. Green explains that "The feeling of impotence is evident. Impotence to withdraw from a conflictual situation, *impotence to love*, to make the most of one's talents, to multiply one's assets, or, when this does take place, a profound dissatisfaction with the results" (Green, 1983, 148, my emphasis). Anne obviously has trouble withdrawing from her early disagreement with Lady Russell over Wentworth; and her passivity accords with her impotence to love. Anne holds back from accepting multiple marriage proposals: from Wentworth, Charles Musgrove, and, in effect, Mr. Elliot.

Green lists "agitation, insomnia and nocturnal terrors" as methods of fighting off anxiety induced by the complex. "Agitation" is the precise word that Austen uses repeatedly to describe Anne's state. After reading Wentworth's love letter, Anne's "overpowering happiness" coexists with "fresh agitation" (Austen, 1995, 158). She is incapable of confidence, even after Wentworth's full written testimony of his inextinguishable passion for her: "her heart prophesied some mischance, to damp the perfection of her felicity" (Austen, 1995, 159). Upon walking with Wentworth and hearing full verbal testimony of his devotion, Anne's felicity is so "high-wrought" that she feels "obliged to find an alloy in some momentary apprehensions of its being impossible to last" (Austen, 1995, 163). And she feels "lively pain" in lacking a family "to receive and estimate [Wentworth] properly" (Austen, 1995, 167). I take such constant agitation, expressed in relation to the complex role of Wentworth in her psychic drama, as a sign of Anne's persistent ambivalence, as well as of her state of lack of lack.

Beyond agitation, for Green, is mirror-identification. The victim of the dead mother complex (similar to Kristeva's melancholic) identifies unconsciously with the "dead mother"—in order "to establish a reunion with the mother" (Green, 1983, 150–51). Hence the victim of the dead mother complex "recathect[s] the traces of the trauma," which is a psychoanalytic way of putting what I have illustrated—i.e., Anne's opening up to Wentworth as a possible husband after all. Anne realizes unconsciously that rather than usurp Lady Elliot's place in her psyche, Wentworth can galvanize the trauma.

Typically, an hysterical dissociation emerges in the victim of the dead mother complex between body and psyche; he/she shows little tenderness or sensuality. While sensuality is not something one expects to encounter in excess, if at all, in Austen's fiction, it is striking how rational Anne and Wentworth, now lovers, are at the end as they rehearse their mutual agonizing past—the very past required for (at least) Anne to enter the relationship, the only sort of past that could have facilitated the union and, in turn, the reunion (with Lady Elliot). Together they caress, instead of each other, the details of their masochistic routes to this stopping place. Seeming as melancholic as she was during the past eight years, Anne defends her (still diseased?) conscience. Anne's "love talk" is self-defense; what she defends is, of course, obedience to a maternal-surrogate.

> I must believe that I . . . was perfectly right in being guided by the friend whom
> you will love better than you do now. To me, she was in the place of a parent. . . .
> I mean, that I was right in submitting to her, and that if I had done otherwise,
> I should have suffered more in continuing the engagement than I did even in
> giving it up, because I should have suffered in my conscience (Austen, 1995,
> 164).

Originally, Anne yielded, as we know well, to the voice of the person "in the place of a parent" (Lady Russell); it makes sense, then, that for Anne to yield now, the person enabling her to yield—obviously, Wentworth—would also have to be "in the place of a parent." *Persuasion* could and would never be explicit about its dead mother complex. Yet an incestuous bond between Anne and Wentworth (like that between Emma and Knightley) is alluded to in the novel's description of Lady Russell's finding "little hardship in attaching herself as a mother to the man who was securing the happiness of her other child" (Austen, 1995, 166). Do Green's words not apply? "It is evident that one is witnessing an attempt to master the traumatic situation. But [this] attempt is doomed to fail" (Green, 1983, 153).

IV.

Jouissance *comes easily to the slave, and it will leave the work [of mourning?] in bondage.*

—Jacques Lacan, "Subversion of the Subject and the
Dialectic of Desire"

Austen's *Persuasion,* then, implies that melancholic desire is the desire of the Other; Lacan defines desire, likewise and in general, in these terms. "Indeed, it is quite simply . . . as desire of the Other that man's desire finds form"; "man's desire is the *désir de l'Autre*"; "it is *qua* Other that he desires (which is what provides the true compass of human passion)" (Lacan, 1977, 312). Lacan's desiring subject acknowledges a lack in the Other and thus acknowledges the desire of the Other. But desire is by no means jouissance. The subject's desire is, in fact, a defense, a prohibition, Lacan states, "against going beyond a certain limit in *jouissance*" (Lacan, 1977, 322). It is castration (and not plenitudinous jouissance) that governs such desire. For as Lacan concludes his last chapter of *Écrits,* "Subversion of the subject and dialectic of desire": "Castration means that *jouissance* must be refused, so that it can be reached on the inverted ladder (*l'échelle reversée*) of the Law of desire" (Lacan, 1977, 324). The phallus embodies "*jouissance* in the dialectic of desire" (Lacan, 1977, 319). Otherwise jouissance is forbidden, pathological.

In *The Lacanian Subject,* Bruce Fink conceptualizes "separation" as the result of the overlapping of two lacks: that of the subject and that of what he refers to as the "mOther." "The mOther must show some sign of incompleteness, fallibility, or deficiency for separation to obtain and for the subject to come to be as $, in other words, the mOther must demonstrate that she is a desiring (and thus also a lacking and alienated) subject, that she too has submitted to the splitting/barring action of language, in order for us to witness the subject's advent." The subject gains a "foothold" within a "divided parent," one whose desire is "ambiguous, contradictory, and in constant flux" but is in any case active (Fink, 1995, 53–54). The subject can then lodge his/her lack in the mOther's place of lack, attempting to fill it. But, to return to *Persuasion,* if Lady Elliot were depressed as well as erotically unfulfilled and inactive, having only very weak sources of contentment to keep her from being totally indifferent to dying, she might be seen as undivided, *lacking desire* rather than possessing the lack that her daughter could otherwise match or fill.

And just as Green places emphasis on triangulation, including of course an active paternal figure, to preclude or offset the dead mother complex, Lacan equates separation with the "paternal metaphor" or "paternal function." It is the mother's desire for the paternal figure that enables triangulation to take place: "Should the mother pay no attention to the father or other member of the household, granting him or her no importance, the mother-child relationship may never become triangulated. Or should the father . . . be unconcerned, tacitly allowing the [child-mother] unity to go undisrupted, a third term [the Name-of-the-Father] may never be introduced" (Fink, 1995, 56). Sir Walter Elliot, although presumably the object of Lady Elliot's desire during her early infatuation, fizzled out as a romantic partner: "Lady Elliot had been an excellent woman, sensible and amiable; whose judgment and conduct, if they might be pardoned the youthful infatuation which made her Lady Elliot, had never required indulgence afterwards." Lady Elliot's relation to her husband apparently turned more protective than anything else: she "had humoured, or softened, or concealed [Sir Walter's] failings, and promoted his real respectability for seventeen years" (Austen, 1995, 4). Having no concern about, or affection for, his daughter even after his wife's demise, "a conceited, silly father" (Austen, 1995, 4) submerged in his narcissism, Sir Walter was furthermore apt to have been unintrusive in, even oblivious to, his wife and daughter's bond. Reflecting such paternal egotism, Sir Walter's dressing-room, full of "large looking-glasses," makes Kellynch Hall a hall of literal mirrors (Austen, 1995, 84).

Fink unpacks two dominant meanings from Lacan's idea that desire is the desire of the Other: first, what we have said—that the Other's desire is the cause of the subject's desire—and, second, that the subject desires to *be* the object of the Other's desire. In the case of the melancholic, however, the problem is of course that the mOther fails to respond. Neglect and abandonment often take the place of desire/love. If the mOther is a "dead mother," her desire is nil, both for her child as well as in general. The child can neither be the object of the mOther's desire nor inherit desirousness from her.

It is only in a nonpsychoanalytic manner of speaking therefore that Green's dead mother would seem to have "desire." Psychoanalytically, Mrs. Elliot's urge or wish would need to be called, instead, a drive, a death drive.

As a result, what the subject suffering from the dead mother's complex accrues as her "desire," if desire is the desire of the mOther, is a death drive. In this case, we might say that the subject's desire is the jouissance of the mOther. Or, more accurately: the subject's jouissance is the jouissance of the mOther. Likewise, such a subject's objet a would be localized in a phantasmatic partner who arouses not the subject's desire (as Fink points out it usually does) but the subject's jouissance, which is what, as I have shown, Captain Wentworth eventually offers to Anne. Lacking lack, Lady Elliot provides such a model of jouissance for her daughter, who in turn anxiously lacks lack; consequently Anne herself acquiesces to the comforting plenitude of death, which in turn she discovers embodied in Captain Wentworth.

Persuasion is by no means the quintessential, or sole, literary illustration of the form of melancholia that I lay out in this chapter. It is for roughly these same reasons, to offer two quick examples beyond Austen, that the heroine of Marguerite Duras's *The Lover* and Ruthie in Marilynne Robinson's *Housekeeping* lack desire and drift in the direction of figures whose rapport with death is strong and compelling (the Chinese lover, in the case of Duras's girl; Sylvie in Robinson's novel). These heroines, too, have overidentified with, overcathected, abandoning mothers who lacked lack/desire. Helen in *Housekeeping*, like the girl's mother in *The Lover*, like Lady Elliot, lacks the lack that enables one to be a desiring subject, a mOther who demonstrates desirousness; they all, instead, pass on to their daughters a weakness for jouissance. "We too," writes the unnamed girl in *The Lover*, speaking of herself and her brothers, "have become strange, and the same sluggishness that has overtaken my mother has overtaken us too" (Duras, 1984, 26). "Their mother never knew pleasure" (Duras, 1984, 39). Instead, they admired, she relates, their "mother's knowledge" about "all that had to do with death" (Duras, 1984, 32). As a consequence, the girl's affair with the Chinese lover is "unto death"—"I asked him to do it again and again. Do it to me. And he did, did it in the unctuousness of blood." "It has been unto death" (Duras, 1984, 43). After Ruthie's mother, Helen, commits suicide in *Housekeeping* by methodically driving off a cliff into the lake, Ruthie fantasizes that her body inflates with water: "Say that the water and I bore the rowboat down to the bottom, and I, miraculously, monstrously, drank water into all my pores until the last black cranny of my brain was a trickle, a spillet" (Robinson, 1980, 162). Again, jouissance is the jouissance of the mOther.

Trauma, writes Fink, is apt to be "the child's encounter with the Other's desire." It can function as "the child's cause: the cause of his or her advent as subject and of the position the child adopts as subject in relation to the Other's desire" (Fink, 1995, 62–63). I am adding, on the model of Lacan's conception of desire, that instead of desirousness the child might psychically inherit an uncontrollable craving for a dangerous jouissance. What can be done? Fink contends that such fantasies must be traversed; the subject must subjectify the trauma, take "the traumatic event upon him or herself," and assume "responsibility for that jouissance" (Fink, 1995, 63).

I want to propose finally that literature about melancholic jouissance—predicated on, or catalyzed by, that of the depressed, psychically dead mother—can enable the traversal of such a crippling, underlying fantasy. For the literary text, *Persuasion* in this case, transforms the trauma into the dialectic of linguistic desire. The dead mother's jouissance manages to fuel narratives about the depressive's vulnerability to the mOther's jouissance, narratives that appear to readers in mourning and suffering from melancholia (as well as possibly to writers in such states) as reflections of their state, but they actually serve as encounters with an Other's desire. I did not betray my lost love object by reading this book, the reader assures herself/himself. In fact, I reencounter her here, restaging the trauma in effect, since this book does its best to represent her in all her fullness—one profound reason why literature of mourning and melancholia is seductive to a depressive. The narrative process, though, however weighed down by the encrypted object now swallowed by the text, can prove to be therapeutic as it lures the reader into what looks like, and certainly verges on, linguistic jouissance but instead refuses jouissance insofar as language necessarily accepts the losses it is founded on, insofar as castration is the condition of language, which necessarily submits to splitting and barring. The apparently reflective melancholic text produces an illusion, a misrecognition; the reader encounters much more than a mirror reflection of his/her state.

The melancholic *text*—e.g., *Persuasion* as well as *Emma*—renders the absent maternal figure amorphously present; it re-presents her. But, as Kristeva stresses, the newfound "object" is not the mother, or her representatives, but symbolization itself. Writing transferentially preserves at the same time as it masters, thus setting mourning in motion. "[L]anguage both performs and defends against the separation that it figures," writes Butler in *Bodies That Matter,* "as a result, any figuration of that loss will both repeat and refuse the loss itself" (Butler, 1993, 70). Now desire can thrive as desire of the Other, as the text demonstrates desirousness.

NOTE

1. Tony Tanner, in "In Between: *Persuasion,*" is persuaded that "a hint of syphilis must be intended." For Gowland's Lotion, "which Sir Walter recommends to Anne 'on the strength of its supposed benefits to Mrs Clay's freckles,' contained 'corrosive sublimate of mercury,' which 'had a particular connection with the old-fashioned treatment of syphilis' " (Austen, 1995, 255).

3

Tales of Beauty: Brookner's, Atwood's, and Drabble's "Feminine Symbolic"

In "[l]ooking over the list of those one could consider 'great melancholics' (Petrarch, Ficino, Tasso, Rousseau, Chateaubriand, Holderlin, De Quincey, Nerval, Dostoevsky, Walter Benjamin)," Juliana Schiesari, in *The Gendering of Melancholia,* is "struck by the notable absence of women, an absence that surely points less to some lack of unhappy women than to the lack of significance traditionally given women's grief in patriarchal culture" (Schiesari, 1992, 3). Worried about such nonrecognition of women's grief, Schiesari lambastes Kristeva for sustaining the gender split between melancholic male artists and depressed ordinary women, in part by including in *Black Sun* just one female melancholic artist, Marguerite Duras, and then attenuating Duras's artistic claim to gendered loss by placing Duras (alone) in an historicizing context, defined by the traumas of Hiroshima and Auschwitz.

One function of this chapter, in light of Schiesari's critique, is to defend Kristeva's theory of melancholia by supplementing her analysis in *Black Sun* with an examination of three contemporary women writers who produce what can be read as melancholic writing and thus achieve the symbolic status of male melancholic artists. The analyses that follow of *Look at Me* (Brookner), *Lady Oracle* (Atwood), and *Jerusalem the Golden* (Drabble) challenge Schiesari's contention that melancholia up to the present day has been "considered to be in excess of a purely normative state of depression; its discourse encodes male eros and male subjectivity" (Schiesari, 1992, 75), although surely it is the case that traditionally women's grief has been slighted. Schiesari herself fails to give not only Kristeva but also women artists (including Jane Austen) the credit they deserve for attributing profound significance to women's grief, for thereby altering the course of the represented history of melancholy, and for bestowing the prestige of an aestheticized melancholia on women. The women writers treated herein capture the glamour, the richness, the exquisite aristocratic quality of various forms of melancholia through its amenability to elegant labyrinthine style.

Yet even as they mark progress by aestheticizing a recognizably Kristevan pathological female melancholia, expressing female loss through literary technique, the women writers I take up here (again like Austen) draw out a specific liability of Kristeva's theory that Schiesari (who stresses Kristeva's self-hatred, misogyny, and matriphobia) happens to miss. To rehearse: one means by which Kristeva recommends that melancholic women enter the symbolic order—through "an other jouissance" effected by a partner, an Other, who invigorates the narcissistic object and displaces it, and who thereby enables "symbolic life" (Kristeva, 1989, 79)—invites an attachment to brutal men, to which the very pathology of melancholia renders women vulnerable in the first place. The women writers of this chapter diagnose a propensity on the part of the female melancholic to favor a domineering man, whom she psychically identifies with her lost and at least in this way neglectful, if not abusive, mother. That the cure for melancholia entails transferential duplication of the neglectful or abusive mother (as both my research and counseling of battered women intimate) poses a problem since the mother's illness-producing behavior is apt to have been cruel; it would seem that any duplication of her would have to duplicate it.

These writers, therefore, ask us to consider the social and cultural contexts in which women's melancholy is "worked out": what happens when the male Other (with whom, according to Kristeva, the melancholic woman unites to enter the symbolic order) takes up his culture's invitation to be domineering or abusive? They also expand our sense of the source of female melancholia by raising the possibility of a social/cultural etiology: why is the mother herself depressed and/or angry, neglectful, abusive? Inverting Jacqueline Rose's objection, in *Sexuality in the Field of Vision*, to the idea that "the social produces the misery of the psychic in a one-way process," since it "utterly divests the psychic of its own mechanisms and drives," the contemporary women writers of this essay inject the social into the psychic (Rose, 1986, 16).

And so we loop back to Schiesari: for Atwood and Drabble especially would seem to agree with Schiesari's general notion that "the lack of adequate integration into the symbolic that Kristeva associates with depression" may not be "the fault of the women involved but rather the fault of the extra-psychic structure found in the social hierarchy of a male-dominated symbolic order" (Schiesari, 1992, 89). Of course Kristevan theory it-self is not utterly asocial; on Schiesari's own account, a particular woman (such as Duras) may be thrown into a melancholia whose source is not en-tirely the woman but also a symbolic order whose issue, at one moment of history, was Hiroshima and Auschwitz. My specific quarrel with Kristeva, then—so that Austen, Brookner, Atwood, and Drabble not only reinforce Kristevan theory but also draw out its problematic implications—is that, with respect to the personal as opposed to the artistic cure, she may not fully apprehend the dangerous circularity of returning women to a patriarchal symbolic order that contributes to the production of female melancholia in the first place. And it is in realizing this that the best impetus of the artistic solution may reside.

Not only do the texts that follow lend the weight of "seriousness" to women's grief that Schiesari assumes is missing in the discourse of melan-cholia. But they (like Austen's novels) also gain weight in holding onto the melancholic object, and thereby put up some resistance to the patriarchal symbolic order, at the same time as they resist asymbolia, first, by being ar-tistic, linguistic, cultural productions (with the necessary access to a signify-ing economy) and, second, by issuing political warnings about melancholic women's vulnerabilities. By including such political content, Austen, Brookner, Atwood, and Drabble do more than merely supplement the list that Schiesari points to—of exclusively male writers whose expression of melancholia serves "as a *discursive and cultural practice* that has given men a cultural privilege in displaying and representing loss so as to convert it into a sign of privileged subjectivity" (Schiesari, 1992, 68). Novels by these women might be said to constitute Schiesari's "feminine symbolic," which "may indeed be a way to re-inscribe women's losses through another type of representation" (Schiesari, 1992, 77), allowing women to express their losses without aggravating them. As Schiesari laments, "women's melan-cholia or depression is thought of as a problematic access to a phallic order that is fundamentally (and uncritically) viewed as desirable" (Schiesari, 1992, 93). What Schiesari prefers instead the authors of this essay move toward putting into effect: "the voicing of women's depression, not as some personal failure to 'differentiate' but as the very site of mourning, or expres-sion, and of community" (Schiesari, 1992, 93).

To pick up on the idea of community: as the focus on aestheticized male melancholia shifts to aestheticized female melancholia, it is easier than it once was to keep in mind that not everyone has access either to melancholia or especially to its aesthetic expression—that it is the privilege of those with the leisure to revel in loss and possibly even to capitalize on it. Part of the "beauty" of Atwood and Drabble's representations of the daughter's fraught overattachment to a neglectful or abusive mother is that they fold in the mother's plugged-up pain. At the same time: although I feel compelled to raise the issue of class by calling attention to a lack of access on the part of economically disadvantaged women to a strategic, or at some level enjoyable, melancholia, I would not want to depreciate such a claim on the part of more "privileged" women. I say this not so much because psychic pain can be excruciating but primarily because the insertion of women's melancholic writing into culture—homeopathically attenuating melancholia while expressing it, unlike Kristeva's other jouissance, which does not so much attenuate melancholia as renovate it—helps to do the work of brightening the black sun hovering over privileged and underprivileged women alike.

I. BROOKNER'S MELANCHOLIC MATERNAL WEB

Why are these patients overwhelmed with self-reproach and inhibitions, why are they subject to exhausting ruminations, physical diseases, constant depression, fatigue, and anxiety? Why do they suffer from disinterest in objectal love? What dulls their creativity and makes them sigh nostalgically: "I might if I could . . . "? It is very rare that the connection between their state of mind and the originating event becomes conscious. To effect this realization is the task of analysis. "He pursued me intensely and I wanted to marry him. But an inner voice said to me: 'You would then have to abandon your dead.' This sad and insistent voice would return and for a long time I heeded its call. The world was an immense desert for me."

—Maria Torok, "The Illness of Mourning and the Fantasy of the
Exquisite Corpse"

Called "a latter-day Jane Austen," Anita Brookner has produced several novels about women's depression and the power of writing to contain it. *Look at Me, Hotel du Lac, The Misalliance,* and *A Closed Eye,* for example, narrate variations on a struggle with melancholia—whose etiology is maternal abandonment and/or neglect. ("The trouble was obviously psychic; the nurse . . . seemed to think the fault lay in a lack of mothering.")[1] Brookner's heroines are graceless losers who agonize over ways of compensating for their loss. They are submerged in gloom, forever subject to "an implosive mood that walls itself in and kills [them] secretly, very slowly, through permanent bitterness, bouts of sadness . . . " (Kristeva, 1989, 29). Brookner's depressives refuse to negotiate, to say, "I consent to lose her" (Kristeva, 1989, 43). Unable to negate their loss, they suspend that negation and collapse back onto the real object of loss, to which they painfully remain attached.

Brookner's heroines consequently latch onto male disciplinarians as if that were a mode of remaining in bondage to the wounding mother; hence this potential bridge to worldly power, to liberation from maternal suffocation, turns out to be sadomasochistic. Brookner's novels reinforce the idea that a woman who loses her mother, especially if that mother subjected her (making her "subjectivity" a function of her attachment to the mother), may be drawn to an abusive erotic partner: having absorbed her mother, the daughter through this strategy turns the usual matricide against herself. One theorist who issues a similar warning is Maria Torok—who, along with Nicolas Abraham, first coined the term encrypt and developed cryptology as a major theoretical area. And it is also the case that Kristeva herself notes that her patient Anne showed manic excitement over "torture that took hold of her in her relationship with her mother and sometimes with her partner in between her depressions" (Kristeva, 1989, 57). In *The Shell and the Kernel,* Torok considers the little girl's difficulty in divesting the mother of her prerogatives, in evicting the mother, as she identifies with both parents. Torok speaks of this difficulty in conjunction with "a special imagoic configuration: a demanding, castrated, and jealous Mother; a Father who is envied, depreciated, and magnified at the same time." When a woman burdened by such imagoes approaches married life, explains Torok, her "affective life remains immature"; she is apt to replay the anal relationship to the mother with her spouse: the "benefit derived from this position is not having to come face to face with the maternal imago and thus being able to avoid the deep-seated anguish at tearing oneself free from her dominion." Women, as a result, accept relationships of dependency on men, "on the imagoic heirs of the anal mother" (Torok, 1994, 70–71).[2]

Brookner's *Look at Me* opens self-sabotagingly with a piece of wisdom that the sheer existence of the novel seems to contradict—"It is wiser, in every circumstance, to forget, to cultivate the art of forgetting. To remember is to face the enemy" (Brookner, 1983, 5).[3] The heroine's dejection and consequent craving for invulnerability—good luck, good health, good looks, no terror, and therefore cancellation of the past—result from her inability to complete mourning for (to "forget") her "enemy": her now literally dead but psychically encrypted mother. Frances comments matter-of-factly that after her mother's death she was "dry-eyed and stony-faced, glad that the ordeal was over" (Brookner, 1983, 26). Her housekeeper, Nancy (a mother surrogate, inherited from her mother), thought that Frances's behavior after the death was "ruthless": she moved about stiffly and practically, stripping her mother's bed, cleaning up, as if nothing had occurred. Yet Frances reflects back on her "terror" over her ailing mother's spasms—and her dread of her ailing mother's wish to kiss her goodnight. Her fear of her mother's death was so enormous that her death had to be denied, as it was at the time and still is: Frances has "changed nothing in the flat"; the nights are "just the same," as is the food. She "fingers the gold brocade curtains, with their tasselled gold tie-backs, and . . . think[s] how [her] mother used to stand at the window, waiting for [her] father to come home. And then [she] knows that [she] will stay" (Brookner, 1983, 27). "Like a commemorative monument," as Torok writes in "The Illness of Mourning," "the incorporated object betokens the place, the date, and the circumstances in which desires were banished . . . ; they stand like tombs in the life of the ego" (Torok, 1994, 114).

The end of *Look at Me* is as frozen as its beginning. After a terrifying walk back through an "endless tunnel" clearly symbolic of a birth canal (it is as if Frances is wading through "viscous substance" [Brookner, 1983, 170]), melancholic Frances collapses into a "state of total regression" (Brookner, 1983, 177), "a mood of lethargy that was almost one of mourning" (Brookner, 1983, 180). But not exactly: having consumed the love object she misses, Frances engages in incomplete mourning or, we might say, *"refuse[s] to mourn,"* shunning "the consequences of mourning even though [her] psyche is fully bereaved. Incorporation is the refusal to acknowledge the full import of the loss, a loss that, if recognized as such, would effectively transform [her]" (Torok, 1994, 127). Instead of a transformative recognition of loss, Frances inhabits her dead mother's flat so fully as her mother that she dons her mother's white nightgown and sleeps in her bed: "It felt quite natural for [her] to be there" (Brookner, 1983, 190). Mrs. Hinton died at home, no doubt in the very bed in which Frances now sleeps. Like Kristeva's patient Helen, Frances has "assimilated her [mother] into [herself]," possessed her, held "her within . . . so as never to be separated from her" (Kristeva, 1989, 75). Her mother is enwombed/entombed in Frances; and at the end Frances reenwombs/reentombs herself (traveling back through the "endless tunnel") in her mother, a double psychic invagination. Torok's insights into the subject of entombment fit Frances perfectly. Words of grief cannot be uttered, scenes of grief recalled, or tears shed— "everything will be swallowed along with the trauma that led to the loss. Swallowed and preserved. Inexpressible mourning erects a secret tomb inside the subject" (Torok, 1994, 130).

Kristeva's Helen is a similar case of "cannibalistic solitude," of "the body as tomb," of "omnipotent devouring" (Kristeva, 1989, 71). Helen consequently undergoes a period of frigidity, which Kristeva explains as "an imaginary capture by the frigid woman of a maternal figure anally imprisoned and transferred to the cloaca-vagina" that bars anyone else from entering (Kristeva, 1989, 77). Frances Hinton, like most of Brookner's heroines, also seems impregnably virginal. Although she is romantically inclined toward Dr. James Anstey, she holds his hand "as confidently as a child holds the hand of its parent" (Brookner, 1983, 95). She is in no hurry for sex, although she expects eventually to do "whatever was demanded" (Brookner, 1983, 98). That Frances resists the idea of sex at the Maida Vale flat—suffused with her dead mother's presence—is a glaring confirmation that her blockage is the result of an incorporated mother. Given what dwells within her, weighing her down and filling her up, the act can occur only on demand; any fulfillment of desire it might bring is not a consideration, for it would be a potentially traumatic ripping out of a deeply embedded "maternal Thing." Kristeva writes that the partner capable of dissolving the mother imprisoned in the melancholic woman acts "neither the father's part, ideally rewarding his daughter, nor the symbolic stallion's." Yet it is "by means of a phallic violence" (Kristeva, 1989, 79) that Kristeva imagines him outwardly displacing the mother; and it makes sense that conquering the all-consuming, death-bearing mother would entail a blow of some sort. Perhaps the purgative effect of phallic violence helps explain why so many women abandoned by mothers (in literature at least) seek, or accept, abusive lovers. (This pattern also turns up in the films *Breaking the Waves* and *Under the Skin*.) Still, the membrane between phallic violence that "destroys the bad but also bestows and honors" (Kristeva, 1989, 79) and purely destructive phallic violence—that sustains, or even deepens, the wound—is permeable. Frances Hinton seems to have trouble with this distinction twice. In her first romantic relationship, she was debased, "enjoyed precisely because she was humiliated" (Brookner, 1983, 122), caught in a cycle of desire and contempt, and rose to the cruelty of it all. Although she claims not to love her new beau James "in the fatal sense"—"he was not a drug, an obsession, like that time of which [she] never speak[s]" (Brookner, 1983, 121)—her fondness for him is linked to his harsh treatment of her. James strikes her as a cruel man: "His general bearing was that of an army officer" (Brookner, 1983, 73). His hands look angry; his tie is severe. Frances sits "on the ground at his feet[,] . . . and his large authoritative hand would stroke [her] face and hair" (Brookner, 1983, 90). "James, in his long, severe overcoat, [thrills] her with delight" (Brookner, 1983, 93).

Yet for all James's "phallic violence" (after he attempts to make love to Frances, her dress is creased, her "collar slightly torn," her "mouth swollen and open, the unaccustomed lipstick smeared all over it" [Brookner, 1983, 127]), he fails to possess her. Prior to his attempt, instead of sitting on a stool that Frances pulls up in front of the fire for him, James occupies her mother's chair, as if he senses what is at stake. Moments later, James recognizes a problem: "Not with you, Frances. Not with you" (Brookner, 1983, 127). No explanation—such as, because of their fidelity to the Thing that points them toward Thanatos, depressives resist Eros—is proferred. The presexual, lightly sadomasochistic relationship that Frances and James maintain facilitates Frances's self-punishment according to the depressive's paradoxical logic: I love the lost object, and therefore I hate it; but in order to retain it, I enclose it in myself; and since it is bad, I become bad. James keeps Frances's wound blissfully festering. To Abraham and Torok, it is, in fact, Freud's "recurrent image of an open wound that is said to attract the whole of a counter-cathecting libido . . . the wound the melancholic attempts to hide, wall in, and encrypt" that epitomizes melancholia (Torok and Abraham, 1994, 135). Yet once sexual advances are made, *Look at Me* implies, the sadistic partner and incorporated mother no longer cooperate but compete for the body of the melancholic woman.

The alternative indication, as physicians put it, is always art. Kristeva proposes that the "artist consumed by melancholia," fighting to overcome the death-bearing mother, mounts a relentless campaign against the "symbolic abdication" blanketing him/her (Kristeva, 1989, 9). She points in particular to "poetic form"—melody, rhythm, semantic polyvalency, the decomposing and recomposing of signs—as a possible " 'container' . . . able to secure an uncertain but adequate hold over the Thing" (Kristeva, 1989, 14). Insofar as literary creation "bears witness to the affect," through the transposition of "affect into rhythms, signs, forms" (Kristeva, 1989, 22), it may help control sadness. To write, to name suffering, exalt it, dissect it "into its smallest components—that is doubtless a way to curb mourning" (Kristeva, 1989, 97). Frances Hinton herself suggests that full-fledged melancholics are gripped by an affliction beyond words, so that her own creative writing along with the amorously poetic *Look at Me* itself testifies that the worst stages of the syndrome have been surpassed. Indeed, Frances uses her writing "to be hard": "to recompose events, to make them sharper, funnier, than they really were" (Brookner, 1983, 44). She spares no feelings but her own, writing to enhance her lot. By the end she works, with pen and notebook, at recovery in the form of revenge: she wants to return to the group that ostracized her only to "make notes for a satirical novel" (Brookner, 1983, 184). The words pour out; she jazzes things up, plays for laughs, seeking fortitude that compensates for humiliation. No apparent crisis of the signifier here.

Frances's writing—like the ponderously delayed narrative of Austen's *Emma* and the lyricism of *Persuasion*—is nevertheless as much an act of allegiance to the mother as it is a means of detachment from her. Theorizing melancholia, in fact, *Look at Me* makes writing-as-homeopathic-antidote one of its subjects. Now representing "the burden of [her] solitude" (Brookner, 1983, 53) and in this way keeping her mother close, Frances's writing had once been a pleasure for her mother to hear read aloud. Her mother's bedroom—where Frances and her mother coalesce at the end—provides the context in which she converts her lost hopes into language. The last voice of the text, uttering the words "My darling Fan" that inspire Frances to pick up her pen and start writing (presumably the novel we have at this instant finished reading), is that of her mother who, wide-eyed, used to say, " 'My darling Fan' . . . 'I think you have a gift.' . . . [and who] encouraged [Frances] to write it all down" (Brookner, 1983, 16). Frances laments that, since her mother died, she has no one with whom to converse about her writing process. To *conquer* her need to write—Frances's "penance for not being lucky" (Brookner, 1983, 84)—then, would appear to be a way of divorcing herself from what she has lost. Writing, the "enemy of forgetfulness," as the text in a depressive refrain keeps reminding us, is (not always undesirable) punishment.[4]

Look at Me seems balanced precariously on the border between negation (of loss) that pries open sign systems (the novel as therapeutic entry into the symbolic) and a refusal to complete mourning that disavows negation by overloading signs with affects—ambiguous, repetitious, alliterative, musical, even at times nonsensical—to the point that language devotes itself to accessing the unnameable (the novel as poetry of penance on the verge of collapse). It contains, in this respect, a fort/da motion that, as Madelon Sprengnether describes little Ernst's fort/da game, "institutionalizes both the act of renunciation and the impulse toward regression that inheres in it" (Sprengnether, 1990, 135).[5] Frances writes to murder time, locked—like the text—in an eternal cycle effected by the almost inconceivable *mise en abyme* ending that points to its beginning and epiphanizes the entire book: "A voice says, 'My darling Fan.' I pick up my pen. I start writing" (Brookner, 1983, 192). She memorializes literarily a regression, verging on asymbolia. Still, intricate writing is being spun out, by Frances and especially by Brookner, despite the fact that, as Sokolsky elaborates: "Melancholy seems to harbor a revulsion against narrative: there is nothing to say, or no point in trying to say it. The great loss or grief the melancholic has suffered cannot be eased by rehearsing it. All efforts to persuade one that anything but an irredeemably lost past matters are regarded with wonder or disdain. The only audience who counts—the one whose loss has precipitated the melancholy—cannot or will not hear the protest that without it is not worth mounting. . . . to recount one's loss would be to vitiate or disperse it" (Sokolsky, 1994, 129–30). Avoiding such vitiation or dispersion while simultaneously "protesting" (i.e., announcing her pain), Frances/Brookner has devised a way of writing publicly for the only audience who counts.

Brookner depicts melancholia as self-perpetuating, as turning "cures" back into nutrition for the disease, as an endless maternal web: the more furiously her heroines spin, the more entangled they seem to get. Yet, regardless of this apparent futility, both as an outgrowth and an expression of melancholia's interminable quality, elegant writing gets produced, the melancholia of women engrossingly articulated. Writing, given its own interminability, turns out to be well suited to reproduce and embody the illness as a way of grappling with loss. If the cause is, in Schiesari's words, "to give the depression of women the value and dignity traditionally bestowed on the melancholia of men," Brookner furthers it (Schiesari, 1992, 93). Brookner recuperates loss aesthetically, achieving as a female artist the very symbolic triumph that Kristeva attributes to her (genderless) melancholic artist, and that Schiesari's male melancholic artist achieves—through an oscillation that both posits and conquers maternal loss. Like Freud's fort/da game (understood as an unending progressive/regressive movement, rather than as pure mastery), writing enables the requisite preservation of loss as a means of achieving liberation from it: "To remember is to face the enemy" (Brookner, 1985, 5).

II. PREMATURE SOCIAL/CULTURAL MATRICIDE

I shall not be discussing here the psychical consequences of the real death of the mother, but rather that of an imago which has been consti-tuted in the child's mind, following maternal depression, brutally trans-forming a living object, which was a source of vitality for the child, into a distant figure, toneless, practically inanimate, deeply impregnating the cathexes of certain patients whom we have in analysis, and weighing on the destiny of their object-libidinal and narcissistic future.

—André Green, "The Dead Mother"

Like Brookner, who presents melancholia as predominantly a psychic prob-lem, whose genesis can be traced to the mother (Thing), Margaret Atwood and Margaret Drabble too focus on wounds inflicted by the mother that result in their heroines' fascination with self-destructive behavior. However, both of these novelists also take into account specific social/cultural condi-tioning that leads the mother to mistreat her daughter, which is not to say that they abandon a psychological etiology. Neither Atwood nor Drabble falls into the trap that Jacqueline Rose describes of choosing between, and therefore polarizing, the social and the psychic. Avoiding a monolithic ex-planation that would render melancholia a simple reflection of either psy-chic or social conditions, Atwood's and Drabble's novels simultaneously point to the deep psychosexual impact of compassionless, contemptuous mothers on their daughters—lack of self-regard that at times produces de-sire for punishment—and socioeconomic factors that can set such a cycle in motion, as well as make it turn vicious.

Lady Oracle begins after the mock death of its depressed heroine, who has feigned her own drowning to "start being another person entirely" (At-wood, 1976, 18). This is Joan's most extravagant act as an escape artist: "the real romance of [Joan's] life was . . . entering the embrace of bondage, slithering out again" (Atwood, 1976, 367)—only to reenter. For repeatedly in *Lady Oracle*, potential escape routes from Joan's mother turn out to be a widening of Frances's (her mother's, her beloved enemy's) net. Joan has unconsciously arranged it so that even revenge against her mother ends up pleasing her or at least preserving her dominance. Because Joan's love for her mother—"could she see I loved her? I loved her but the glass was between us, I would have to go through it. I longed to console her. . . . I would do what she wanted" (Atwood, 1976, 362)—is not reciprocated, Joan embeds Frances within herself so as not to lose her. In André Green's terms, she "nourish[es] the dead mother, to maintain her—perpetually embalmed" (Green, 1980, 162); in Joan's terms, "She'd never really let go of me because I had never let her go" (Atwood, 1976, 363). But the lack of reciprocity makes the embedded object "a bad self." And so, following the logic of the depressive based on her identification with the maternal object, Joan reasons, "I am bad, I am nonexistent, I shall kill myself" (Kristeva, 1989, 11)—which in a sense she does several times by cancelling, and then reproducing, her identity.

That the modes by which Joan attempts to retaliate against Frances end up being self-destructive forms of allegiance to her, allowing the forbidding mother to thrive within the cowering daughter, is borne out in *Lady Oracle* by Joan's alimentary, sexual, and verbal appetites. Her mother's attitude toward her weight is initially presented as unforgiving. At thirteen, Joan is "eating steadily, doggedly, stubbornly, anything [she] can get. The war between [herself] and [her] mother is on in earnest; the disputed territory is [her] body" (Atwood, 1976, 73). Otherwise making her miserable, Joan's considerable weight is her "refutation," her "victory" over her mother; and as such, it gives her "a morose pleasure" (Atwood, 1976, 78). Fighting with her mother one day, though, Joan is struck by the idea that Frances has determined even Joan's only weapon against her, when Frances asks, " 'What have I done to make you behave like this?' " (Atwood, 1976, 94). Joan is annoyed that her mother appears to be "taking all the credit for herself," and thinks defensively, "surely I was behaving like this not because of anything she had done but because I wanted to" (Atwood, 1976, 94). Frances undermines Joan's agency originally by producing Joan's ostensibly rebellious reaction and then later by egging her on. At the end she tries to spoil Joan's diet by leaving cookies and pies around so that Joan realizes that "in a lesser way she had always done this" (Atwood, 1976, 136). It is after Joan's announcement that, upon losing eighteen more pounds, she is moving out, as if dissolving herself so that there will be nothing left for her mother to control, realizing now that the excess was created precisely as something to contain, that Frances stabs Joan in the arm with a paring knife. Then Joan acts "as if [she] herself had inflicted the wound" (Atwood, 1976, 137). For she is determined to blanket her mother's ferocity toward her, as well as fused with her mother, and so dedicated to self-annihilation. André Green's work on the psychically dead mother again seems applicable. He discusses mirror identification with the object, "a mimicry, with the aim of continuing to possess the object (who one can no longer have) by becoming, not like it but, the object itself" (Green, 1980, 151). The subject conserves the "dead" mother through a kind of psychic cannibalism. (It makes perfect sense at least theoretically that Green was Kristeva's training analyst.)

Joan's attempts to find compensation for her unloving mother in an erotic attachment backfire by entangling her in abusive relationships that cement the masochistic position in which her mother placed her. Joan's mother warns her so adamantly about "lurking pervert[s]," "exhibitionists," and "bad men" (Atwood, 1976, 54) that it seems plausible that Frances ironically instills in Joan a rebellious desire for them. "Bad men," to whom Joan turns to thwart her mother, in turn imitate Frances in damaging Joan. As a girl walking to Brownies, Joan almost hopes "that the bad man would really come up out of the ravine. . . . Even my mother would be sorry" (Atwood, 1976, 62). But when the "daffodil man" actually emerges and unveils his flaccid flesh and Joan is later rescued either by the same or another mysterious man, it is Joan who is in for two complementary doses of torture: fear of men *and* violence from her enraged mother, who slaps her across the face, apparently for dallying.

Two of the men Joan hooks up with (the Polish Count and the Royal Porcupine) may as well be figures in her costume gothics (as an escape artist, she creates escapist art), centered on the ravishment of women by rapacious villain-heroes. The third (Arthur), whom she marries, actually turns up in her writing, his name occasionally slipping in metaleptically as a substitute for Lord Redmond, who is literally a lady killer. Two of Joan's lovers (the Count and Arthur) are tidy, methodical, dictatorial. Even the Royal Porcupine (drawn aesthetically to dead animals), whose fantastic qualities are meant to counter Arthur's sobriety, eventually becomes openly hostile to Joan. Revealing an ominous repetition compulsion, all three relationships sustain Joan's warped bond with her mother. In criticizing Joan's clothes and writing, making her exceedingly self-conscious, trying to make her feel like a village idiot, and reaping pleasure from her defeats, Arthur especially seems to reembody Frances.

Joan knows that the pulp fiction she writes "exploit[s] the masses, corrupt[s] by distracting, and perpetuate[s] degrading stereotypes of women as helpless and persecuted" (Atwood, 1976, 34). Still, she needs her trashy prose to keep her mother near but under control: she longs "for the simplicity of that world, where . . . wounds were only ritual ones" (Atwood, 1976, 316). It is for this reason—aesthetic sublimation—that Charlotte (Joan's heroine) finds herself *"wishing that his hand had remained on her throat just a moment longer"* (Atwood, 1976, 144), that all the Lady Redmonds are excited by the deadly maze (there must be temptations, threats, wounds, albeit ritualized), and that *Lady Oracle* itself is a maze—Atwood's version of Kristeva's "poetic form" capable of transposing affect into rhythms and signs. Like the female masochism providing the sublimated subject matter of Joan's costume gothics, the polyphonic configuration of *Atwood's* novel—comprised of present time, various past times, gothic romances, dreams, daydreams, and spiritual visions—restores the maternal Thing, in discontinuous narrative form, capturing the "black sun's incandescence." "Together," Joan writes of her mother and herself, "we would go down the corridor into the darkness" (Atwood, 1976, 362). Joan's/Atwood's plunge into the maternal abyss, the darkness at the end of the tunnel, enacted paradoxically for the sake of excavation in the form of representation, results in an aesthetic containment of female melancholia. Psychic disturbances must be transformed through *"linguistic activity,"* Kristeva reiterates in *New Maladies of the Soul*, "into a form of sublimation or into an intellectual, interpretive, or transformational activity" (Kristeva, 1995, 29). At the same time—moving beyond the parameters of Kristeva's theory of black sun, as well as Green's theory of the psychically encrypted dead mother—*Lady Oracle* examines what catalyzes Joan's mother's cruelty toward her daughter, which in turn catalyzes Joan's attraction to harsh men. And the novel's finding is, again, the cruelty of men or, culturally speaking, the patriarchal ideology of a fifties-style marriage and family. Joan's mother's "terrible anger" is expressed in the razor blade sharpness with which she cuts out of her photograph album the faces of Joan's father and a "white-flannelled man" to whom she was "more or less engaged." Frances appears "young and pretty, laughing gaily . . . , clutching the arms of her headless men" (Atwood, 1976, 201). She only becomes a "monster" (Atwood, 1976, 70) after being incarcerated in the Delacourt "plastic-shrouded tomb from which there was no exit" (Atwood, 1976, 201). In "The Dead Mother," Green correspondingly illustrates the brutal alteration of the maternal imago, before which "there is an authentic vitality present in the subject, which comes to a sudden halt, remaining seized from then on in the same place," by noting photos—only of "the young baby in the family album," which "show him to be gay, lively, interested, carrying much potentiality, whereas later snapshots show the loss of this initial happiness." In both cases, "love has been lost at one blow" (Green, 1980, 150)—Green concentrating on its loss for the child, Atwood on its loss for the mother.

Frances's monstrosity grows after she is pressured to marry a man who impregnated her, argues her out of an abortion, but then abandons her during the pregnancy as well as the child's (Joan's) first five years, for a military career. Joan even realizes the likelihood that her mother regards her "as a reproach" because Frances had nothing more to do with her life than redecorate her bedroom, throw insipid parties, take odd jobs. "She used to say that nobody appreciated her, and this was not paranoia. Nobody did appreciate her, even though she'd done the right thing, she had devoted her life to us, she had made her family her career as she had been told to do. . . . My mother would say that my father didn't love her, and I believed my mother" (Atwood, 1976, 200). While Green shows no interest in the social roots of the "dead" mother's behavior, again he makes a relevant point: that often the subject (as we saw in *Persuasion*) is "caught between a dead mother and an inaccessible father, . . . because he leaves the mother-child couple to cope . . . alone" (Green, 1980, 150). Unmistakably an absent man, Joan's father may even be a murderer (the text raises the possibility that he murdered Joan's mother, thus literalizing hypothetically the metaphor that he/men/the system "killed" her). Atwood gives the mother-daughter sadomasochistic cathexis a cultural footing: Joan cannot commit "matricide," since in a sense culture has beaten her to it.

Blaming the stunted growth of the daughter's subjectivity on the mother's patriarchal maternal role, Irigaray, in "And the One Doesn't Stir without the Other," puts Atwood's ideas into lyrical theory. The daughter swallows ice with her mother's milk, becomes more captive the more she loves, feels engulfed, all because the frantic mother cannot afford to lose the sole proof of her life's worth. Irigaray's wise daughter comprehends that she too therefore risks being "abducted from [herself]. Immobilized in the reflection he expects of [her]" and "[t]rapped in a single function—mothering." Irigaray's moving last words capture a plea of all the female melancholics analyzed thus far: "what I wanted from you, Mother, was this: that in giving me life, you still remain alive" (Irigaray, 1981, 66–67). This is the melancholic daughter's plea in part because once the mother becomes a "dead mother" the daughter is subject to a paralyzing entombment. For, again turning to Green, the "*essential characteristic of this* [the child's] *depression is that it takes place in the presence of the object, which is itself absorbed by a bereavement*. The mother, for one reason or another, is depressed" (Green, 1980, 149).[6] Jouissance is again, therefore, the jouissance of the mOther.

Clara Maugham, in *Jerusalem the Golden*, regrets that her mother joined the ranks of the living dead. Hence Drabble follows Brookner and Atwood in proposing a writing solution to depression; also like Atwood, Drabble looks hard at the social/cultural roots of the mother's despair. She considers, in particular, constraints of class. Can a working-class daughter burdened by a "dead" mother afford to be blocked professionally, romantically, by a maternal encryptment? If not, what sort of delusory world must she, disavowing such entombment (too expensive a luxury), seek to enter?

Clara's very name signifies the poisoned state Mrs. Maugham was in at the time of Clara's birth, since it was bestowed maliciously ("Mrs. Maugham did not like the name any more than Clara") as penance for Clara's "existence and her sex" (Drabble 1967, 9). Mrs. Maugham continues to punish Clara in resenting Clara's academic achievements, disallowing her daughter pleasure and emotion, and refusing to acknowledge Clara's beauty. Guided by "many fixed and rigid rules" (Drabble, 1967, 53), she induces guilt and fear. Clara sums up the double bind that Mrs. Maugham has put her in when her mother offers a concession, a visit to Paris: "By letting me go, she is merely increasing her power, for she is outmartyring my martyrdom. I die from loss, or I die from guilt, and either way I die" (Drabble, 1967, 70). During and after college, Clara imagines her mother sucking her back to Northam, dragging at her sleeves and hems. Her visits home are infantilizing: they "reduce her to exactly the same stage of trembling, silent, frustrated anxiety that she had endured throughout her childhood" (Drabble, 1967, 97).

Clara nevertheless in the end evades the melancholia that her hopeless mother's overbearing treatment primes her to suffer. In part through her own recognition of, and delight in, her surprising physical beauty, as well as the charms of high culture (hymns, literature, academic life, travel, the Denhams), and the pursuit of men (mainly Gabriel Denham, married, inaccessible) who enable her to advance socially and culturally, Clara bypasses the melancholic's slough of despond. Clara "wished to feel herself attached to the world" (Drabble, 1967, 197); putting up a hard fight, she refuses to "live a living death," to have wounded flesh, "bleeding or cadaverized" (Kristeva, 1989, 4). Such a morbid scenario *is* represented, however, in *Jerusalem the Golden* by a nightmare Clara has of dying, thus collapsing Clara and her "dead" and dying mother (who at the time of the dream is hospitalized with a fatal cancer) and playing out the melancholic's wish for union with the death-bearing mother. But, in actuality, Clara wills "herself to survive, because she did not have it in her to die" (Drabble, 1967, 239). Here would appear to be a Kristevan success story.

Yet *Jerusalem the Golden* is by no means oblivious to the self-destruction that Clara seems bound to enact. Her dream of dying represents the melancholic's plunge not taken, but the melancholic's plunge *is* taken by Phillipa (Gabriel's wife), as if the novel were a dream and Phillipa a displacement of Clara. Burdened by an at times overpowering malaise, Phillipa finds herself, and can be found, weeping just about anywhere. She suffers equally from injustice and a broken nail: "she was so deeply wounded that pain came to her simply, as itself" (Drabble, 1967, 167). Regarding herself as a maimed member of a female line (Phillipa imagines her wounds reborn in, and reborne by, a daughter), as incommunicably distressed, Phillipa (rather than Clara) inherits Mrs. Maugham's deadness of tone. Mrs. Maugham greets Clara's announcement that she plans "to do French" with a grunt, "Suit yourself" (Drabble, 1967, 54), just as Phillipa, when faced with Gabriel's Parisian business trip, scarcely responds, "Go if you want. . . . It's all the same to me" (Drabble, 1967, 189). As if to underscore a *cultural* transmission of female suffering, the text again connects Mrs. Maugham and Phillipa when, in Paris, Clara grieves over her mother's ravaged life, and Gabriel drinks her tears in empathy, "for he too felt the weight of those empty, rolling, joyless years, years without hope and without pleasure, for they were his own wife's years unrolling there in Clara's eyes, and rolling down her face" (Drabble, 1967, 201).

Although a full account of Phillipa's distress is never offered (for all we know, she suffers from loss of the maternal Thing grounded in her biological mother), it is the woundedness of Phillipa's maternal body that is flaunted. Her "body was covered with scars, the blue-white scars of childbearing. And she had been stitched and sewn. She had been too narrow, and they had remade her badly" (Drabble, 1967, 170). Drabble's erasure of Phillipa's past leaves us to concentrate on her scars as the sign of entrapment, to reinvoke Irigaray, "in a single function—mothering." The text likewise features Mrs. Maugham's metamorphosis from sanguine to sour at the moment of marriage. Clara's premarital mother appears in a photograph smiling bravely, gaily, radiantly "with hope and intimacy," whereas her face has been seized with "rigid misery" by the time of the wedding photos. Mrs. Maugham's premarital exercise books are full of prose that seems to burst passionately into verse—"O let us seek a brighter world/ Where darkness plays no part" (Drabble, 1967, 227)—as if on a semiotic/symbolic seesaw, gracefully poised. But married life yanks the poetry out of Mrs. Maugham's expressions. On the day of her husband's funeral, Mrs. Maugham herself condemns her marriage, uttering (of course tearlessly) to Clara nothing else but a stark: "Well, he's gone and I can't say I'm sorry" (Drabble, 1967, 35). Kristeva's other jouissance supposedly liquifies "the melancholy object blocking the psychic and bodily interior" especially when the partner effecting it gives "the major gift [that the mother] was never able to offer: a new life" (Kristeva, 1989, 78). "Within feminine fantasy," Kristeva theorizes, "such a jouissance assumes a triumph over the death-bearing mother, in order for the interior to become a source of rewards while eventually becoming a source of biological life, childbearing, and motherhood" (Drabble, 1989, 79). But such theoretical antidotes to melancholia in the case of Mrs. Maugham as well as that of Phillipa look like contributing causes. Rather than assuage melancholia, wifedom and motherhood seem to produce it.

Drabble (like Atwood, and Austen in *Persuasion*) contributes to the theory of melancholia that the "inadequate" mother herself was no doubt in pain and that therefore what the daughter is invited to enclose within herself, and reproduce as herself, is not only the mother-as-punisher but also the mother-as-punished. Moreover, if women's woe is imagined to begin with marriage and childbirth, then perhaps the most intimate female connections are between mothers and other mothers (as the linkage of Mrs. Maugham and Phillipa demonstrates), in which roles all generations of women may receive, as if genetically, the female/maternal curse. But, on this model, it is also the case that they may not: insofar as biographical contingencies rather than biological or psychological exigencies are at the root of melancholy, mothers and daughters *can* be cheerful.

Jerusalem the Golden, alive to this possibility, makes a point of not indicting marriage or motherhood categorically: Denham fecundity is enviable. While Mrs. Maugham's refrigerator lacks milk, Mrs. Denham—a famous novelist and so liberated from Irigaray's single function of mothering—likes to hear a baby suck. The difference can be understood as a matter of class. The Denham children disport themselves "in classy sunhats on the beaches of southern Europe" (Drabble, 1967, 128), while Clara grows up amid "insidious industrial grime" (Drabble, 1967, 123). Love itself—between Candida and Sebastian Denham, between parents and children, and among siblings—flourishes, on the thrilling brink of incest, under the aegis of money. Clara learns from the Denhams that love is a socioeconomic production, as is its opposite. She announces to Gabriel that she is "all nerve," "hard," that "there is no love in [her]. . . . [For S]he had not been taught to love, she had lacked those expensive, private lessons" (Drabble, 1967, 193). The implication is that the daughter's melancholia can be averted by social and economic stability, especially when the mother—exceeding her maternal role, though by no means abandoning it—contributes to that foundation.

Yet, in bringing the question of class to bear on the subject of melancholia, *Jerusalem the Golden* also seems to imply that, if the possibility of liberation from melancholy is a function of the degree to which a woman can sidestep the implications of the mother's pain, then the working class may have its advantages. In light of Clara's eventual forced entry into the world of desire—founded on her repudiation of death, her refusal to allow the melancholy Thing (which certainly surrounds and threatens to suffocate her) spoil her pleasure—melancholia begins to look like a bourgeois extravagance, one that an ambitious working-class girl cannot afford, a kind of consumerism in the realm of the psychic. Sokolsky exemplifies this idea of melancholia as an elitest luxury through Anne Elliot's "deprecatory stance" in *Persuasion,* which "arises from a sense of exclusivity that makes her own social exclusion a point of pride. The melancholy that distinguishes Anne in the first part of the novel derives partly from the isolation of being a rare bit of psychic goods. Her refinement of sensibility, her capacity for exquisite sensation, the tenacity of her attachments, all price her out of the emotional market" (Sokolsky, 1994, 132). It is not of course that all bourgeois women must be melancholic (Candida Denham is not) or that working-class women cannot be (Mrs. Maugham seems depressed). It is, rather, that the bourgeois family is apt to be a place where melancholy (a function of assumed entitlement) may flourish. If her mother is absent or cruel, the bourgeois daughter has the leisure to shop for substitutes.

The working-class daughter frantically tries to flee. Shunning a "final, exhausting, bleeding martyrdom" (Drabble, 1967, 98), Clara plans to enter "a bright and peopled world," a neverending metonymic chain of "amusement" (Drabble, 1967, 239). *Jerusalem the Golden* itself springs from a pre-

oedipal phase based on denial of the negation of the maternal Thing—
chapters 2 through 4 loop back into Clara's past, disrupting chronology at
the outset, as do Clara's periodic reflections on her Northam past—to an
antioedipal opening up of the realms of desire. Clara leaps from a feeling of
maternal suffocation to an insistence upon nonabsorption by the death/loss
on which any progress would psychoanalytically seem to depend. The text
presents the desire expressed in the last few pages of *Jerusalem the Golden*
as emphatically not triggered by pain or lack of satisfaction, but as a simple,
unfounded desire to desire. Clara at the very end refuses to acknowledge her
losses even as she assumes that somehow she will be a desiring subject.

Clara's subjective break is ostensibly problem free. Upon leaving Gabriel,
she feels "strangely . . . light: weightless, almost . . . a whole moral inheri-
tance of doubt had dropped away from her." She sits on the bus "with a
kind of placid blankness" (Drabble, 1967, 218), nonchalant about what
will happen to her, nonchalant specifically *about illness:* "she did not at all
care if she was going to be sick all over the bus. It was all the same to her"
(Drabble, 1967, 219). (Clara vomits throughout the book after intense pleasurable experiences with one Denham or another, as if physically striving to
make room in her psychic body for something other than Mrs. Maugham.)
Upon leaving her mother, Clara glides into a postmodern Deleuzean, tech-
nological open space. Entering a world of "pure multiplicity . . . irreducible
to any sort of unity" (Deleuze, 1977, 42), Clara prefers a "wide road,"
"lanes of traffic," "headlights," "speed," "movement," "glassy institutions
where [she and Gabriel] would eat eggs and chips and put coins in fruit ma-
chines and idly, gratuitously drink cups of nasty coffee, for the sake of it,
for the sake of amusement, and all the lights in the surrounding dark"
(Drabble, 1967, 239) to sitting at her dying mother's hospital bedside or
mourning her eternally. Clara refuses to feel guilty, to be "harnessed to the
yoke of daddy-mommy," to play the role of the melancholic whose "abject
desire to be loved, . . . whimpering at not being loved enough, at not being
'understood'" Deleuze mocks (Deleuze, 1977, 269). As if reacting to *Black
Sun*, Deleuze attacks the "sniveling desire to have been loved," what he calls
"sick desire," which must be castrated twice: "once in the family, in the familial scene, with the knitting mother; another time in an asepticized clinic
in the psychoanalytic scene" (Deleuze, 1977, 334). Similarly iconoclastic,
Clara attempts to sweep aside the "mommy spider web" (Deleuze, 1977,
112).

Is Drabble (then) a Deleuzean? In fact, I think that Drabble is as worried
about Clara's plunge into postmodern glitter as Kristeva would be—and as
much as she would be worried about a plunge into a maternal abyss. Clara's
realization that "desire was in every way preferable to possession" (Drabble, 1967, 188) might seem healthily liberating if the possession referred to
were her mother's overpossession of her. But if it refers to her ability to ca-

thect her libido onto anything else, besides that mother, whether the object be an activity or a person, Clara would seem to be in trouble, i.e., acting out a liberation that (like so many of Joan's attempts at freedom in *Lady Oracle*) only reveals the grip of the maternal Thing after all. It is no accident that the one relationship Clara develops is with an inaccessible married man. Despite her cool air, Clara knows, and admits, that she is still in the clutches of her past and only acting ("acting out"?) otherwise: "I can't be free, but there's no reason why I shouldn't be thought to be free, is there?" (Drabble, 1967, 237). Or, as she discloses to Gabriel in their Parisian hotel bed, where she *attempts* to act on the Kristevan injunction to obtain through a man "a view of other things [other jouissance], a sensation of other ways of being[;] she wished to feel herself attached to the world" (Drabble, 1967, 197): "I am chased, I am pursued, I run and run, but I will never get away, the apple does not fall far from the tree" (Drabble, 1967, 193).

Jerusalem the Golden finally has us wondering whether the working-class heroine forced to bypass melancholic indulgence does not risk "soullessness," as she speeds headlong into a postmodern world, uninterested in psychic wounds, and therefore in treating them. "In the wake of psychiatric medicines, aerobics, and media zapping, does the soul exist?" is a provocative question with which Kristeva opens *New Maladies of the Soul*. Kristeva condemns "today's men and women—who are stress-ridden and eager to achieve, to spend money, have fun, and die—[who] dispense with representation of their experience that we call psychic life. Actions and their imminent abandonment have replaced the interpretation of meaning" (Kristeva, 1995, 3, 7). Read as a reflection of these sentiments, *Jerusalem the Golden* is a text that deliberately ends with a mindless repudiation of all attachment to the maternal Thing, seeking emergence without immersion, a fending off, a resistance, without any trace of acceptance, and thus achieving lightness of being. In linking Mrs. Maugham and Phillipa, Drabble points to a cultural transmission of female melancholia that finds its way to expression; in presenting Clara as an evader of such pain, Drabble points to the working-class daughter's worse predicament of being unable to register, articulate, and thereby ease her suffering. Social constraints are shown to contribute to the production of psychic pain and then (enhancing the cruelty) to bar its expression.

For it seems likely that so long as Clara refuses to face her loss, her mother/maternal Thing will only lodge itself more deeply beneath Clara's performance of autonomy. Even theatricality, as Butler proposes, may be constituted by what it disavows and embeds: "one might ask . . . after the disavowal which occasions the performance and which performance might be said to enact, where performance engages 'acting out' in the psychoanalytic sense." Performance "may be related to the problem of unacknowledged loss. . . . [P]erformance allegorizes a loss it cannot grieve, allegorizes the incorporative fantasy of melancholia whereby an object is phantasmatically taken in or on as a way of refusing to let it go" (Butler, 1997, 145–46).

By drawing out the socioeconomic emphases in Atwood and Drabble, I have by no means meant to dismiss Kristeva's psychoanalytic approach to melancholia, or its narrative correlatives. One of my primary aims in presenting all three analyses has been to extend Kristeva's conception of female melancholia by locating its symbolization in more women writers than Duras. In *Lady Oracle* and *Jerusalem the Golden*, socioeconomic factors, however, provide an emendation that leads us to acknowledge a coproduction. Psychic and social etiologies are interimplicated.

Given the compound roots of such severe malaise, all the women writers examined here question the efficacy of romantic heterosexual relationships, marriage, childbirth, and motherhood as routes to symbolic life. In *Black Sun*, Kristeva recommends giving birth as a counterdepressant. In "Stabat Mater," she extols the masochistic jouissance of that experience: *"My body is no longer mine, it doubles up, suffers, bleeds, catches cold, puts its teeth in, slobbers, coughs, is covered with pimples, and it laughs"*; *"a mother is always branded by pain, she yields to it"*; *"motherhood destines us to a de-mented* jouissance *that is answered, by chance, by the nursling's laughter in the sunny waters of the ocean"* (Kristeva, 1989, 167, 179). The *"opaque joy"* that Kristeva feels while caring for her infant, in fact, *"roots"* her in her mother's bed: *"Alone: she, I, and he"* (Kristeva, 1989, 172)! But how does becoming a maternal body, which plops the daughter back into the mother's bed, counter addiction to the mother's (maternal) body, or serve, as Butler words it, as "a defense against libidinal chaos" (Butler, 1990, 86)? On both sides there is jouissance; on neither side desire that would serve as such a defense. How can maternity, source of the pleasure of the damned, outside the terms of the law, assuage melancholia, itself interlaced with masochism?

If Kristeva's masochistic passion for pain is offered as a homeopathic cure for the melancholic addiction to pain, Brookner, Atwood, and Drabble (as well as Austen) warn that the melancholic addiction is apt to begin in, or at least be reinforced by, the administration of the so-called cure. Opting instead for an artistic homeopathic solution, they spin out aestheticizations of melancholia that communicate this very, political point. Simultaneously holding onto while transferring to language the maternal Thing, a "writing cure," these writers propose, is preferable to male domination. By making their heroines writers who put their relationship to pain into language, Brookner and Atwood amplify this point.

Such entry into the symbolic, I am suggesting, entails only a partial decathexis from the "inadequate" maternal object; ideally, it may even make her palatable, forgivable. Through writing, the less than perfect mother, no matter how cruel, may be duplicated without the reinfliction of abuse. In addition, the sources of the mother's own despair and/or anger may be taken into account, so that she may therefore be held onto, instead of abjected, with diminished daughterly resentment, creating a healthy space—a "feminine symbolic"—between asymbolia and the patriarchal symbolic arena, as well as a useful shield against the patriarchal symbolic. For why should the depressive daughter wish to become a full-fledged member of the very club that ostracized and degraded her mother and in turn at least coproduced in the first place the daughter's psychic trouble? Desertion, new wounds, inflicted vengefully against the already wounded mother, only make female melancholic matters worse: if maternal wounds (a sense of cultural devaluation, if not something more particular or personal) are responsible for maternal resentment toward or neglect of the daughter, then supplementing them only enhances the vicious cycle. Such duplication of destruction—one abandonment enacted to punish another—implies the mimetically depressing collapse of feminist cultural critique and sympathetic bonds (of forgiveness) among women.

Kristeva is in a sense one step ahead of me here, having located in melancholic art a "psychic organization of forgiveness" that assists the artist in bypassing complacency through "a subliminary hold over the lost Thing." Perhaps forgiveness for the neglectful mother becomes a real possibility because melancholic art can bestow forgiveness on the suffering daughter, by "removing the guilt from revenge, or humiliation from [a] narcissistic wound, which underlies depressed people's despair" (Kristeva, 1989, 97). Aestheticizing the daughter's pain, then, sets in motion two waves of compassion, or rather, since the daughter's self-forgiveness is both cause and consequence of her forgiveness of the mother, an inflow and outflow, in a cycle of forgiveness that is not vicious.

NOTES

This chapter is a reprint of Frances L. Restuccia, "Tales of Beauty: Aestheticizing Female Melancholia," *American Imago*, vol. 53, no. 4 (Winter 1996), pp. 353–83. © 1996 The Johns Hopkins University Press.

1. I quote here from *The Misalliance*, in which a Brookner melancholic (Blanche) fixes on a wordless little girl (Elinor) whose natural mother died when she was one month old and whose putative mother feels that the three-year-old has encroached on her glamorous life. The nurse diagnoses Elinor's condition as maternal neglect that jeopardizes the daughter's access to language. Corroborating her hypothesis, Elinor toward the end of the novel begins to sputter words—"Something about Grandma. Going to Grandma" (Brookner, 1986, 185)—that seem predicated on her expectation of being at least grandmothered. But Elinor's breakthrough is not cause

for unadulterated joy; the text is saturated with sadness over "The cruelty of the world in apportioning children to the wrong mothers"—misalliances that plunge Blanche into a vast mourning on behalf of all children whose mothers are cold. "Mothers like [Sally Beamish] as Blanche knew only too well, induce bewilderment, loneliness" (Brookner, 1986, 102). Anita Brookner, *The Misalliance* (New York: Harper & Row, 1986) 44.

2. Dusty Miller, in *Women Who Hurt Themselves*, notes the tendency of the TRS (Trauma Reenactment Syndrome) woman to find a partner "similar to the abusive parent, . . . because of her loyalty to the abuser. . . . " The TRS woman's perception of intimacy, to Miller, is organized by the "idea that violence equals connectedness" (Miller, 1994, 136). Dusty Miller, *Women Who Hurt Themselves* (New York: HarperCollins, 1994).

3. The heroine (a reference librarian at "a medical research institute dedicated to the study of problems of human behavior" [Brookner, 1983, 5]) of this masochistic, melancholic narrative feels that she could "write a treatise on melancholy," which is, she has noticed, "usually portrayed [in old prints] as a woman, dishevelled, deranged, surrounded by broken pitchers, leaning casks, torn books. She may be sunk in unpeaceful sleep [Brookner's heroines are incorrigible insomniacs], heavy limbed, overpowered by her inability to take the world's measure, her compass and book laid aside." Frances observes that, while melancholy men seem "to be striking a bit of a pose," women "look as if they are in the grip of an affliction too serious to be put into words" (Brookner, 1983, 6)—a gender difference that Kristeva (alert to the issues Schiesari raises) corroborates with reference to the *"sociologically proven fact"* that there is a *"greater frequency of feminine depressions,"* which she conjectures may *"reveal an aspect of feminine sexuality: its addiction to the maternal Thing and its lesser aptitude for restorative perversion"* (Kristeva, 1989, 71).

4. Frances Hinton strikingly resembles Kristeva's patient Didier, whose "mother's death had made only a small impact on him." She had been "the only person allowed to look at his paintings"; he "kept [her] apartment the way she had left it" (Kristeva, 1995, 12). "Ever since his 'audience' had died, his mother's apartment was closed off, and Didier dared not lay a finger on it or sell it." His sexuality is voyeuristic, "one in which sadomasochistic scenarios gave him the most pleasure" (Kristeva, 1995, 12, 42).

5. Or, as Irigaray writes about the girl's relation to the mother: it is "not to be mastered by the *fort-da*. The mother always remains too familiar and too close. . . . Furthermore, the sexual movement fundamental to the feminine is much closer to gyration than to the gesture like little Ernst's. . . . The girl tries to reproduce around her or inside herself a movement whose energy is circular, and which protects her from dereliction, from immediate effraction, from depression, from loss in itself" (Irigaray, 1989, 133). Luce Irigaray, "The gesture in psychoanalysis," trans. Elizabeth Guild, in *Between Feminism and Psychoanalysis,* Teresa Brennan (New York: Routledge, 1989).

6. Abraham and Torok also of course are typically concerned with cases in which a child's inchoate passions encounter "a parent's own conflictual or paralyzed history of desire" (Abraham and Torok, 1994, 103).

4

⁓〜

Conjurings: Mourning and Abjection in *Story of O* and *Return to the Château*

I.

Taking account of subjectivity means identifying and addressing not only the complex of identities constituting one's location in culture but also the multiple and often conflicting values, drives, desires, enjoyments, anxieties, and defenses that both derive from and help produce this location and that constitute the psychological roots of social and cultural formation.

—Mark Bracher, "Editor's Introduction," *Journal for the Psychoanalysis of Culture and Society*

Especially the figure of the depressed daughter's depressed mother alerts us to the necessity of considering "location in culture," but a focus on cultural location alone is as impoverished as the psychic unsupplemented by the social. An elegant diagnosis of the inadequacy of historicism may be found in *Read My Desire* by Joan Copjec, who defines historicism broadly as "the reduction of society to its indwelling network of relations of power and knowledge" (Copjec, 1994, 6). In a nutshell, to Copjec, historicism "wants to ground being in appearance and wants to have nothing to do with desire"; it disbelieves in repression and "proudly professes to be *illiterate in desire*." Copjec urges analysts of culture to improve their literacy in desire, so that they may read what is "inarticulable in cultural statements" (Copjec, 1994, 14).

I was reminded of Copjec's critique of the blindness of Foucauldian analysis in reexamining Kaja Silverman's essay *"Histoire d'O*: The Construction of a Female Subject."* Although she is a brilliant psychoanalytic critic elsewhere, in her piece on *Story of O*, Silverman gets carried away with proving that the novel exposes the pornographic discursive production of a woman through the intricate exercise of power: O's "body is constituted through the regimen to which it is subjected— . . . it is the consequence of a specific discursive operation" (Silverman, 1985, 332). "Phallic meaning" defines O (Silverman, 1985, 336); O is not permitted at any point "to participate in the production of meaning." The "whipping of O serves a very precise and important signifying function . . . : it constitutes her body as 'readable' through a system of writing." Silverman asserts that the marks on O's body, a writing surface, "signify O as the masochistic subject" (Silverman, 1985, 337)—a subject, I would point out, that really is, in Silverman's reading, an object, since any agency O might appear to possess is only (to Silverman) the result of internalizing, in Foucauldian fashion, "the external structure within which her body is organized" (Silverman, 1985, 340). Yet, in fact, O's conscious consent is underscored in both *Story of O* and its sequel: O must "consent in the real sense of the term," for "nothing would be inflicted upon her by force . . . ; she could refuse, nothing was keeping her enslaved except her love and her self-enslavement" (Réage, 1965, 122); O confesses "quite candidly that she was happy she had consented to the rings, and that her lover whipped her every day" (Réage, 1971, 144–45). But to Silverman, O's cooperation is merely a function of the male power structure.

At one point Silverman does refer to O's assumption of "the sadistic position," for O relegates several men to the masochistic position and also "plays the part of aggressor and mistress-of-ceremonies" in supervising "linguistic, visual and erotic transactions into which she enters with other women." But this acknowledgment of O's taste for cruelty only leads Silverman to the non sequitur that "Sir Stephen thus effects a complete psychic structuration of O. He links her . . . to the self-destructive desires of the masochistic subject" (Silverman, 1985, 342). Silverman is unwilling to grant O agency as sadistic or masochistic subject. But what is worse is that she finally dilates O's story into "the history of the female subject—of the territorialization and inscription of a body whose involuntary internalization of a corresponding set of desires facilitates its complex exploitation" (Silverman, 1985, 346). Silverman collapses O's sadism with her masochism, masochism with patriarchal objectification, and O as object with the female "subject" *tout court.*

In a way Silverman's assumption that O's masochism implies a lack of agency comes as no surprise, since in "Masochism and Male Subjectivity" Silverman by and large follows the old guard on the question of whether masochism is specifically a male pathology. Krafft-Ebing, Freud, Helene

Deutsch, Theodor Reik, and Gilles Deleuze sustain the fundamental paradox that masochism tends to be seen as constitutive of femininity and yet is enacted for strategic purposes exclusively by men. Of course, the trouble with such an outlook is not only that it naturalizes women's submission and suffering, thus enhancing their vulnerability to abuse as well as undergirding the power structures that depend on it, but it also encourages the co-optation of any wish on the part of women to seek enjoyment and/or power through masochistic means as merely more evidence of their essentially masochistic nature. In this conception, while women are imagined as natural lovers of pain, they are excluded from its perverse allure and force.

Silverman is no doubt right to argue that because masochism is an accepted part of female subjectivity, its capacity to have any potency is radically reduced. The difficulty with conceptualizing female masochism as deviant or perverse is, as Silverman clarifies, that "it represents such a logical extension of those desires which are assumed to be 'natural' for the female subject. Because there is so little cultural resistance to it, it does not generally assume any of the poetic or narrative complexity of pathological male masochism, nor manifest as marked a heterocosmic impulse. Nor does it usually threaten anything but its victim's capacities and health, failing for the most part to put power and privilege at risk" (Silverman, 1988, 59).

Yet Silverman herself, in "Masochism and Male Subjectivity," is uneasy about absolutely closing down the possibility of a female (pathological) strategic masochism with the view that women's potentially subversive masochistic energies are subsumed by the normative conception of women-as-subordinate. Toward the end of "Masochism," she discovers a threat posed by the few cases of female masochism that Krafft-Ebing includes in *Psychopathia Sexualis,* conceding that "There may . . . be occasions on which a woman's masochistic fantasies and sexual practices challenge gender[,] . . . heterosexuality, class, or race" (Silverman, 1988, 59). Silverman reads Krafft-Ebing's Case 86—about a woman who pays frequent visits to medical assistants at the General Hospital in Vienna for gynecological exams, during which the woman resists, the doctor continues his "investigation" until the end, and the woman thus experiences sexual excitement culminating in intense orgasms—as a way of achieving bliss inimical to the medical establishment. Case 86 reverses the usual doctor-patient power relation and, to Silverman, subordinates "medicine's discursive ends to [the patient's] libidinal economy," as this female patient prefers "the speculum to the penis, and pleasure to profit" (Silverman, 1988, 60). In Krafft-Ebing's Case 84, the female masochist requires a female disciplinarian who in some of her fantasies is a schoolmistress and, in others, is represented by cruel, uneducated female warders of a mental institution. Here authority and power are shifted to a mother-figure; and insofar as the mother assumes the identity of the masses, the shift is to Silverman "doubly subversive" (Silverman, 1988, 61).

Yet, in her Foucauldian analysis of O, Silverman doesn't consider that resistance or release like that operating in these exceptional examples might be operating in *Story of O*. As I hope to demonstrate, however, something like what appears to be getting worked out in Case 84—where the disciplinarian must be a mother-figure who inflicts pain and punishment within a female masochistic fantasy—would seem also to be at work in *Story of O*. Part of why I think so is based on the author's having lyrically, if incoherently, written (here no doubt *is* poetic complexity of the pathological masochism of a woman) that

> once having taken into account the fair share played by the fantastic and fanciful, and by the endless repetition, in the assuagement of obsessions (the endless repetition of pleasures and brutality being as necessary as it is absurd and impossible to achieve) everything blends together faithfully, dreamed or experienced, everything unfolds as being commonly shared in the universe of a like madness—and if you manage to look at them squarely—horrors, wonders, dreams, and lies—everything there is conjuration and release. [Réage, 1971, 22–23]

In *Masochism: An Interpretation of Coldness and Cruelty,* Gilles Deleuze elaborates a meticulous psychoanalytic scheme followed by male masochists, whose goal is to deprive the father of his symbolic function—more specifically, to exorcise the father encrypted within the son. It is interesting (in conjunction with *Story of O*) that Deleuze takes a *"literary* approach": as he writes, "it is from literature that stem the original definitions of sadism and masochism" (Deleuze, 1971, 13). Deleuze locates the clinical specificities of masochism in the literary values peculiar to Leopold von Sacher-Masoch; the heroes of Masoch's fiction produce Deleuze's model, predicated on the idea that through disavowal of the father the masochistic son atones for his likeness to him. As a literary paradigm of female masochism, how might *Story of O* compare with *Venus in Furs?*[1]

No psychoanalytic paradigm for female masochists has been widely accepted.[2] But in *Coming to Power: Writings and Graphics on Lesbian S/M,* one can find persuasive testimony to the therapeutic (one might even say strategic) value of lesbian sadomasochistic practices. In "If I Ask You to Tie Me Up, Will You Still Want to Love Me?" Juicy Lucy values sexual S/M as "a healing tool" (*Coming to Power,* 1987, 29). She was a battered woman for years and now claims "the right to release & transform the pain & fear of those experiences," any way she pleases (*Coming to Power,* 1987, 30). She describes S/M as "passionate, erotic, growthful, consensual, sometimes fearful, exorcism, reclamation, joyful, intense, boundary breaking, trust building, loving, unbelievably great sex, often hilariously funny, creative, spiritual, integrating, a development of inner power as strength" (*Coming to Power*, 1987, 31). Through lesbian S/M, Juicy Lucy faces what she calls her "hidden side," rather than deny it as she had done, and thereby reclaims herself, defusing in the process the terror and powerlessness she had experienced through former rapes and beatings. Jayne, in "Impromptu S/M," describes submitting to the whip with immense relief, and soaring, "like a bird in flight, freed of the earth's pull" (*Coming to Power*, 1987, 193).

It is Susan Farr who best conveys the psychological seductiveness of lesbian S/M. She starts her piece, "The Art of Discipline: Creating Erotic Dramas of Play and Power," by pointing out that our society accepts systematic violence "where consent is absent (woman battering, rape, war), but issues stringent taboos against consenting adults exploring the complexities of power and sexuality within highly controlled situations" (*Coming to Power*, 1987, 183). Such exploration seems to entail various ways of finding an outlet for frustration, anger, jealousy, and even guilt as well as producing the obligation to give comfort and love, which means for both women also receiving such gifts. "The person who has been spanked feels vulnerable and in need of warmth and comfort; the person who's delivered the spanking needs to offer strength and love. Also, the person who's done the spanking needs to be reassured that she's done a good thing even though she's hurt her lover" (*Coming to Power*, 1987, 185). When Susan gives her lover, Rae, a whipping after Rae has been unfaithful, Rae's guilt is alleviated at the same time as Susan's negative feelings get expressed; their emotional burdens get mutually lifted. A needed expiatory ritual is enacted, as the lovers share excruciatingly intimate knowledge of one another. Concluding, Susan quotes from *The Velveteen Rabbit*: "When you are Real, you don't mind being hurt" (*Coming to Power*, 1987, 190).

The main point for me here, in coming to terms with *Story of O,* is that especially consensual S/M (although perhaps all sadomasochistic practice must be consensual at some level, or else it is battering) can fulfill a psychic need, if not provide a form of psychoanalytic transference. Consequently, we ought to ask, what psychic forces, in addition to institutional forces, propel O's masochism? My aim is by no means to supplant but to supplement Silverman's work on O, that is, to show what has led up to O's status as a product of pornographic discourse, to O's "phallic meaning." In *Return to the Château*, O herself poses her version of this question: "In the dark, chained to the hook above her bed . . . in the dark and unable to sleep, O asked herself for the hundredth time why, whether or not she derived any pleasure from it, someone, no matter whom, from the fact that he penetrated her, or simply opened her with his hand, beat her or only made her strip naked, had the power to make her submit to his will" (Réage, 1971, 137).

Jessica Benjamin curiously notes at the start of *The Bonds of Love* that the more sophisticated feminist thinkers tend to "shy away from the analysis of submission, for fear that in admitting woman's participation in the relationship of domination, the onus of responsibility will appear to shift from men to women, and the moral victory from women to men" (Benjamin, 1988, 9). But women, Benjamin wants to say loud and clear, often participate in their own submission. Hence Benjamin launches her chapter "Master and Slave" with the penetrating question of "How . . . domination [is] anchored in the hearts of those who submit to it." Basically, she sees the fantasy of domination as a cry for recognition. As if speaking to Silverman's reading of *O* that elides the psychic dimension of the text, Benjamin urges her reader to comprehend submission as "the *desire* of the dominated as well as their helpless fate" (Benjamin, 1988, 52). She reads the novel as an allegory of the urge for attention, rather than one of "a victimized woman, too weak or brainwashed or hopeless to resist her degradation." We need to "explain what satisfaction is sought and found in submission, what psychological motivations lead to oppression, humiliation, and subservience." The perhaps unpleasant facts "that people really do consent to relationships of domination, and that fantasies of domination play a vigorous part in the mental lives of many who do not actually do so" must not be denied (Benjamin, 1988, 55). Benjamin sees O's submission as complicit with her deepest longings.

I want to draw on all of these general insights in *The Bonds of Love* for my own analysis of *Story of O*. Ironically, however, as soon as Benjamin becomes more particular, reading O's masochism as "a search for recognition through an other who is powerful enough to bestow this recognition" (Benjamin, 1988, 56), she stops short. *Why* does O crave recognition through the power of the other to the point that she is driven to submit to the repeated torture of her body? Why is O willing to suffer egregiously for the sake of connection first with René and then Sir Stephen? Why is O obsessed with "exist[ing] for [Sir Stephen]"? Why is she terrified of abandonment and loss? The novel is the most moving engagement I know with the fear of abandonment and loss. Although she does not account for it, Benjamin acknowledges this richness: "O's desire for connection increasingly assumes the symbolic and ritual character of a devotion. . . . O's story, with its themes of devotion and transcendence, is suggestive of the surrender of the saints. The torture and outrage to which she submits is a kind of martyrdom, seeming 'to her the very redemption of her sins' " (Benjamin, 1988, 60).

Benjamin distinguishes shrewdly between O's direct relation to pain (O hates it) and her gratification from having endured it: *Story of O* clarifies that O "liked the idea of torture, but when she was being tortured herself she would have betrayed the whole world to escape it, and yet when it was over she was happy to have gone through it" (Réage, 1965, 156–57). Benjamin interprets this gap to indicate that through being abused by an Other O gets the feeling of being reached, connected, recognized. Yielding such crucial rewards, physical pain is highly desirable ("When you are Real, you don't mind being hurt"). Engagement in a sadomasochistic relationship, in other words, can provide an alternative to psychic rupture. This avenue of thinking leads Benjamin to invoke briefly M. Masud R. Khan's *Alienation in Perversions,* in which he describes a case where sadomasochism "substituted for a deep depression based on very early abandonment and loss" (Benjamin, 1988, 61).

And here, in a footnote in *The Bonds of Love,* is buried the key question: what early abandonment and loss might be at the core of *Story of O* and its sequel? Although the novels yield little that allows one to answer this question, it seems to nag at Benjamin, for she proceeds by asking why O's search for recognition culminates in submission instead of in a mutual relationship. Why is there no intersubjectivity between O and her lovers? Then Benjamin enters dangerous waters, sailing off on Bataille's theory of eroticism as "the perilous crossing of" the "sea of death" (Benjamin, 1988, 63). There is excitement in the risk of death. But would not such excitement in such risk of death be universal? This part of Benjamin's discussion lacks specificity. The master's authority "inspires love and transforms violence into an opportunity for voluntary submission" (Benjamin, 1988, 64). But (still) why? This is in fact a critical question for Benjamin, for unlike Freud, who believes that domination is inevitable, she advocates intersubjectivity, subject-subject (rather than subject-object) relations.

Benjamin perceives O as a masochist to whom the most intolerable, terrifying outcome is abandonment. In so doing she takes us many steps further than Silverman in examining the psychopathology as well as the meaning of the text. But it is almost as if what she needs in order to comprehend why this is the ultimate phobia of the book is so massive and therefore so buried that the very book whose therapeutic task may be to release the pain of abandonment can barely face it enough to do so. Is such working against itself a sign of a text in the throes of masochism?

In any case, that abandonment (whatever its etiology) is what ultimately terrifies O *can* be perceived and documented in both novels. In *Story of O,* upon hearing that René has phoned Sir Stephen instead of her, O calls softly "in the solitude of her room, 'I love you, do whatever you want with me, but don't leave me, for God's sake don't leave me' " (Réage, 1965, 93). When René seems indifferent toward O, "everything was choked and smothered within her" (Réage, 1965, 95). Not whipping but nonchalance is her torture. (The text even gives an explanation of why, curiously through a theological analogy: because "she was guilty. Those who love God, and by Him are abandoned in the dark of night, are guilty, *because* they are abandoned. They cast back into their memories, searching for their sins" [Réage, 1965, 95]. To be abandoned, then, is necessarily to be guilty. Consequently, O looks for her sin, and comes up with the sin of wantonness, which leads her to submit to further punishment in order to furnish proof that she belongs solely to René, proof that she is not abandoned [i.e., guilty], which in turn exposes further wantonness, in a vicious cycle. O's punishment, the only potential mode of redemption for her sin, is also her sin: hence she unceasingly yields to blows with "abominable servility" [Réage, 1965, 96].) As a child, O had read: "It is a fearful thing to fall into the hands of the living God." But now she disagrees: "What is fearful is to be cast out of the hands of the living God" (Réage, 1965, 96). On the diegetic level, this translates into: when René is delayed, O suffers attacks of terror, feels subjected to a "gas chamber" (Réage, 1965, 97). In *Return to the Château,* upon feeling that Sir Stephen has abandoned her, sent her to Roissy to get rid of her, O's tears flow until she is coaxed (by Noelle) to dry them, as she does "with both her fists, the way children do when they've been scolded" (Réage, 1971, 95–96).

Beyond the fact that abandonment terrifies O, herein lie a couple of useful clues to the real object of the fear of abandonment, suffused throughout both novels. The reference to O as a child wiping her tears points to a childhood trauma. We can come to this conclusion also by noting that in effect O's training in violent eroticism (what we would assume to be adult activity) results in a devolution to girlhood. When O returns to her job (after her stay at Roissy) in the fashion department of a photography agency, the models notice an alteration in her dress. She now wears sweaters and pleated skirts so often that they seem to be a "uniform," just as she and Jacqueline wore "uniform blouses" when they attended the *lycée* (Réage, 1965, 101): " 'Very little-girl-like,' one of the models said to her one day" (Réage, 1965, 63). Dining with René and Sir Stephen one evening, O drinks a grapefruit juice that René orders for her, while the men imbibe a martini and whiskey. For dessert, O is allowed the ice cream she requests, with an abundance of almonds and whipped cream. At Samois, Anne-Marie addresses O as "my child" (Réage, 1965, 143); upon being released into Paris with Sir Stephen, "[h]atless, wearing practically no make-up, her hair completely free, O looked like a well-brought-up little girl, dressed as she was in her twirled stripe or polka dot, navy blue-and-white or gray-and-white pleated sunskirts and the fitted bolero. . . . Everywhere Sir Stephen escorted her she was taken for his daughter, or his niece, and this mistake was abetted by the fact that he, in addressing her, employed the *tu* form, whereas she employed the *vous*" (Réage, 1965, 168–69). At the end of *Story of O,* O's "offending [pubic] hair" is removed (Réage, 1965, 198); in *Return to the Château,* we learn that O has a physical anomaly that precludes pregnancy. O becomes a girl, a child.

Another albeit more circuitous route to the idea that *Story of O* and its sequel hover over a childhood trauma is from the theological references to abandonment in *O* to what M. Masud R. Khan has to say about God in his chapter "From Masochism to Psychic Pain," which will bring us back to the quite pertinent case that Jessica Benjamin footnotes. As if supplying direct insight into the references to God in *O*, Khan explains that it is the "need in the human individual for his or her psychic pain to be witnessed silently and unobtrusively by *the other,* that led to the creation of the omnipresence of God in human lives." With the disappearance of God, and therefore the disappearance of such an almighty witness, Khan proposes, "the need has rapidly increased for psychotherapeutic interventions to alleviate these pathological masochistic states" (Khan, 1979, 210–11). We might deduce from all this that *Story of O* laments the loss of such a witness, an Other who could alleviate masochistic suffering, a craving possibly brought on by the withdrawal of such a witness.

What is fascinating about Khan's chapter in relation to *O* is that he slides from this discussion of the loss of God to the case of a female depressive who, as a teenager, inspired by a film in which a gunman spanks a can-can girl, concocts and obsessively retells to herself a story of a man who pulls her across his lap "to spank her for her prankishness." The man does not actually commit the act, but he causes her nevertheless, in the fantasy, to depart "humiliated, enraged and vengeful" (Khan, 1979, 216). This story makes the girl "come alive" (Khan, 1979, 216). Likewise, as a woman she gains vitality upon discovering that her parents died in a car accident and that "[w]hen the police arrived, they found the parents dead and a child alive in her dead mother's *lap*" (Khan, 1979, 217, my emphasis). Khan concludes that the woman "had all her life unconsciously sought that lap to come alive again so that she could live" (Khan, 1979, 217). The case teaches him that in "masochistic fantasy or practice there is always a kernel of psychic pain, that has been lived and lost, and instead, proliferations of screen-fantasies take its place" (Khan, 1979, 217). Here a woman fantasizes about experiencing pain on the lap of a man as a way of returning to the lap of her dead mother. What is the kernel of psychic pain whose place "screen-fantasies"—in the form of *Story of O* and *Return to the Château*—take? What is being worked through aesthetically?

II.

The question remains as to the ordeal . . . that abjection can constitute for someone who . . . presents himself with his own body and ego as the most precious non-objects; they are no longer seen in their own right but forfeited, abject. . . . Such are the pangs and delights of masochism.

—Julia Kristeva, *Powers of Horror*

While no paradigm of female masochism has been constructed with the kind of definitive properties featured in Deleuze's model of male masochism, we can turn to Kristeva's *Powers of Horror* to analyze the masochism of *Story of O* and *Return to the Château*. Pairing this theoretical text with these literary texts seems appropriate given that Kristeva ties abjection to masochism, since abjection is indicated by a crossing of borders normally left intact for the sake of stabilizing the subject, and the line between inside and outside is traversed in both directions by pleasure and pain. Abjection manifests itself through an uncertainty of borders demonstrated by perversion, anal eroticism, defilement—as well as by residues such as sperm, blood, tears, all matter issuing from orifices (one connotation of "O").

Drawing her ideas from *Leviticus*, Kristeva writes that, culturally speaking, flow is impure. Anything that breaks boundaries—"flow, drain, discharge" (Kristeva, 1982, 103)—poses a threat. What exits the body gives rise, through open orifices, to abjection. "Any secretion or discharge, anything that leaks out of the . . . body defiles," blood especially (Kristeva, 1982, 102). "Blood, indicating the impure, . . . inherits the propensity for murder of which man must cleanse himself. But blood, as a vital element, also refers to women, fertility, and the assurance of fecundation. It thus becomes a fascinating semantic crossroads, the propitious place for abjection where *death* and *femininity, murder* and *procreation, cessation of life* and *vitality* all come together" (Kristeva, 1982, 96).

Story of O and its sequel contain an excess of various sorts of liquidities, and so might be called abject texts, on the grounds that, as Bataille writes, abjection is "the inability to assume with sufficient strength the imperative act of excluding abject things" (Kristeva, 1982, 56). These novels are full of outpourings of tears that befoul; sperm that merge with the liquids of O's mouth, vagina, and anus; and blood from wounds inflicted all over O's body (" 'I'd like to whip you till I draw blood. Do I have your permission?' 'I'm yours,' O said" [Réage, 1965, 107]). O's thin body is "marked by thick, purple welts like so many ropes spanning the shoulders, the back, the buttocks, the belly, and the breasts, welts which sometimes overlapped and crisscrossed. Here and there a little blood still oozed" (Réage, 1965, 109).

O's bodily boundaries are literally and continuously opened up and broken down, potentially anywhere. Her labia are pierced; her buttocks (like those of cattle) branded. In *Powers of Horror*, Kristeva explains that the "abject confronts us . . . with those fragile states where man strays on the territories of *animal*" (Kristeva, 1982, 12). At the end of *Story of O*, O crosses over from the very category of human to that of animal, or crosses, combines, the two categories, as she metamorphoses into an owl: "O stared at them with eyes that, beneath her plumage, were darkened with bister, eyes opened wide like the eyes of the nocturnal bird she was impersonating, and the illusion was so extraordinary that no one thought of questioning her, which would have been the most natural thing to do, as though she were a real owl" (Réage, 1965, 202). Rather than being rejected, the abject in *Story of O* and *Return to the Château* beckons and engulfs.

But abjection is always paradoxical: the same horrifying thing that seduces simultaneously instills horror and fear, and hence a need for containment and release. We have identified the dominant phobia in *Story of O* and *Return to the Château* as that of abandonment and loss. If we invoke Kristeva's insights into phobia, we can further zero in on the idea of an early childhood trauma at the heart of these texts. For phobia, to Kristeva, "best allows one to tackle the matter of relation to the object" (Kristeva, 1982, 33). Phobia stages the instability of the object relation; presumably what is wanted is that relation stabilized, through intersubjective reciprocity. Not only is intersubjectivity lacking, but there is incorporation, blockage, consumption, of the mother by the daughter, and vice versa. Kristeva presents a case of a little girl whose phobia (analyzed during Anna Freud's seminar) of being eaten up by dogs develops in relation to a separation from her mother.

The masochism of abjection, then, would seem to originate in incest, especially in the incestuous longing of a daughter for a mother, of a daughter who may have "swallowed up . . . a maternal hatred"; instead of maternal love, there is "emptiness" (Kristeva, 1982, 6). Yet *Story of O* has been taken to establish (and scorned for establishing) the general principle that what women need is "a good master, one who is not too lax or kind: for the moment we [men] make any show of tenderness they draw upon it. . . . In short, that we [men] must, when we go to see them, take a whip along" (Réage, 1965, xxv), implying that the masochism of O is specifically that of a woman in relation to aggressive men. These are sentiments from Jean Paulhan's notorious preface to *Story of O,* titled "Happiness in Slavery." However, even though it turns out that the book was written as an erotic love letter for him, and even though he observes that "the story of O has deep roots" (Réage, 1965, xxv), Paulhan may have missed the object of the phobia of abandonment that he took to be himself alone.

My thesis is that O and its sequel are the literary products as well as representations of a masochistic incorporation of an Other—a possession previous to the advent of subjectivity. At the same time, these novels (like *Emma* and *Persuasion* as well as *Look at Me, Lady Oracle,* and *Jerusalem the Golden*) come to terms with the maternal entity and through this confrontation begin the mourning process. The abject that was the mother is regurgitated in *Story of O,* through which thwarted incestuous desire—or what would again be more accurately termed jouissance—is first expressed at a distance (via men) and then dealt with head-on.

Leaving aside for now the move in *Story of O* and *Return to the Château* back to a father figure (Sir Stephen) and then to a mother figure (Anne-Marie), we can assume at this point in our analysis of the relationship between maternally abandoned women and abusive men that O's vulnerability to her lover René itself has a parental history and motive behind it. Providing further quite pertinent psychoanalytic theoretical support for this idea, Maria Torok in *The Shell and the Kernel* connects a girl's "anal relationship to the mother," which causes her to have trouble tearing herself free from the mother's dominion, with dependency on a man, who serves as the anal mother's heir (Torok, 1994, 71).[3] Brutal anal intercourse pervades O.

One might therefore suspect that O's submission to René, as well as to all the other abusive men, especially at Roissy, who stand in for René, serves O's need to displace aggression toward the "mother" onto herself, as Kristeva would lead us to believe, for loving and, because the love is unreciprocated, hating her, for therefore needing to embed "the mother" within herself in order to punish her, by hurting herself. Only O's case seems more acute. Her maternal vision conjures up ferocity and (sharing the anality of Torok's patient's enthralling mother) fecal matter. Visiting the south of France for the first time, O finds the "mirror-like sea [mer = mère] . . . hostile. . . . 'The sea doesn't smell like the sea,' she thought. She blamed the sea for washing up nothing more than an occasional piece of wretched seaweed which looked like dung, she blamed it for being too blue and for always lapping at the same bit of shore" (Réage, 1965, 180).

While Kristeva's melancholic/depressed woman achieves a certain unhealthy balance in bonding with her lost, neglectful, or abusive mother by acquiescing to severe discipline or even to abuse from a male partner, O exemplifies Kristeva's "deject," the woman whose abjection tugs on her so strongly that she literally opens her bodily borders, so that not even the "stability" of encryptment remains as a form of cohesiveness and support. In such a case, as Kristeva elaborates, "It is as if the skin . . . no longer guaranteed the integrity of one's 'own and clean self' but . . . gave way before the dejection of its contents. Urine, blood, sperm, excrement . . . show up"; and this immersion gives the "deject" the "full power of possessing, if not being, the bad object that inhabits the maternal body" (Kristeva, 1982, 53–54). In a thoroughgoing takeover, the abject/mother would seem to seep in osmotically from outside to settle, to make herself at home, within the daughter. Needing such maternal inhabitation to avoid the alternative of rejection and loss (as well as to alleviate the guilt of the original abandonment), the daughter yields to cruel men who liquify her so that she may merge with the "bad object," instead of retaliating against it.

In a sense, like Deleuze's male masochist who sets up a female dominatrix to assist him in transforming a threatening, punishing paternal law into bliss, O "uses" sadistic men to assist her in punishing herself, so as not to alienate, or destroy, the miring maternal object/abject, whose love she craves, and all aggression toward whom she hopes to conceal. (In both cases a form of incest would seem to be the psychic goal.) René and all the other violating men further provide the service of opening O up and thereby facilitating her access to the abject. Sir Stephen especially makes rapid progress in a tight area: "he forced her from behind, to rend her as René had said he would. . . . He went at it again, harder now, and she screamed. . . . [H]e remarked to her that what he had spilled in her was going to seep slowly out tinted with the blood of the wound he had inflicted on her, that this wound would burn her as long as her buttocks were not used to him and he was obliged to keep on forcing his way" (Réage, 1965, 89). Abjection is here an uncertainty of literal boundaries, an intermingling of the residues of blood and sperm at the abject site of the anus.

The loss of O's identity is foregrounded on the first page of *Story of O:* René removes O's leather handbag, in which she keeps her "identification papers." O is stripped first of her identity, then of her clothes. Next, certain body parts, including O's orifices, are confiscated: "Your hands are not your own, nor are your breasts, nor, most especially, any of your bodily orifices, which [René announces] we may explore or penetrate at will" (Réage, 1965, 15–16). The purpose of this threefold stripping and exploitation, as René explains it, is less for the men's pleasure than for O's "enlightenment" (Réage, 1965, 17), less even to make O suffer than to make O feel, through her suffering, that she is "fettered," "totally dedicated to something outside [herself]" (Réage, 1965, 17). Of course, the power of men, mainly driven to rape O, is what René ostensibly has in mind; but if we consider his statement in the light of *Powers of Horror*, we might imagine this "something outside" of O's self to be "an archaic authority, on the nether side of the proper Name" (Kristeva, 1982, 75), the abject, to which O is more than pleased to dedicate herself.

O is drawn to the underside of subjectivity and the symbolic order: "nothing had been such a comfort to her as the silence, unless it was the chains. The chains and the silence, which should have bound her deep within herself, which should have smothered her, strangled her, on the contrary freed her from herself. . . . Beneath the gazes, beneath the hands, beneath the sexes that defiled her, the whips that rent her, she lost herself in a delirious absence from herself which restored her to love and, perhaps, brought her to the edge of death" (Réage, 1965, 38–39). Even here we return to the mother or "maternal Thing" (at least if we are thinking within Kristevan circles), for Kristeva locates death "in the chasm of the maternal cave" (Kristeva, 1982, 24), the place where, propelled by an initial loss, drives that repetitively wander ultimately find their home. Through the self-destruction of abjection, O is "resorbed . . . into communication with the [deadly] Other" (Kristeva, 1982, 127).

The ellipsis of this last quotation replaces Kristeva's question: "is that grace?" (Kristeva, 1982, 127). *Story of O* might lead us to think so. For imagining at one point that René will leave her, O cries out silently: "let the miracle continue, let me still be touched by grace" (Réage, 1965, 97). As O is "ceremoniously soiled with saliva and sperm," even as she feels "herself literally to be the repository of impurity, the sink mentioned in the Scriptures," "those parts of her body most constantly offended . . . seemed . . . to have become more beautiful and . . . ennobled." O gains in dignity as her body parts hook up with those of violating others, as her mouth closes upon anonymous members, the tips of her breasts are fondled by multiple hands, and the "twin, contiguous paths" between her thighs are "wantonly ploughed." She is "illuminated . . . , as though from within" (Réage, 1965, 44). Just as the "mystic's familiarity with abjection is a fount of infinite [masochistic] *jouissance*" (Kristeva, 1982, 127), O greets the "[b]lessèd darkness" (after Pierre covers her eyes with a black velvet blindfold) with "joy" (Réage, 1965, 47). For, an Other has settled in O's place (she has become Other), for whom she had to destroy and thereby lose herself. Perhaps *Story of O* is after all, as André Pieyre de Mandiargues proposes in his prefatory essay, a novel that "we should not hesitate to categorize as a mystic work. . . . [B]eneath the guise and methods of eroticism, the subject is the tragic flowering of a woman in the abdication of her freedom, in willful slavery, in humiliation, in the prostitution imposed upon her by her masters, in torture, and even in the death which, after she has suffered every other ignominy, she requests and they agree to" (Réage, 1965, xvi–xvii).

To plumb the depths of *O*, then, one must concentrate on more than O's masters, on more than O's need for recognition from them. Especially René lacks the weight necessary to provoke the *ascesis* or spiritual transformation (to transplant Mandiargues's terms) of this novel. That O "considered herself fortunate to count enough in [René's] eyes for him to derive pleasure from offending her, as believers give thanks to God for humbling them" (Réage, 1965, 84) is absurd. Upon entering section II, however, we encounter a weightier (older) male figure, Sir Stephen, who is "a far more demanding but also a far surer master than René. Yet, with Sir Stephen too, O prostrates herself in a way that seems out of proportion to Sir Stephen's worth: "The word 'open' and the expression 'opening her legs' were, on her lover's lips, charged with such uneasiness and power that she could never hear them without experiencing a kind of internal prostration, a sacred submission, as though a god, and not he, had spoken to her" (Réage, 1965, 57). It might seem plausible that through Sir Stephen O seeks a paternal power that can facilitate her entry into the symbolic order. "The paternal agency alone," writes Kristeva, "to the extent that it introduces the symbolic dimension between 'subject' (child) and 'object' (mother)," can place the subject "in a symbolic chain." "Otherwise, what is called 'narcissism' [and Kristeva conceives of abjection precisely as a crisis of narcissism] . . . becomes the unleashing of drive as such, without object, threatening all identity, including that of the subject itself" (Kristeva, 1982, 44). But the mother still must be vomited up, in order not to foreclose the Name of the Father; and there are several ways in which Sir Stephen, especially in his role as sadistic violator of O, not only fails to supplant the mother but duplicates her.

Sir Stephen serves both as a surrogate maternal object (he works in tandem with Anne-Marie at Samois) and as a potential erotic subject beyond her—in relation to whom O tests out her "desires," but to whom she in the end always submits herself as punishment for those "desires" ("let him take her, if only to wound her! O hated herself for her own desire" [Réage, 1965, 82]). What Sir Stephen's dual position therefore reiterates is the appeal of the abusive male for the abandoned, neglected, or abused daughter. The experience of other jouissance with an abusive male comfortably preserves the bond to the abject. For he is not the original abject and so does not have the psychic force that would enable him to cannibalize her. Yet he behaves like the abject—by prying open orifices and merging with the deject through their various liquid leakages and ejections, by hurting her—and so does not tear her away.

My analysis thus far may seem to impose a maternal abject on O as well as on the text itself, mainly as a way of explaining O's acquiescence to subjection. In large part that is because I have taken into account the move in both *Story of O* and *Return to the Château* to Anne-Marie, a friend of Sir Stephen (his age), a kind of witch with black hair streaked with gray. In section III, at Samois, where Anne-Marie resides and presides, O experiences the most unbearable punishments of all. Upon meeting O, Anne-Marie topples her over an ottoman, orders her not to move, and seizes her nether lips: "This is how they lift the fish at the market, O was thinking, by the gills, and how they pry open the mouths of horses" (Réage, 1965, 144). Anne-Marie instructs O to wear corsets that barely allow O to breathe: "now her waist was scarcely larger than the circle formed by her ten fingers; Anne-Marie ought to be pleased" (Réage, 1965, 150). And O is whipped viciously at Samois until she grovels, until she begs for mercy, for "that was precisely what Anne-Marie intended wringing from her lips." When O can bear no more, Anne-Marie dictates, "She can scream for five minutes" longer (Réage, 1965, 156); upon meeting this demand, O complies with Anne-Marie's further request that O express gratitude.

Especially the culminating role of Anne-Marie, curiously neglected in *Story of O* criticism, leads us to read *Story of O* and *Return to the Château* as narratives of abjection based on some sort of misfire of maternal identification, resulting in the incorporation of a devouring mother. After O thanks Anne-Marie for having her gruesomely whipped, O suspects not that Anne-Marie is interested in making a spectacle of her power but that she wishes to establish "between O and herself a sense of complicity" (Réage, 1965, 156). And O seems glad to oblige her, admitting to Anne-Marie that "she was happy to have gone through it, happier still if it had been especially cruel and prolonged" (Réage, 1965, 157). Anne-Marie coaxes O to become an accomplice in Anne-Marie's crimes against O (her punitive devouring of O), and O joins in (accepts the punishment). For through an abjection that dissolves her identity, O can experience jouissance, as the absent mother thereby becomes present to her. Kristeva writes: "[O]ne joys in it [*on en jouit*]. Violently and painfully." "A passion," the abject is a "repulsive gift that the Other, having become *alter ego*, drops so that 'I' does not disappear in it but finds, in that sublime alienation, a forfeited existence. Hence a jouissance in which the subject is swallowed up but in which the Other, in return, keeps the subject from foundering by making it repugnant. One thus understands why so many victims of the abject are its fascinated victims—if not its submissive and willing ones" (Kristeva, 1982, 9). Through abjection, the abject and deject coalesce. In fact, O accepts complicity with Anne-Marie to the degree that O takes intense pleasure in striking Yvonne (another girl at Samois) "as hard as she could" (Réage, 1965, 162)—which act could simultaneously be explained as self-laceration, since we are told that O "resembled Yvonne. At least one was led to suspect as much by the way Anne-Marie felt about them both" (Réage, 1965, 162). O identifies with Anne-Marie consistently here as part of her campaign to beat herself.

The end of O plays out a complex masochistic fantasy about the mother who torments her "child" *and* allows that "child" to express incestuous love, sometimes both at the same time. Anne-Marie declares that she is "going to open [O] every day" (Réage, 1965, 162). She oversees, if not enacts, the branding of O: "O felt one of Anne-Marie's hands on her buttocks, indicating the exact spot for the irons. . . . One single, frightful stab of pain coursed through her, made her go rigid in her bonds and wrenched a scream from her lips. . . . When they unfastened her, she collapsed into Anne-Marie's arms. . . ." (Réage, 1965, 166–67). Yet Anne-Marie is also "all kindness and gentleness with O, kissed her on the mouth and kissed her breasts, and held her close against her for an hour . . ." (Réage, 1965, 164). She solicits O for sex: "O, who was sleeping with her legs together, was awakened by Anne-Marie's hands probing between her thighs." Because Anne-Marie wants O to caress her, "With her lips, O brushed the hard tips of her breasts, and her hand ran lightly over the valley of her belly. Anne-Marie was quick to yield" (Réage, 1965, 163).

Still, even here, at the climax of incestuous mother-daughter sexual relations, Anne-Marie tortures O by making her feel excluded, unwanted, substitutable. Anne-Marie's pleasure is "anonymous, impersonal"; O is merely its instrument. At this excruciating peak of potential intimacy, Anne-Marie expresses indifference: "It made no difference whatever to Anne-Marie that O admired her face, . . . her lovely panting lips, nor did she care whether O heard her moan when her lips and teeth seized the crest of flesh hidden in the furrow of her belly. She merely seized O by the hair to press her more closely to her, and only let her go in order to say to her: 'Again, do it again' " (Réage, 1965, 163–64). Anne-Marie runs "her hand softly, and at great length, over O's rear," as if she were a sweet mother affectionately stroking her young child, but in the end "No one possessed Anne-Marie" (Réage, 1965, 164). Abjection not only has roots in incest, but incest regenerates it. Where else would a masochist wish to go but to the fertile spot that would produce more pleasure in pain?

While *Story of O* proceeds past these encounters between O and Anne-Marie (in the final section, O dons the owl costume and attends a party; then in one ending Sir Stephen abandons her, and in the other O chooses to die), *Return to the Château* mounts to a final confrontation between the two women. It is as if the sequel adjusts the deceptive emphasis of *O*—on O's submission to male masters—by concluding with Anne-Marie, thus unveiling what is behind such prostration to men, exposing at last, as Lacan writes in *Écrits*, that "A dream involving punishment may very well signify the desire for what the punishment is repressing" (Lacan, 1977, 257). Because Sir Stephen is suspected of murder at the end of the sequel, he is not expected to return, which apparently puts O's relation to Samois in an entirely new light. " 'You're free now, O,' said Anne-Marie. 'We can remove your irons, your collar, and bracelets, and even erase the brand. You have the diamonds, you can go home" (Réage, 1971, 187). O is perfectly unresponsive. She sheds no tears, displays no bitterness, utters no sound. In the novel's penultimate paragraph, there is only blankness. In the ultimate paragraph—" 'But if you prefer,' Anne-Marie went on, 'you can stay here' " (Réage, 1971, 187)—there is perhaps a leaning in the direction of O's hanging on. Or we might say there is ambiguity.

Yet what is ambiguity but a sign of abjection, the blurring of borders between positions? Like incest and the masochism/abjection to which it gives rise, ambiguity transgresses clear borders, refusing to exclude. "[A]bjection is above all ambiguity," Kristeva pronounces, "Because, while releasing a hold, it does not radically cut off the subject from what threatens it" (Kristeva, 1982, 9). *Return to the Château* concludes with a mother-daughter confrontation that stages ambiguity that *conjures up* the maternal devourer even as it offers the possibility of *conjuring* her away. Abjection is embodied in the text's very meta-abject style.

III.

At [a certain] level of downfall in subject and object, the abject is the equivalent of death. And writing, which allows one to recover, is equal to a resurrection.

—Julia Kristeva, *Powers of Horror*

What makes Kristeva's theory of abjection even more pertinent to *O* and its sequel is that she assumes that the eroticization of abjection may function to stop the hemorrhage and that writing—perhaps in particular erotic writing?—may provide the control of aesthetic sublimation. The doubleness implicit in the idea of conjuration brings us to the question of the writing of abjection—specifically to writing that releases without a radical break, that conjures away through conjuring up. "In the symptom, the abject permeates me, I become abject. Through sublimation, I keep it under control" (Kristeva, 1982, 11).

On the last page of *Return to the Château,* Anne-Marie looms large, even as she offers O the option of leaving. The lack of obscurity surrounding the maternal figure would seem to suggest at least some therapeutic progress— progress dependent upon immersion in the abject, the return *to* the Château, the return, that is, to the repressed. That cures must ground themselves in wounds is the crux of psychoanalytic transference; it is equally the principle by which the writing of mourning must abide. Kristeva views narrative as a caring mother, as "the most normal solution": with "the recounting of suffering," "fear, disgust, and abjection crying out" are "quiet[ed] down, concatenated into a story" (Kristeva, 1982, 145).

The writer of abjection "is a phobic who succeeds in metaphorizing in order to keep from being frightened to death," so that he/she may be revitalized by language (Kristeva, 1982, 38). The more phobic Kristeva's little girl-client fearful of dogs (because she has been separated from her mother) becomes, the more she talks—which leads Kristeva to see verbalization, or language, as a counterphobic object. To Kristeva, the girl, at some level, thinks: "Through the mouth that I fill with words instead of my mother whom I miss from now on more than ever, I elaborate that want, and the aggressivity that accompanies it, by *saying*" (Kristeva, 1982, 41).

Signs of abjection are apt to be both an indication of inhabitation by the mother and of the subject's breaking free. The verbalization/writing of abjection simultaneously preserves "what existed in the archaism of preobjectal relationship, in the immemorial violence with which a body becomes separated from another body in order to be—maintaining that night in which the outline of the signified thing vanishes and where only the imponderable affect is carried out" (Kristeva, 1982, 10). Abject verbalization or writing also enacts "the violence of mourning for an 'object' that has always already been lost," an "alchemy that transforms death drive into a start of life, of new significance" (Kristeva, 1982, 15). Elegant writing (*O* is known for its felicitous style) ultimately transforms the punishment of abjection into its aesthetic pleasure. That is: *O* and its sequel express the jouissance of masochistic abjection and convert it into linguistic desire.

But who is the writer? My final focus runs the risk of reduction even as it attempts to supplement, if not clinch, my Kristevan analysis of these texts. As John de St. Jorre, in "The Unmasking of O," made clear in the *New Yorker* in August of 1994, "Pauline Réage" turns out to be Dominique Aury, eighty-six years old at the time of the article. Her lover had indeed been Jean Paulhan, now long dead, to whom Aury wrote *Story of O* as "an extended love letter," because she feared he "was going to abandon her" (writes de St. Jorre) (de St. Jorre, 1994, 43). But just as we can locate deeper forces at work in *Story of O* and *Return to the Château* than those instigated by men, we can find within the *New Yorker* article itself a more subterrranean figure than Paulhan propelling Aury's erotica.

After Aury's father (born in London) and mother had Dominique in 1907, "Her mother decided that she did not want to bring her up, and gave the newborn infant to her mother-in-law. Dominique grew up as a solitary child in her grandmother's house in the country and developed a passion for books" (de St. Jorre, 1994, 44). Here we have in blatant biographical terms a strong possibility of the sort of "primal repression" that Kristeva identifies as the source of abjection. The abject "takes the ego back to its source on the abominable limits from which, in order to be, the ego has broken away—it assigns it a source in the non-ego, drive, and death" (Kristeva, 1982, 15). Kristeva names two causes that effect the narcissistic crisis of abjection, one of which Aury clearly experienced: "The *lapse of the Other*" (Kristeva, 1982, 15).[4]

Aury seems to have tried to travel back in various ways to the mother who gave her away. "Dominique Aury," itself connotative of orality, turns out to be a pseudonym "derived from her mother's maiden name" (de St. Jorre, 1994, 44). During the time in which she was widely recognized as Paulhan's mistress, Aury was living with her parents. And for the material of *O*, which she wrote down in "school-exercise books," Aury drew upon sexual fantasies that "had begun during her lonely adolescence" (de St. Jorre, 1994, 45). Aury admits to "repeated reveries, . . . slow musings just before falling asleep . . . in which the purest and wildest love always . . . demanded . . . the most frightful surrender." In such reveries "childish images of chains and whips" were somehow constraining but "beneficient";

they protected her "mysteriously" (de St. Jorre, 1994, 45). When de St. Jorre asks Aury if, in her fiction, she were not perpetuating male fantasies, Aury is perplexed.

Instead of presenting and fulfilling fantasies of sadistic men gratified by women in pain, *Story of O* to Aury expresses "that other, obscure life that is life's consolation, that other life unacknowledged and unshared" (de St. Jorre, 1994, 45). *She* seems to acknowledge the mystical dimension of her writing (Aury had an interest in French religious poetry), in a way that chimes with Kristeva's sense of the mysticism of "those in despair"—"mystics—adhering to the preobject . . . mute and steadfast devotees of their own inexpressible container. It is to this fringe of strangeness that they devote their tears and jouissance. In the tension of their affects, muscles, mucous membranes, and skin, they experience both their belonging to and distance from an archaic other that still eludes representation and naming, but of whose corporeal emissions, along with their automatism, they still bear the imprint" (Kristeva, 1989, 14). (Here *Black Sun* itself bleeds into *Powers of Horror.*)

We also learn from the *New Yorker* piece that Aury discovered in Sade psychoanalytic meaning related to this mysticism and in turn to *Story of O* and *Return to the Château.* For Sade helped Aury to "understand that we are all jailers, and all in prison, in that there is always someone within us whom we enchain, whom we imprison, whom we silence" (de St. Jorre, 1994, 46). This paradox of the jailed jailer strangely expresses the psychic situation at the heart of these novels of an identificatory cannibalizing of an abject Other who in turn cannibalizes the cannibal. (And if cannibalism seems antithetical to mysticism, one only need think of the Eucharist.)

Kristeva can be helpful here too in bringing out a transubstantiating effect of the "melancholy cannibalistic imagination." Such "cannibalism" accounts for the "passion for holding within the mouth (but vagina and anus also lend themselves to this control) the intolerable other that I crave to destroy so as to better possess it alive. Better fragmented, torn, cut up, swallowed, digested . . . than lost." Such cannibalism is "a repudiation of the loss's reality and of death as well. It manifests the anguish of losing the other through the survival of self, surely a deserted self but not separated from what still and ever nourishes it and becomes transformed into the self—which also resuscitates—through such a devouring" (Kristeva, 1989, 12). Does O "cannibalize" this Other orally, vaginally, and anally in the form of abusive male others, swallowing, ingesting, and digesting it, to repudiate its loss and transform it into nourishment? The *New Yorker* article concludes with a moving peaen to this recovered lost object/abject. Aury's final focus is on her linkage to someone with whom she communicates, not publicly, but "through depths of the imaginary with dreams as old as the world itself" (de St. Jorre, 1994, 50), on that maternal Thing she conjures up so as not to be sucked down.

But what, asks Derrida, in *Specters of Marx: The State of the Debt, the Work of Mourning, and the New International,* in more detail, in all its complexity, "is a 'conjuration' "? (Derrida, 1994, 40). The double meaning that Derrida lays out in fact suits *Story of O* and its sequel perfectly. A "conjuration" signifies "the magical incantation destined to *evoke,* to bring forth with the voice, to *convoke* a charm or a spirit" (Derrida, 1994, 41). On the other hand, a conjuration is "a matter of neutralizing a hegemony or overturning some power," "to conjure it away," "to exorcise: to attempt both to destroy and to disavow a malignant, demonized, diabolized force, most often an evil-doing spirit, a specter, a kind of ghost who comes back or who still risks coming back *post mortem*" (Derrida, 1994, 47–48). Hence "conjuration and release," the terms Aury poetically employs, is a redundancy, since to conjure is both to elicit and exorcise. The redundancy economically reiterates that the act of releasing (conjuring away) necessitates a convoking (conjuring up). And it is the very capacity of language for doubleness, as I have tried to demonstrate, that is the primary reason why writing is an appropriate context in which such conjurings can operate: for writing can transferentially preserve at the same time as it masters, thus setting mourning in motion. Dominique Aury writes similarly in "A Girl in Love" (an exquisite account of the writing of *Story of O,* placed at the beginning of *Return to the Château*) that "prison itself can open the gates to freedom . . . free this unknown creature whom we have kept locked up" (Réage, 1971, 15).

Story of O and its sequel give the appearance of being merely pornographic discursive productions of a woman by a patriarchal power structure. "Phallic meaning" would seem to define O; and whipping does appear to serve as a kind of inscription on her body that renders her body "readable." But such a reading misses the masochistic jouissance of these texts. One of my aims has been to show that if O's need to pursue jouissance as a way of returning to the lost maternal Thing is acknowledged, that is, if we consider why O pursues the jouissance of abuse, then we can better understand how it is that she became a product of pornographic discourse. We can more thoroughly comprehend what not only allows but also upholds the sadomasochistic social structure that defines a woman such as O in terms of phallic meaning. The trouble with Silverman's reading of O is that it is only half the story. What I have tried to unveil is meant to explain how O arrives at the point of figuring in Silverman's Foucauldian conception. As Copjec points out in the opening chapter of *Read My Desire,* "desire may register itself *negatively* . . . the relation between . . . social surface and desire may be a negative one" (Copjec, 1994, 14).

And yet, as most of this chapter has attempted to illustrate, there is also a great deal more than such a negative relation between social surface and desire, or in this case jouissance, operating in O and its sequel. Heeding Copjec's injunction to analysts of culture "to become literate in desire, to learn how to read what is inarticulable in cultural statements" (Copjec, 1994, 14) in relation to O and its sequel also means discovering the way that writing of abjection performs the hard work of mourning for a lost maternal Thing, spinning masochistic jouissance into the desire of the text.

NOTES

This chapter is a reprint of Frances L. Restuccia, "Conjurings: Mourning and Abjection in the *Story of O* and *Return to the Château*," *Gender and Psychoanalysis,* vol. 3, no. 2 (April 1998), pp. 123–53. © 1998 International Universities Press, Inc.

1. I spell out Deleuze's theory of masochism in the final chapter, "Petticoat Government," of my book on Joyce (*James Joyce and the Law of the Father* [New Haven: Yale, 1989]), in which I read Joyce's writing as part of a masochistic strategy to secure his own liberation from patriarchy, as a way of beating the ghostly presence of the flogging fathers/Fathers of Dublin out of himself in an effort finally to achieve forbidden pleasure.

2. Gaylyn Studlar, in her book *In the Realm of Pleasure: Von Sternberg, Dietrich, and the Masochistic Aesthetic* (Urbana: U of Illinois P, 1988), has attempted to expand Deleuze's theory so that it might yield an aesthetic inclusive of the female film spectator. And in "Of Female Bondage" (in *Between Feminism and Psychoanalysis,* ed. Teresa Brennan [New York: Routledge, 1989]), Parveen Adams takes the freedom of lesbian sadomasochism to be freedom from the phallus altogether. Adams imagines lesbian S/M—perverse and not pathological—as a new, improved materialization of the unconscious life that it effects.

3. Freud provides general reinforcement of this notion in "Female Sexuality," where he refers to the repetition in a woman's married life of her "bad relations" with her mother. "With many women," Freud comments, "we have the impression that their years of maturity are occupied by a struggle with their husband, just as their youth was spent in a struggle with their mother" (*Standard Edition,* 21 [London: Hogarth Press, 1931], 23–31).

4. The other cause that Kristeva mentions is, as she notes, contradictory: "*Too much strictness on the part of the Other,* confused with the One and the Law" (Kristeva, 1982, 15).

5

⁓

Redirecting Spectacles of Domestic Woman Abuse: *I, Tina* and *Defending Our Lives*

I. TINA'S MOURNING

[T]he melancholic lives in the immobility of a paradoxical having, that of a love emptied of all desire.

—Jacques Hassoun, *The Cruelty of Depression*

If we attempt to heed Joan Copjec's injunction to analysts of culture "to become literate in desire, to learn how to read what is inarticulable in cultural statements" (Copjec, 1994, 14) as we decipher the meaning of Tina Turner's autobiography *I, Tina,* we make discoveries similar to those in *Story of O* and its sequel. That is, we locate an abused woman clinging phantasmatically to the lost maternal object and pursuing in turn an other jouissance through such abuse. We also find an enabling negation of loss as that pursuit is captured in the representative form of Tina Turner's autobiography itself. This pattern of a duplication of pathological jouissance at the level of the story and completed mourning or desire at the level of the text—a two-tiered pattern we have located in classic novels, contemporary women's fiction, mystical pornography—now surfaces in the autobiography of a rock star.

Tina Turner presents herself in *I, Tina* as a victim of maternal abandonment and as a result tenaciously in search of substitutes. Born in 1939 to parents who found her intrusive, who only grudgingly tolerated her, who later in the century (Tina speculates) would have aborted her, Anna Mae

Bullock grew up in an atmosphere of continuous domestic strife, in which (*I, Tina* implies) her father battered her mother and her mother fought back as strenuously as she could. Anna's childhood lacked "easy affection, solicitous commitment"; in her home she "felt frozen out, barely there" (Turner, 1986, 7–8). Her autobiography tells the tale of her survival despite the fact that she "had no love from [her] mother or . . . father from . . . birth" (Turner, 1986, 10). Zelma Bullock was a cold mother, who provided "no foundation" for her daughter (Turner, 1986, 12); nonetheless, that daughter adored her, down to taking pleasure in observing her mother's pretty features and breathing in her sweet feminine aroma.

This epitome, in her daughter's eyes, of feminine womanhood abandoned Anna twice, first for two years when she took a war-related job with her husband (Anna was three) and seven years later more absolutely when she suddenly ran out on the whole family. Zelma's flight threw into relief her daughter's ambivalence: "That's when it really hit me how much I loved my mother—and how much I hated her, too. I guess I was learning how close love [pleasure?] and hate [pain?] can be." Tina conveys the heavy loss on which her life was from then on predicated by reconstructing a poignant scene of herself as a sorrowful young girl awaiting her vanished mother's return: "I wanted her to come back for us. . . . I waited, and waited, and she never did. I used to go to the mailbox every day, but there were no letters. I used to cry and cry. . . . I was so hurt. I had wanted her love for so long, and now I would never have it. How many years had I watched her . . . in the kitchen on Sundays, sitting in the window, just staring out? Then one day she wasn't in that window anymore. And she was never in it again. Gone. I cried and cried, but it didn't do any good. It never does, you know" (Turner, 1986, 25).

This is the vacuum into which Ike Turner eventually rushed. But first, prior to her deadly car accident, Anna Mae's cousin Margaret—"closer to [Anna Mae] than her own mother"; "cousin, sister, mother—my heart" (Turner, 1986, 20)—served as Anna Mae's surrogate mother. Margaret instructed Anna Mae on sex—"She really was like my mother. She told me what sex was . . ." (Turner, 1986, 31)—as if Anna Mae conceived of her mother as an untapped fount of sexual enjoyment. Margaret's lessons were not only theoretical but also phenomenological: she showed Anna how to "tongue-kiss." So when Tina Turner explains that it was not sexual but "kissing your first cousin," we are led to think, given Margaret's maternal surrogacy, that it was instead a sublimated form of "kissing your mother." And insofar as it was maternal kissing, Margaret paved the way from Zelma to boy-lovers. Tina spells out this psychic concatenation that accommodates her losses: "I had lost Margaret . . . . There was an empty space there. But as I say, you're always given someone, and about a year after Margaret died, I met the first real love of my life" (Turner, 1986, 37). If pain and pleasure had not coalesced for Anna by this time, at least pleasure was worth the price of pain. Anna Mae lost her virginity in the backseat of a car, where "it hurt so bad. . . . I was just dying, God. . . . It was like poking an open wound" (Turner, 1986, 44). It would seem that at this early stage Anna was primed for an abusive lover, who could sustain her bond with, her bondage to, her "open wound" from, her neglectful, absent mother.[1]

Tina and Ike themselves testify to the incestuous nature of their pairing: each saw the other as a sibling. In Ike's crude terms: "The first time I went with her, I felt like I'd screwed my sister or somethin'. I mean . . . we really had been like brother and sister" (Turner, 1986, 74). Ike built the "foundation" that Zelma failed to provide; he offered "a kind of family love" (Turner, 1986, 73). As a result, when Ike first tried to touch her, Anna was appalled: "God, this is horrible. I can't do this" (Turner, 1986, 73–74). Anna Mae Bullock (too) bears out Kristeva's notion expressed in *Black Sun* that maternally addicted daughters resist erotic attraction to the opposite sex. Maternally addicted daughters spend their psychic energy elsewhere: in the case of Tina, on balancing herself *between* asymbolia and management of her grief. Hence Tina describes herself as "addicted" to *love* (rather than desire), admitting that she "would have been lost in [her] life at that point without [Ike]" (Turner, 1986, 74); hence Tina communicated with Ike semiotically, as she says, "through music" (Turner, 1986, 72); and hence Tina in a sense failed to resist Ike's violence. For it enabled her to continue the self-punishment necessary to cover her hatred for her encrypted mother—displacing it onto herself—and thus to sustain the punishing maternal relation.

In a speech in which Tina relates a scene of Zelma's violence toward her, Ike's violence too is uncannily conjured. At some level Tina conflates their aggressive behavior: "She hit me a backhand lick to the side of my face, and when I saw it had given me a nosebleed, I nearly hit back. She said, 'So you been singin' with Ike Turner'—and the way she said it sounded like a banner headline: PISTOL-WHIPPING IKE TURNER. Because that was the reputation he had. . . . Ike would go *whunk-whunk-whunk* . . .'" (Turner, 1986, 63). Ike served as a perfect mother substitute in being similar to Zelma (each is violent) and, since Zelma's violence against Anna Mae was meant to alienate her from Ike, as a means of revenge, thus allowing Anna to sustain the tie to Zelma as well as to express (and cover) her resentment. Ike helped Anna/Tina to secure a hold over the mother inhabiting her, even as he exempted her from experiencing desire that would ultimately threaten her primary allegiance to the mother whose loss she refused to negate. Tina insists that he was not her type, not physically appealing to her: "His teeth seemed wrong, and his hair-style, too . . . when he got closer, I thought, 'God he's ugly' " (Turner, 1986, 49). It was his music that entranced her. Tina Turner therefore fits Kristeva's portrait of the melancholic for whom "no erotic object could replace the . . . preobject confining the libido or severing the bonds of desire" (Turner, 1986, 13). Rather than being Tina's object of desire, Ike sustains maternal jouissance.

In fact, Tina Turner eventually, as an adult-child, moves in with her mother, and in a sense shares her bed. Toward the end of her written story, Tina composes "I Am a Motherless Child"; yet her work allowed her to rectify her motherlessness. By the eighties, Tina provided her mother with a home and thereby established for herself as well the home she lacked and craved. "One of the things I always wanted was to have a home and now I have one. I bought my mother, my family, a house. Now we all have a home. My mother is there. That was a dream of mine" (Turner, 1986, 249). Perhaps one explanation (besides Buddhism) for why Tina is able to seem unembittered at the end of her story, even to admit in her epilogue that "Ike Turner gave [her her] start" (Turner, 1986, 247), is that by making her into Tina Turner, Ike gave Anna Mae the means by which she could transform an absent punishing mother into a present receptive one, fulfilling an unconscious aim.

Hinting at her preoedipality, despite her performance image as "Sexy Tina" and "Wild Tina" (Turner, 1986, 130),[2] Turner expresses wonderment over the fact that "the bedroom where [her] mother is now was [her] master bedroom, and the bedroom where [her mother] was when she came is now the room [Tina] use[s] when [she] stays with [her] mother" (Turner, 1986, 249). This apparent game of musical beds restores Zelma to the master's position—Tina paradoxically takes charge, or mothers, in an effort to have a mother—while it also comes close to suggesting that they occupy the same bed, as if one. The bright white suit, with shoulder pads, that Tina Turner sports on the cover of *I, Tina* also implies Tina's continued need for maternal fusion. For when Zelma returned, after a long absence, from St. Louis to the backwoods of Tennessee, and reunited with Anna Mae—because of the death and funeral of Zelma's own mother (Mama Georgie)—Zelma was wearing "a white suit with big shoulder pads" (Turner, 1986, 46). As Tina Turner herself states it: "nothing can really take the place of a girl's mother" (Turner, 1986, 30).

But having put her mother in her "proper place," having generously situated Zelma to be a mother, albeit a diminished, yet at least no longer an abandoning one, Tina can sign her epilogue with the words *"Love, I, Tina"*—which seem to float on the page, reconfiguring themselves provisionally as *I Love Tina*? That is: the preoedipal would seem finally to be surpassed. Tina here is like a little girl who said to Lacan "sweetly that it was about time somebody began to look after her so that she might seem lovable to herself," which illustrates for Lacan "the mainspring that comes into play in the first stage of the transference" (Lacan, 1973, 257). Maternally neglected and abandoned, Anna Mae Bullock rediscovers her mother in an incestuous male partner, from whom she gradually extricates *herself* through various artistic acts that enable her transferentially—since Ike substitutes for Zelma—to extricate herself from her mother. (I take, by the way, this suggestion that Tina transfers Zelma onto Ike to be psychoanalytically appropriate, especially given that Lacan writes that whenever someone plays the role of the subject supposed to know, "whether or not an analyst, the transference . . . is established" [Lacan, 1973, 233].)

By entering the realm of signs and creativity, by actively entering the world of capitalism—by modeling stockings for Hanes, cowriting *I, Tina* as well as through her musical performance—by naming (signifying) her suffering through art, Tina Turner secured a subliminary grip on the lost Thing. Moving beyond Kristeva's other jouissance, with all its liabilities, Tina Turner dances (one is tempted to say, literally) on the border between negation of the "maternal Thing" and denial of that negation, in a desperate but successful effort ultimately to avoid descent into the abyss, i.e., psychic breakdown. Completing her mourning process, she resists collapse into asymbolia and enters into "the arena where the world's power is at stake" (Kristeva, 1989, 30).

II. IKE TURNER: MODERN POLICEMAN/PRE-NINETEENTH-CENTURY KING

The physical pain is so incontestably real that it seems to confer its quality of 'incontestable reality' on that power that has brought it into being.

What assists the conversion of absolute pain into the fiction of absolute power is an obsessive, self-conscious display of agency.

—Elaine Scarry, *The Body in Pain*

Substituting for Zelma, Ike began the process of repossessing Anna Mae as soon as he took her on, at sixteen years old, as a singer in his band. We learn from *I, Tina* that Ike adorned her with sequined dresses, long gloves and rings to wear over them, shoes, stockings with seams, a fur stole. He bought her a gold tooth and had a cavity filled. By "taking care," Ike "make[s] you become his. He had to own you" (Turner, 1986, 64). He put Anna Mae in the limelight; he made her a star by enabling her to sing in public. And after so much generosity (Tina and her baby son by Raymond Hill, the saxophone player, even moved into Ike's house), Ike felt entitled to rename her, to mold her into his fantasy Wild Woman. Ike was "fixated on the white jungle goddesses who romped through Saturday-matinee movie serials—revealingly rag-clad women with long flowing hair and names like Sheena,

Queen of the Jungle, and Nyoka . . . . Nyoka, Sheena-Tina! . . . Ike's own personal Wild Woman" (Turner, 1986, 77–78).

By this time Ike had battered Tina into battered women's syndrome. In *I, Tina*, Tina addresses the battered woman's $64,000 question with a typical answer: "Why didn't I leave him? It's easy now to say I should've. But . . . I already had one child, and I was pregnant with another by him. Singing with Ike was how I made my living. And I was living better than I ever had in my life." (Turner, 1986) Not only is it a matter of economics (which it remains for Tina throughout, as well as after, her relationship with Ike—she went on food stamps and into monstrous debt upon leaving him later on); but she also possessed the battered woman's typical faith, implying a sense of failed responsibility, that she could fix everything: " 'Well, Ike is my husband, and we have our children, and I'll make our life good, and happy' " (Turner, 1986, 137). Tina was, as the rest of the autobiography clarifies, indeed a self-punishing fool in love, indoctrinated to think that it was up to her to restore a relationship with a man overpowered by a fiercely controlling temperament. And once Ike had conditioned her in effect to blame herself—a mode of self-destructive thinking endorsed by the surrounding culture that so readily accepted through Ike's songs the batterer's sexist ideology—Tina had a hard time thinking outside of her new "subjectivity." ("A Fool in Love," "You Shoulda Treated Me Right," and "Think It's Gonna Work Out Fine" loosely reflect Lenore Walker's three phases of battering: "The tension-building phase; the explosion or acute battering incident; and the calm, loving respite" [Walker 1979, 55].) "Whatever she—a twenty-year-old country nobody from Nut Bush, Tennessee—had achieved so far in her young life was due to him," the editor (Kurt Loder) sums up, with (I think) insufficient sarcasm or wisdom about the loss (or lack thereof) entailed in the metamorphosis of Anna Mae.

Capable of more insight into her complex identity than Kurt Loder (to what extent is she *no longer* "a nobody"?), Tina Turner at times was able to distance herself from "that woman who went out onstage—she was somebody else" (Turner, 1986, 130). Yet, during the divorce proceedings, willing to relinquish all financial claims while shouldering more than her share of financial burdens, all Tina wanted was "her" name. She had been so radically transformed that the title of her autobiography can only hope to signify her by foregrounding the "I" in Tina, even as this "I" invokes her violent maker. "I was like [I was Ike?] a shadow. I almost didn't exist" (Turner, 1986, 130). Readers can find exasperating, in fact, Tina Turner's apparent failure to extricate herself from Ike. She keeps Ike's name; the covers of *I, Tina* maintain her image as Ike's Wild Woman.

But perhaps the most insightful realization we could come to here is that the psychological constituents of Tina's newly constructed identity make a peeling away of Tina from Anna Mae impossible. Since one of the psychic benefits of the production of "Tina Turner" was the preservation, through Ike, of Anna Mae's bonds of love to Zelma, "Tina Turner" is psychically imbricated with Anna Mae; and there is no one else to be. Becoming Tina Turner, the battered woman/wife of violent Ike, was enabled by the preoedipal attractions of this "new identity." Here we have an example of Diana Fuss's idea in *Identification Papers* that "Identification inhabits, organizes, instantiates identity" (Fuss, 1995, 2). Anna Mae's identification with her mother—her incorporation or assimilation of her, upon losing her—led Anna Mae to become Tina Turner, i.e., to become repossessed by Ike. Such an identity also was, in other words, instantiated by the identification with Zelma. Anna Mae/Tina is a psychic double bind.

At the time of her marriage, then, Tina's identity was being constituted by two collaborating sources. Like the typical batterer, Ike bestowed "identity" on his victim in part by prohibiting interaction with others that might interfere with his disciplinary procedures. (Ike so much resembled the police that he was known for fining people he employed for various lapses, such as missing a snap on a dress.) It was not until Phil Spector took an interest in Tina alone, and she visited his mansion to record "River Deep," that she was able to go anywhere without Ike. Ike's girlfriends were the sole people Tina could befriend, since "There was no life outside of the house and the studio and the road. . . . I couldn't even go to a movie on my own. If I had to go to the market or something, I'd have to tell [Ike] first—and he still might come and check up on me" (Turner, 1986, 127). Shopping became Tina's only escape, although on tour with the Rolling Stones, she possessed no money of her own with which to shop. Ike denied Tina's girlish request for a five-dollar-a-week allowance; she had to "steal" from Ike's wad of cash to purchase a wig she wanted.

Of course Foucault's disciplinary power is institutional and not wielded by an individual; still, it is as if Ike invented Bentham's panopticon for his own personal use. He had the audacity to expand his disciplinary control and punitive power by installing within his new music studio (Bolic) a closed-circuit TV system that monitored all of the studio's spaces, including its restrooms. Ike's "panopticon" instilled in his employees, colleagues, whoever came into the studio, the sensation that someone was watching them all of the time, as indeed someone might have been. While Ike recorded, he could click dials to check out goings-on in various rooms: naked women predictably were favored targets of Ike's Benthamite gaze. Although not living on site, Tina was irregularly but often summoned to wait on Ike at Bolic in whatever way he wished. Referring to herself and another of Ike's women (whom Ike also beat and by whom he had a daughter), Tina remarks, "we were prisoners, you know?" (Turner, 1986, 168). Ann Cain broaches the subject of the psychological etiology on Ike's side: "Ike really did love Tina. But he was always afraid of losing her—of losing *control* of

her. And he felt that the only way he could keep her was to lock her up"
(Turner, 1986, 179). Tina's being locked up, imprisoned, I am suggesting,
helped her (another Sadean jailed jailer) to secure her own maternal prisoner.

Invisibly suffused within the TV waves of his panopticonic prison network, Ike was also decidedly "there," often reigning as fully and visibly as
Foucault's pre-nineteenth-century sovereign—as the King of the Kings of
Rhythm.[3] Batterers certainly enhance their ability to provide jouissance to
abused daughters desperately seeking it by engaging in literal violence beyond their disciplinary strategies. The *punishment* component of male
power within the modern disciplinary network simply cannot be neglected
in an analysis of violence against women. As preposterous as it may seem to
have to assert that, the recent Foucauldian emphasis on discipline has
helped to exclude battered women from contemporary anti-exclusionary
political theory in the humanities (despite the fact that passages can be
found in Foucault's writing itself that point to the "very real" "oppressive
effects of power relations" [Oliver, 1998, 115]).

On her final day with Ike, flying to the Dallas concert, Tina imagined him
imagining himself as royalty when he insisted on a certain seating arrangement, "with me and Ann on either side and him lying across us. We had
always had to put up with this whether he slept or not, just so he could lie
there like some kind of king, right?" (Turner, 1986, 188). On this horrific
day of Tina's final rebellion, Ike behaved as if he were a king seeking to
inflict excessive pain, to mark and bloody the body of his offender, and to
make of that body a public spectacle. Ike pounded Tina with several of his
backhand licks and blows with his shoe, so that the left side of her face was
"swollen out past [her] ear and blood was everywhere—running out of [her]
mouth, splattered all over [her] *white suit*" (Turner, 1986, 189, my emphasis). She had to walk from the taxi to the Hilton reception desk as a battered
bloody spectacle, "with one eye swollen almost shut" (Turner, 1986, 189).

Restoring Zelma, Ike typically inflicted peculiar bodily punishment on
Tina for others to witness. He was driven to mark and scar her body and to
have those marks show, to brand publicly his victim with infamy—his own
transferred. Foucault's comments on the pre-nineteenth-century torturer's
intentions fit Ike: torture traces "on the very body of the condemned man
signs that must not be effaced"; the "very excess of the violence employed
is one of the elements of its glory: . . . that the guilty man should moan and
cry out under the blows is not a shameful side-effect, it is the very ceremo-
nial of justice being expressed in all its force" (Foucault, 1979, 34). (The
batterer's compulsion to publicize his brutality is epitomized by the fact that
photographer Donna Ferrato has been able to capture with her camera *live*
scenes of domestic violence: one of her photos includes a mirror reflecting
her startling presence in the corner of the bathroom in which a husband

slaps his wife.) Like the body of Foucault's condemned man, Tina's body published her crime (to have been abandoned?) and carried its punisher's signature. One of Ike's habits was to beat Tina with shoes and shoe trees (and then to rape her) so that she "always had a cut on [her] head somewhere, always had bruises" (Turner, 1986, 91), even while performing on stage, where she struggled to sing through "cut and swollen lips" (Turner, 1986, 92). Just before a show, Ike punched her in the face, broke her jaw, and Tina had to "go on and sing anyway, with the blood just gushing in [her] mouth" (Turner, 1986, 144). Domestic violence could hardly get more spectacular.

In his obsessive psychological manipulation of Anna/Tina, Ike seems keenly aware of the superior power of the mind compared to the power of physical violence, cognizant that (as Foucault writes, in *Discipline and Punish,* quoting Sevran) "despair and time eat away the bonds of iron and steel, but they are powerless against the habitual union of ideas" (Foucault, 1979, 103). In particular, the feminism that was beginning to pervade society threatened Ike; he was eager to fight that ideological fire with his own, backed by an economy of suspended rights. Nevertheless Ike used physical violence to ground and substantiate his retrograde notions. The wounding of Tina's body seems to have provided Ike, as it provides Scarry's torturer as well as the typical batterer, with verification of his power, voice, and identity: "the torturer's growing sense of self is carried outward on the prisoner's swelling pain" (Scarry, 1985, 56). Ike seems to have gained from Tina's contraction, which fortified her melancholic state, his own expansion. Especially when he felt his power slipping, Ike resorted to physical abuse; certain momentary injuries (usually imagined) were sufficient to cause him to feel, and act on, the necessity of immediately restoring his sovereignty.

I have been arguing that the psychologically regressive power of a batterer (a restoration of matriarchal power) implies an historically regressive power (a restoration of monarchical power). The batterer's physical assault provides a reminiscence of the presubjective maternal bond. This reversal of the Foucauldian historical arrow, however, is not only a peculiar horror but also a horrible feminist opportunity. Return modern power to the moment it intersects premodern power, and it is returned to the moment of its undoing. The self-contradiction of premodern power is reentailed every time a batterer publicly reverts to it, so that he crowns himself king only to risk, at the moment of imperial triumph, his own beheading. My aim here is to point to a mode by which battered women and their advocates can regain, and have been regaining, control over their bodies and psyches. The batterer's reliance upon spectacular punishment offers battered women a chance to resignify their predicaments and pain. At the same time, they work against their melancholic condition of asymbolia, however it is acquired, so that their own representation serves as both a political and therapeutic act.

Foucault provides the paradigm of such reappropriation and transformation. Historically, as he explains in *Discipline and Punish*, public executions began to be undermined as the carnival atmosphere surrounding them began to accommodate, if not inspire, the inverting of rules, the mocking of authority, and the metamorphosis of criminals into heroes. Especially when a conviction was regarded as unjust, in particular if a man had been unjustly put to death, the people refused to support such penal practices. The accessibility of the spectacle left room, in other words, for rebellion that grew to become unignorable social disturbance. Public intervention became possible in the open air, as, especially for the poor, it could not occur in court. The "great spectacle of punishment ran the risk of being rejected by the very people to whom it was addressed." A solidarity grew up between petty offenders and spectators: "out of the ceremony of the public execution, out of that uncertain festival in which violence was instantaneously reversible, it was this solidarity much more than the sovereign power that was likely to emerge with a redoubled strength" (Foucault, 1979, 63). During one punitive display in Avignon at the end of the seventeenth century, compassion moved the crowd to hurl stones at the executioner, fall on him, and beat him; children carried off the smashed gallows and threw it into the Rhône. The unmoored quality of spectacle seems to have given rise to a two-sided discourse, as crowds managed to wrest for the alleged criminal the glory that the sovereign intended to wrest (out of the spectacle) for himself—and thus to the possibility of the redirecting of spectacle.

It therefore seems crucial to keep up the current surge of representations of woman abuse—the more spectacular the better?—in an effort to capture the hold of spectacular violence against women on pain, to keep the public eye riveted on manifestations of such pain, and thus to use art as a counter to the signature of the power that men inscribe on the female body—all of this without fretting too much over our possible theoretical complicity with the powers-that-be, due to our necessary dependence upon forms of representation (an argument taken up at length in chapter 6), as if we were battered women thought to be a party to our abuse.[4] For, as Scarry writes, "[t]he failure to express pain . . . will always work to allow its appropriation and conflation with debased forms of power; conversely, the successful expression of pain will always work to expose and make impossible that appropriation and conflation" (Scarry, 1985, 14).

The batterer's silencing and shrinking of the battered woman is facilitated by her propensity for silence and containment if she is already melancholic. But even if she is not, he produces the condition of melancholia by incarcerating her through discipline, physically entombing her in a restricted space, pounding her body into muteness, and instilling fears—so that in either case, previously melancholic or not, she needs the bridge of representation to reenter the symbolic order, to resubjectify herself, to enable, through the medium and mediation of signification, her own desiring subjectivity. Especially a text such as I, Tina, with its popular appeal, can perform such work of mourning on individual and collective levels at once.

III. EYE, TINA

I was getting to the point where I was ready to start talking back— because I was just tired of being scared, tired of being hit and tortured, tired of everything.

—Tina Turner, I, Tina (my emphasis)

Moving from silence into speech is for the oppressed, the colonized, the exploited, and those who stand and struggle side by side a gesture of defiance that heals, *that makes new life and new growth possible.*
  It is that act of speech, of "talking back," that is not mere gesture of empty words, that is the expression of our movement from object to subject—*the liberated voice.*

—bell hooks, Talking Back (my emphases)

Spectacle would seem to entail the unleashing of its agent's control, to be untethered by a single producing gaze while open to the apprehension of multitudes—the multiplicity of angles of vision being what defines a spectacle. Its privileging of the audience seems to lend spectacle an egalitarian openness that narrative, more grounded, more powerfully authorized, lacks. If we consider, in particular, spectacles of bodies in pain, we realize that it is the very ability of spectacle to seize on the prediscursive phenomenon of pain, resistant to representation, that renders spectacle itself so seizable. Narratives attempting to express the pain of woman abuse seem inevitably to border on the nonnarrative to do so, as we have witnessed through the semiotic dimension of the texts examined so far. Perhaps, then, the ripeness of spectacle to appropriation, the ease with which it may be translated into multiple discourses, to be claimed by the very audience the spectacle was meant to awe and thereby frighten into submission, helps explain why the topic of woman abuse has been, over the past decade or so, taken up artistically in especially visual, nonnarrative media. There would seem to be a compatibility between spectacular domestic violence and the specular forms that this artwork assumes to combat that violence: e.g., clothesline displays of T-shirts honoring and recording the horrors of battered women; art exhibitions of wrecked automobiles dotted with written tags indicating eerie linkages between battered women's attempts to escape as well as survive and the autos themselves; milk carton art; photography; nonlinear film. It is as if the specular/spectacular aspect of such art were necessary to wrest—to transfer—from spectacles of violence their grip on women's pain, to tap into them for the sake of transmutation, to recover the pain generated by such violence.

That this is a major direction of artistic expression of woman abuse validates the stress in feminist film theory on the capacity of nonnarrative artistic modes to spur resistance. The relation of conventional film's complex expression and wide circulation of "woman as spectacle—body to be looked at, place of sexuality, and object of desire" to "women's cinema," which defetishizes that body (de Lauretis, 1984, 4), might be said to parallel the relation of spectacular woman abuse to the visual art that engages this topic. Teresa de Lauretis, in *Alice Doesn't*, encourages the turning of dominant discourses inside out, having concluded that "the only way to position oneself outside of that discourse is to displace oneself within it" (de Lauretis, 1984, 7), which is in effect what feminist artists of highly visual art forms are doing on behalf of battered women, as they resituate victims of theatrical male violence within feminist theater. The victim is in a sense extracted and released from one spectacle and deposited into another, an alternative spectacle whose function is to protect her from further abuse—in part by publicizing it and thereby producing unignorable social disturbance. For the sake of grounding male empowerment, the battered woman's body is bloodied, wounded, ripped open and thus turned into spectacle. Using strategic homeopathy in aesthetic acts of mourning, artists of domestic woman abuse sabotage this male spectacularizing of the woman's exposed (even internally, insofar as it is wounded) body and the resulting power, as well as pleasure in that power.

With this theoretical speculation in mind, I want to look at how *Defending Our Lives* (winner of the 1994 Academy Award for best short documentary) ambivalently deploys spectacle to arrest violence against women. *Defending Our Lives* is needless to say visually oriented, in part for the sake of mirroring, to displace, spectacular violence, even as it seems deliberately to preclude sight in particular of the wounded female body (though a couple of anonymous exceptions flash by at the beginning, and several battered *faces* are shown), or for that matter of the female body *tout court*. Throughout the documentary we witness bulky, sometimes colorful police bags that enclose women's dead bodies being hauled out of homes, in a kind of pageant; coffins too appear, encasing bodies, which again we do not see. No further pleasure or power will be taken in/from these women's wounds, the documentary seems to insist. *Defending Our Lives* lets us visualize primarily, and strangely, talking heads, as if dramatizing a literalization of hooks's representational "talking back." In listening to the four featured women incarcerated for the killing of their boyfriends and husbands, we concentrate on the neck up; we are lured into their minds, as they lapse back onto the ghastly vivid images they labor to translate into words.

Yet *Defending Our Lives* is spectacular in its atemporality: a frozen qual-

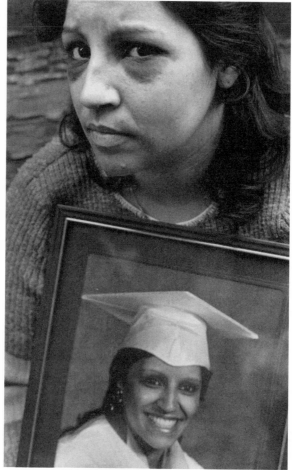

Copyright Donna Ferrato/Domestic Abuse Awareness, Inc.

ity dominates the documentary, which in a sense refuses to progress. It begins with two shots from a photograph included in Donna Ferrato's *Living with the Enemy*—the former of a smiling school graduate, wearing a graduation cap and gown and glowing with promise; the latter (which contains the former) of her face blackened with bruises—and ends with the photo of her face blackened with bruises, so that photos, themselves frozen in their frames, seem to frame the stasis of the film situated between. Such stasis "between" is largely effected by the splicing of the six presentations that comprise the documentary: all beginnings of the women's accounts are first presented consecutively, then all middles, then all ends, as if synchronically stacked, rather than each account being diachronically carried out, without interruption, from beginning to end. In this way suspense is cut down, if not off. Within each of the four incarcerated women's speeches, too, fragments, which sometimes do not seem perfectly to follow what precedes them, tell the fractured tale.

Pleasure in sustained narrative is voided, enabling the traumatic event that terminated a prolonged painful period of time—the death of the batterer—to be isolated and grasped. *Defending Our Lives* can be read as an artistic embodiment of the static moment of killing. The documentary itself seems enmeshed in the timeless, unforgettable moments of torture culminating in the moment of killing, as if that consummation still consumed everything, as if no release from such trauma could ever be bestowed on the women. When one enters the world of battering from the woman's side, in short, one enters a peculiarly timeless, speechless, depressing realm: battering promises a life of interminable pain with no spatial, temporal, or verbal exit. Even the moment of killing one's batterer must be replayed with never diminishing vividness in the mind of the woman who killed. In the film Patty Hennessy, who shoots her husband three times yet somehow fails to topple him (Brian continues to stand), verbally captures the transcendent moment: "It was like time was standing still"; "he was . . . this unbeatable thing." Meekah Scott, who recites a litany of twenty names of women killed by their batterers in Massachusetts in the past eleven months (of 1991), conveys this same sense of unbeatableness. This sense is ironically underscored when she announces at the end of her recitation that she too could have been one of the statistics, except that—she says limply, affectlessly, ambiguously—"I fought back." Although out on appeal at the time of the filming of the documentary, Meekah Scott was sentenced to prison for eight to twelve years for killing her batterer. A battered woman, as Cynthia K. Gillespie writes, learns that "[n]o matter how hard she tries to please him or appease him, fight back against him, or apply social sanctions to stop his violence, he will always beat her again" (Gillespie, 1989, 154). Silence, melancholic asymbolia, the Thing-like quality of death—all seem locked into place. The documentary therefore, I am suggesting, must be equally static to grasp, to transfer the pain. Here too we have a kind of matching, or overlapping, of two forms of jouissance—one violent, the other aesthetic—the latter designed to convert the jouissance of the former to desire, that is, to textual desire on which desiring subjectivity may eventually be predicated.

The point that no victory has been won, that the batterer is unbeatable, that even upon being killed he is simply reincarnated, is clinched as *Defending Our Lives* suggests the isomorphism of the batterer's and the (still thriving) system's treatment of the women victims. Like batterers who hold their victims hostage, the legal system isolates especially women who kill their abusers; within the confines of their *re*incarceration—while the men are reincarnated, the women are reincarcerated—it controls just about every aspect of their lives, fulfilling the batterer's dream. Lisa Grimshaw's husband, Tommy, tied her up and to her bed, leaving her for *hours*; the legal system isolated her in an eight-by-fifteen foot room for three and a half-*years*, the majority of that time awaiting trial. Also like batterers, the police fail to protect the women in the first place; lack of police protection becomes a refrain within *Defending Our Lives*. And despite the homage it pays to the family ideal, the criminal justice system (again like the batterer) damages the family, in severing mother and (innocent) child or children, who are likewise doubly abused. Lisa Grimshaw and Patty Hennessy do their best to protect their sons from their batterers (Tommy threatens to cut their baby out of Lisa's body, when she is six-months pregnant), and Patty Hennessy shoots her husband for being on the verge of acting on his threat to deprive her forever of her son (he taunts her with: "You better kiss Tim good-bye cause you're never gonna see him again"). It goes without saying that both mothers lose close contact with their sons upon being imprisoned, and Timmy (Patty Hennessy's child) is sent to live with her batterer's family (now she has no choice but to kiss Timmy good-bye). Like a consciously collaborating partner, the court easefully and legally carries out the batterer's former threats.

One function, then, of the documentary's formal lack of movement, of its seeming to be stuck spectacularly in a time whose violence had appeared to overcome time is to establish—acknowledge, represent, and thereby confront—the depth of these women's entrenchment in their violent pasts. To put this perversely: any woman with a psychic appetite for self-laceration as a way of inverting matricidal drive upon herself, of playing out the death of herself instead of the mother, would be quite unconsciously satisfied by such violence. The muteness, destruction, the evil, the deadliness that characterize jouissance, the melancholic's pathway to the all-consuming mother could easily be rediscovered in the jaws of such violence. Likewise, these qualities are imposed on the battered woman no matter what her psychic taste, constructing her as melancholic, causing the abyssal condition of clinical depression, like it or not.

But the flexibility of spectacle, i.e., its discursive duplicity, comes in handy at this nadir, giving spectacle transferential power, and therefore the power to mourn. "Where the wound had been given, there must the cure be found, if anywhere" (Austen, 1972, 97). My argument is that it is because *Defending Our Lives* is isomorphic with the batterer's as well as the system's violence that it can recover female pain, effect a redeployment of male power, and talk back, reverse discourse. For one thing, having ruled out the (feminist) male gaze of desire, *Defending Our Lives* substitutes the gaze of bruised children watching mothers being brutalized and vice versa. Filled with photographed images of distraught children, Donna Ferrato's *Living with the Enemy* makes this same exchange. Paging through, we see an eight-year-old boy pointing in intense anger at his father being arrested, and screaming " 'I hate you. Never come back to my house.' " (Ferrato, 1991, 32–33); a little girl, her eyes full of fear and suspicion, who had seen her father burn and stab her mother, keeping "her eye on the street, frightened her father would find them before they could get away" (Ferrato, 1991, 62); and a three-year-old boy on a tricycle hysterically howling—his Munch-like mouth wide open—gazing up at his father dragging away his undressed mother (Ferrato, 1991, 146–47). Take a look from *that* sociopolitical position, both the documentary and Ferrato's photographs urge the viewer, so that, again, looking is deprived of its pleasure—scopophilia turned into scopophobia.

Homi Bhabha's meditations on and politicization of Lacan's "evil eye," in *The Location of Culture*, seem relevant, if not to the eyes of these children then at least to the unflinching, piercing gaze of Ferrato's camera as well as to *Defending Our Lives* and *I, Tina* (pun intended) themselves.

> The play of the evil eye is camouflaged, invisible in the common, on-going activity of looking—making present, while it is implicated in the petrifying, unblinking gaze that falls Medusa-like on its victims—dealing death, extinguishing both presence and the present. There is a specifically feminist representation of political subversion in this strategy of the evil eye. The disavowal of the position of the migrant woman—her social and political *invisibility*—is used by her in her secret art of revenge, *mimicry*. In that overlap of signification—in that fold of identification as cultural and sexual difference—the 'I' is the initial, initiatory signature of the subject; and the 'eye' (in its metonymic repetition) is the sign that initiates the terminal, arrest, death:
>
> > as even now you look
> > but never see me . . .
> > Only my eyes will remain to haunt,
> > and to turn your dreams
> > to chaos. (56)

IV. GAZING BACK AT THE LAW

*As soon as the subject becomes aware that the other gazes at him . . . ,
the fascination is dispelled.*

—Slavoj Zizek, *Looking Awry*

While signifying pain is certainly an antidote to depression, silence, disempowerment, and desirelessness, speaking back to the law, critiquing it, and consequently altering it are perhaps the most effective ways that battered women have of pulling out of their asymbolia and situating themselves at

the center of the symbolic order. In the form of imitative spectacle, its version of Bhabha's mimicry, *Defending Our Lives* is able to express grief as well as seize male force—as preliminary to its legally informed rebuttal to an antiquated patriarchal judicial system. A key point of *Defending Our Lives* (foregrounded in the title) is that Shannon Booker, Eugenia Moore, Patty Hennessy, and Lisa Grimshaw killed in self-defense. Each woman clarifies that it was unequivocally, inevitably, going to be "me or him."

Mimicking her batterer's deep tone of voice, Eugenia Moore states four times, "He was gonna kill me," in a way that conveys the reality of obliteration she faced. Her boyfriend, Alfred, who commonly carried a butcher knife, snuck up on her in a grocery market parking lot, hit her on her lower back, reiterating his threat to kill her. Eugenia stabbed him, because, as she stresses, "he came to murder me." (She receives a life sentence.) Patty Hennessy, trapped between a fence and her husband's van charging at her like a wild bull, plainly and convincingly states that she "thought [she] was dead . . . this is it. He's finally gonna kill me, like he says he's gonna." In her final confrontation with her (at this time) ex-husband Brian, she "knew he was going to kill [her] that day. I mean he had told me so. It was like the final frontier. This was it. . . . It was me or him." After luring her home, José said to Shannon, "Bitch, before you leave, I'll kill you" and threatened her with a gun. Although he had threatened to kill her before, "this night," she testifies in the film, "was more fearful than ever." These women show that their experiences for the most part fit the legal paradigm of self-defense. (Perhaps Patty Hennessy's frontier allusion is even meant to suggest an analogy between her conditions and those that prevailed in the Wild West that directly informed our self-defense laws.) And insofar as there are gaps between their experiences and that paradigm (apparently the courts thought there were), *Defending Our Lives* points to the inapplicability of the archaic law of self-defense to women terrorized by their mates.[5]

The documentary thus addresses the legal requirement that killing in self-defense be "reasonable," by establishing the necessity of the killings ("it was me or him") through the women's unlugubrious, articulate, controlled accounts (no emotional excess clouds this rational defense) of the mad*men* with whom they had to contend. (In her essay "violence in intimate relationships," bell hooks notes the paradox that "People within patriarchal society imagine that women are hit because we are beyond reason," while "[i]t is most often the person who is hitting that is beyond reason, who is hysterical, who has lost complete control over responses and actions" [hooks, 1989, 85].) Legally, any person is "entitled to kill another if that person reasonably believes that he or she is in imminent danger of death or, at the very least, serious bodily injury at the hands of the other" (Gillespie, 1989, xi). Although each of the incarcerated women in *Defending Our Lives* has undergone a unique tragedy, and one should beware of conflating them, there is no question but that all four reasonably believed that they faced either "imminent danger of death" or at the very least "serious bodily injury." Their guilty verdicts therefore blatantly illustrate Cynthia Gillespie's point that "when a woman kills a man, especially a man with whom she lives intimately, we are loath to acknowledge that she was acting in self-defense" (Gillespie, 1989, xi).

To think that "a woman might justifiably defend herself from her own husband" was—is?—to think the "unthinkable" (Gillespie, 1989, 39). How different is our modern cultural unconscious from Medieval consciousness on these matters? Contributing to the preservation of Foucault's king in another guise, our courts even maintain the "castle doctrine," stemming from the "ancient idea that a man's home is his castle, the place where he has a right to expect safety" (Gillespie, 1989, 82).[6] In a nutshell, premodern spectacular punishment is alive and well largely because the legal system protects it (a point we will reencounter in chapter 6 as it is elaborated and underscored in Drabble's *The Needle's Eye*). It is not merely that law enforcement and criminal justice fail. Domestic abuse is, in a systematic fashion, institutionally supported, women who resist or fight back institutionally punished.

In subtly documenting this Foucauldian point (while keeping gender well in mind), *Defending Our Lives* offers its viewer an education in *contemporary* Medieval law, transforming in the process pain into symbolic power, in an effort to open up sign systems to female sites of mourning—for the overwhelming myriad losses that the women of the documentary have suffered. That is to say: spectacular gazing back at the world in reflection of the insidious ways in which the social and especially the legal system colludes with individual batterers might be seen as the commencement of a process of public mourning. Until battered women have articulated their pain, their passage beyond asymbolia will remain obstructed, their ability to be desiring subjects impaired. Until their losses are negated via entry into discourse—legal discourse in particular—battered women will remain depressingly disempowered.

V. THE DEMISE OF BATTERING

[B]odies never quite comply with the norms by which their materialization is impelled. Indeed, it is the instabilities, the possibilities for rematerialization, . . . that mark one domain in which the force of the regulatory law can be turned against itself to spawn rearticulations that call into question the hegemonic force of that very regulatory law.

—Judith Butler, *Bodies That Matter*

By building on Kristeva's theory of melancholia, I have suggested a connection, traced through the various texts analyzed so far in this study, between disturbed mother-daughter cathexes and the daughters' vulnerability to abuse by a male partner. Through my work as a battered women's counselor, I have also witnessed in my clients Kristevan mother-daughter relations enabling both disciplinary and spectacular forms of male power. The most extreme case was a woman who felt paralyzed in the face of her batterer's torture of her two children, especially her little girl, by her sense that he was an avatar of *her* abusive mother, thus turning her into the helpless little girl. The boyfriend beat the little girl with a board so severely that for a long time she could not walk. It was not until he attempted to drown the little girl in the toilet that the mother snapped out of her identification with the child.

But while Kristevan melancholia may be a common precondition, whether it is a prerequisite for domestic woman abuse would be impossible to say; such power certainly appears to have a tenacious way of locating cultural vulnerabilities where psychological ones are at least not visible. As a psychoanalytic/cultural critic, one hopes to integrate a psychoanalytic perspective with cultural analysis, to do as penetrating an inquiry into the psyches of battered women as possible, attempting to unearth why some women avoid battering while others do not. But that work must be done without contributing to the pernicious but flourishing campaign against victims. At the same time, while psychoanalysis misleads insofar as it tends to make victims responsible for violence that is socially pervasive, a sociological analysis fails to distinguish between batterers and nonbatterers, victims and nonvictims. It is the case that women sometimes participate (consciously and unconsciously) in their own subjection. As a result we need to keep in mind Benjamin's question in *The Bonds of Love* of "How is domination anchored in the hearts of those who submit to it?" (Benjamin, 1988, 52) as well as Copjec's injunction to read the inarticulable, which in this study has been melancholic jouissance and, more importantly, the textual desire depathologizing that jouissance in a textual traversal of the melancholic's fundamental fantasy.

Breines and Gordon's shrewd critique, in "The New Scholarship on Family Violence," of the dichotomy "expressive" versus "functional" violence shows that domestic violence *can* be expressive for the individual who commits it and functional for the society that sanctions it. Therefore, when depression and domestic woman abuse do manage to converge (as in the life of Tina Turner), the battered woman would seem to be up against futility, her psyche playing felicitously into the rough hands, metaphorically speaking, of a systemic production of the "battered woman," as well as into the literal rough hands of her sovereign. When this is the case, it might even be that the regressive maternal attachment on the part of the female victim exacerbates the insecurity of the batterer whose role becomes maternal substitute rather than full-fledged partner, and thus sets in motion regressive forms of power. Ike's position in Tina's psychic and erotic life, for example, was another's displaced; he was king, so to speak, because he could not be queen. A psychic regressiveness might spark a social regressiveness, fortified by a regressive medieval legal system.

Yet, whatever the *interplay* of psychological and cultural forces, especially insofar as it is spectacular, such power is itself susceptible to a mournful takeover—a takeover that, as I have tried to convey, depends on mourning, that is, on a move to signification through negation/acceptance of loss on behalf of all domestically abused women. For the melancholic woman's tendency to find the jouissance of the Other in the form of abusive violence psychically satisfying alerts us to the production of the very conditions of melancholia for the battered woman, predisposed to "enjoy" such abuse or not. As a result, I have tried to show that it is instability—such as that of spectacle—as Butler optimistically has pointed out, that enables resignification. Scarry's idea that expression of pain precludes its conversion into the torturer's power may be superseded. Certain forms of expression of women's pain—epitomized by *Defending Our Lives* as well as by *I, Tina*, whose very existence signifies Tina Turner's progress in mourning the loss of her mother and thereby entering the arena of signs—can themselves become agents of appropriation and transformation in an effort to reconfigure power. As talking/writing cures become talking and gazing back, at the same time as talking and gazing back function as a talking cure, we can begin to imagine the demise of battering.

NOTES

1. Jessica Benjamin likewise assumes susceptibility on the part of a daughter to erotic submission, since, in a masochistic role, she is apt to reenact an "early identificatory relationship to the mother"—whether or not the mother is less than perfect (Benjamin, 1988, 79).

2. bell hooks's assertion that in *I, Tina* Tina Turner "presents a sexualized portrait of herself—providing a narrative that is centrally 'sexual confession' " seems part of hooks's campaign in *Black Looks* against representations of women in art and advertising (hooks, 1992, 66). hooks specifies that "Turner's fictive model of black female sexual agency remains rooted in misogynist notions" (hooks, 1992, 68). Turner herself (however) considered her reputation as sexy as a veneer: "that was the beginning of the sex-symbol thing—'Sexy Tina,' 'Wild Tina,' all that. If the people had only known" (Turner, 1986, 130). I also think that hooks misunderstands the song title "What's Love Got to Do With It?" which she assumes subordinates "the idea of romantic love" and praises "the use of sex for pleasure as commodity to exchange," missing its expression of the battered woman's attitude that

"love," marriage, family, etc. turn out to have very little to do with love (hooks, 1992, 69). Tina Turner puts the title in a quite specific context, clarifying this reading: " 'What's love got to do with it?' You know? Because here I was, pregnant by Ike Turner, who's gone back to his wife, and now she's getting suspicious. . . . I mean, this was not my idea of love at all" (Turner, 1986, 82).

3. Foucault promotes Kantorowitz's conception of "The King's Body" as "a double body," involving the "transitory element that is born and dies" as well as "another that remains unchanged by time and is maintained as the physical yet intangible support of the kingdom": "around this duality . . . are organized an iconography, a political theory of monarchy, legal mechanisms that distinguish between as well as link the person of the king and the demands of the Crown, and a whole ritual that reaches its height in the coronation, the funeral and the ceremonies of submission" (Foucault, 1979, 28–29).

4. Here I allude to Armstrong and Tennenhouse's argument that writing is "a form of violence in its own right," that reading and speaking as well are implicated in power in that they are exclusive, necessarily reconstructing the world "around the polarities of Self and Other" (Armstrong and Tennenhouse, 1989, 25).

5. That "the law of justifiable homicide often cannot be made to fit the kinds of situations that female victims of male violence find themselves in and the ways that they often must act to defend themselves" is Cynthia Gillespie's thesis in *Justifiable Homicide* (Gillespie, 1989, xi). Current self-defense law pertains to men, extending as far back in history as the English Medieval Period, when killing one's husband was considered not as self-defense but as an act of treason, punishable by burning at the stake—"a horror that persisted at least until 1793" (Gillespie, 1989, 37)— since a woman was a "subject" to her "lord." Self-defense law evolved over centuries mainly with regard to: 1) "sudden assault by a murderous stranger," and 2) "the fist fight or brawl" that spins out of control (Gillespie, 1989, 4). Two masculine assumptions about the circumstances underlay the law: that the combatants were of more or less "equal size, strength, and fighting ability" and that they were unknown to each other, fighting "in a public place from which one or both could withdraw or escape" (Gillespie, 1989, 5). Eventually the following criteria shaped the law: death must seem imminent (the threatened harm must be serious enough); a weapon can be used only if one is being used by the perpetrator; mutual combat precludes overpowering one's assailant and necessitates a full effort to retreat.

6. One might assume that such a doctrine would assist battered women, in exempting them from the legal requirement to retreat. But practically what it has done is to oblige women to flee from any king with whom she has "shared" the castle: "the notion that somehow a woman shouldn't be permitted to kill her homicidal husband in *his* castle, but should flee from it instead, is a very persistent one," writes Gillespie (Gillespie, 1989, 83). One might assume, then, that at least a woman could stand her ground against an assailant who is just visiting. Yet exceptions to the castle doctrine have been made for violent men (nobles?) who have "permission" to be in the castle. "The result has been one bizarre case after another in which a woman's right to defend herself—and quite literally whether she would go to prison or go free—hinged not on whether she reasonably believed her life was in danger but on whether the man she killed had a key to her apartment, slept over, or kept clothes in her closet, and thus had implied permission to go there when he wished" (Gillespie, 1989, 84).

6

~~~

Literary Representations of Battered Women: Spectacular Domestic Punishment

Discourses are not once and for all subservient to power or raised up against it, any more than silences are. We must make allowance for the complex and unstable process whereby discourse can be both an instrument and an effect of power, but also a hindrance, a stumbling-block, a point of resistance and a starting point for an opposing strategy.

—Michel Foucault, *The History of Sexuality* (Vol. I)

I. POWER AND PAIN

If Nancy Armstrong and Leonard Tennenhouse are right about the intrinsic violence of representation, then Kathy Acker's martyr in *Blood and Guts in High School,* the woman who gets tied up with ropes, beaten a lot, "all gooky and bloody and screaming," full of "angry hurt pain inside"— like the typical victim fresh from battering who cannot communicate anything to anyone—can *never* express herself, or have her plight expressed by another (such as Acker), without that expression being implicated in the dominant power structure (Acker, 1978, 99). A logical extension of a deterministic strain of Foucauldianism as well as of feminist theories that insist upon the inescapable masculinity of the symbolic register, Armstrong and Tennenhouse's theory assumes that victims who manage somehow to find their way to expression become members of the ruling class, while authors who express their characters' victimization acquire power at their charac-

103

ters' expense. For, as they argue in their introduction to the collection *The Violence of Representation,* writing is "a form of violence in its own right"; reading and speaking too are implicated in power in that they are exclusive, in that they necessarily reconstruct the world "around the polarities of Self and Other" (Armstrong and Tennenhouse, 1989, 2, 7). As a result "whenever we speak for someone else[,] we are inscribing her with our own (implicitly masculine) idea of order" (Armstrong and Tennenhouse, 1989, 25).[1]

Women's as well as feminist discourse is by no means exempt from the colonizing that Armstrong and Tennenhouse indict. They have abstracted the logic of their theory deliberately from a text written by a woman—Brontë's *Jane Eyre*—in which Jane overcomes certain "Others" (Mrs. Reed, Mr. Brocklehurst, Blanche Ingram, Mr. Rochester, "Others" one might have thought worth overcoming; Bertha is conspicuously missing) in order to become a heroine, as well as to attain the status of narrator. Thus Jane suppresses difference and participates in the violence of representation. Even as Jane's power assumes benevolent forms, such as supervision and education, it is a kind of imperialism, rendering her claim to victim status illegitimate. Imperialism represents what is "culturally other as a negation of self," just as (this analogy presumes) Jane does in carving out her "deep" self. Jane Eyre, in Armstrong and Tennenhouse's estimation, "is the progenitrix of a new gender, class, and race of selves in relation to whom all others are deficient. No less is at stake in granting such an individual power to author her own history" (Armstrong and Tennenhouse, 1989, 8).[2]

One can deduce from this reaction to Jane the hopelessness of academics—who are "directly involved in the violence of representation"—ever sidestepping power over those for whom they may wish to put power to beneficent use. To Armstrong and Tennenhouse, there is no refuge, no getting outside the hegemony: not in the "deepest recesses of the female psyche" or on "the loftiest pinnacles of art" (Armstrong and Tennenhouse, 1989, 25). All writing, speaking, reading beings—academics in particular—are "[c]ondemned to power" (Armstrong and Tennenhouse, 1989, 26). The only thing we can do (consequently) is to recognize the kinship between the violence of Jane Eyre's discourse and our own. We are, in Armstrong and Tennenhouse's essay, likewise compared to hospital staff who participate in the construction of the battered woman by refusing to inquire into the cause of her injured body. Armstrong and Tennenhouse end their introductory piece by turning to Teresa de Lauretis's commentary on the institutional complicity in battering of medical and other " 'helping professions' (such as the police and the judiciary)"; de Lauretis looks at how women who are seeking help are boomeranged right back into the role of the battered victim (de Lauretis, 1989, 241). Academics (to Armstrong and Tennenhouse) victimize similarly: "like the medical personnel in de Lauretis's study, we are, in naming, also constituting information as an event, transaction, or relationship. We are positioning it within our culture and in relation to ourselves. . . . We exercise the very form of power which . . . gained centrality as part of modern imperialism" (Armstrong and Tennenhouse, 1989, 26). Imperialists, Jane Eyre, emergency medical staff (deliberately oblivious to the battering that drives their patients to them), academics, writers, readers, speakers—all are complicit in the suppression of difference in the violence of representation.

Following Armstrong and Tennenhouse's logic, it would seem that if academics are as guilty of committing the violence of representation as de Lauretis's medical personnel, then de Lauretis (as an academic) is as guilty of committing the violence of representation as the medical personnel whose representational violence she brings to our attention. Even more extravagantly, a writer apparently writing on behalf of abused women would seem to enact semiotic violence, through representation, on par with the empirical violence "out there" in the world. Their "ultimate goal," Armstrong and Tennenhouse assert proudly, "is to demonstrate that the two cannot in fact be distinguished" (Armstrong and Tennenhouse, 1989, 9).[3]

Armstrong and Tennenhouse's contention that all expression is acculturated and that therefore all discourse maintains "a pattern of dominance" (Armstrong and Tennenhouse, 1989, 25) itself suppresses crucial cultural/political differences. Their theory of representation elides the possibility of "the Other" speaking, as it "condemns" the *speaking* "Other" to power, which she really does not possess, that would wipe out her "Otherness" if she possessed it. Armstrong and Tennenhouse's theory prematurely elevates expressive "Otherness" to a particularly insidious form of powerful sameness; the ubiquity of power that they assume suffuses discourse cancels their occasional nod of acknowledgment of variable positions. Their opening claim that the topics of class, race, and gender "have lost their oppositional edge," now that they have been cannibalized by literary critical studies, can itself be seen as blunting that sharp edge (Armstrong and Tennenhouse, 1989, 1). Perhaps it is in the context of such assertions of centripetal sameness that Mae Henderson, around the same year (1989), felt compelled to propose a model of reading "that seeks to account for racial difference within gender identity and gender difference within racial identity" precisely in an effort to establish a more complicated paradigm of "Otherness." Henderson plays out various kinds of relationships of otherness, in which the black woman writer participates from a privileged position: "The engagement of multiple others broadens the audience for black women's writing, for . . . black women, speaking out of the specificity of their racial and gender experiences, are able to communicate in a diversity of discourses" (Henderson, 1990, 136–37).

While it cannot be denied, as Scarry elaborates in *The Body in Pain,* that pain eludes, if not resists, language, and while pain is therefore especially amenable to appropriation by persons in power, nonetheless the women writers treated in this chapter manage unopportunistically to articulate the plight and pain of battered women, to expose the complicity of various institutions with batterers, and to censure the insidious process of the social construction of the battered woman. Armstrong and Tennenhouse's theory refuses to distinguish between power congruent with the dominant ideology—including literature complicit in battering—and power on the side of the powerless—including literature that works on behalf of battered victims, literature that fights back/talks back/spectacularly gazes back. Not to make such a distinction is like equating batterers who destroy their victims with victims who defend themselves by destroying their batterers. Not to do so, in other words, is to theorize in sync with a court system (which still has not universally recognized battered women's syndrome) that has been one of the major institutions active in the construction of the battered woman.

To discourage women from representing their abuse (which is what I take to be a logical outcome of Armstrong and Tennenhouse's theory, even if it is not their intention) is also to enforce the batterer's incarceration of the battered woman in her atemporal, spatially restricted, silent domestic prison. And insofar as language is inaccessible to her, she is deprived of the negation of loss required for desiring subjectivity. In effect such abuse casts her into depression and precludes the possibility of her mourning her losses through signification. But the language that Armstrong and Tennenhouse read as violent, contrary to their argument, offers the battered woman a chance to acknowledge, mourn, and thereby accept what she has lost, to rebuild subjectivity destroyed by the pain of domestic woman abuse.

In Zora Neale Hurston's short story "Sweat," Delia Jones's husband, Sykes, keeps a diamondback rattlesnake in their kitchen to terrify her, to incite her to leave their home, and perhaps in the hope that it will escape its cage someday and bite, even kill, her. But when Delia flees from the escaped venomous snake and in turn chooses not to warn her husband that he is walking directly into its path, her passive violence against him is hardly synonymous with his active violence against her (he has abused her for fifteen years). Hurston's achievement, in fact, is to present their *modes* of violence as reciprocal, so that we can distinguish between their *positions* of violence. Again, to invoke Foucault himself: "everyone doesn't occupy the same position; certain positions preponderate and permit an effect of supremacy to be produced" (Foucault, 1980, 156). And the idea of equating Sykes's violence against Delia with Hurston's writing—certainly meant to decry Delia's oppression by Sykes—only italicizes the crudeness of a theory of representation that remains too abstract, that fails (whether it means to or not) to take into account the specific cultural positioning of the supposed perpetrator. The only violence in "Sweat," besides Sykes's, is Sykes's redirected.

Literacy and culture, in fact, are themselves sufficiently hoarded values that to make a claim to them is not necessarily to join the dominant class but can be yet *another* mode of redirection, Butler's term for which would be resignification, and David Halperin's Saint Foucault's term for which would be "reverse discourse." Ironically, given that Armstrong and Tennenhouse offer what they take to be a Foucauldian perspective, Halperin writes in *Saint Foucault* that Foucault scoffs at the idea that his *History of Sexuality* claims "that a 'reverse discourse' is one and the same as the discourse it reverses" (Halperin, 1995, 59). "After all," writes Halperin, translating Foucault into queer theory, "a reverse discourse, as Foucault describes it, does not simply produce a mirror reversal—a pure one-to-one inversion of the existing terms of the discourse it reverses" (Halperin, 1995, 59). "It is a reversal that takes us in a new direction" (Halperin, 1995, 60). This is the political version of my earlier psychoanalytic idea that a melancholic reading literature about melancholia seems to be peering into a mirror, yet the experience pulls that reader into the symbolic nevertheless. We are therefore led to the possibility of progress through writing on both psychic and political fronts.

In *Specifying,* Susan Willis points out that literacy and education are vital to the black underclass and that in the fiction of Alice Walker they are embraced as part of the very "process of liberation." Walker's "radical understanding of education lies at the heart of literacy campaigns from revolutionary Angola to Grenada and Nicaragua. Clearly, the ability to raise questions, to objectify contradictions, is only possible when Celie begins writing her letters. Similarly, for Meridian, education (*notwithstanding its inspiration in liberalism*) and the academic institution (*notwithstanding its foundation in elitism*) offer the means for confronting social and sexual contradictions that she, as a black teenage mother, would not have been able to articulate—either for herself or anyone else" (Willis, 1987, 126–27, my emphases). The "feminist subject," as Teresa de Lauretis proposes in *Technologies of Gender,* both inhabits and stands outside of the dominant ideology (including the "ideology of gender")—women are "at once within and without representation" (de Lauretis, 1987, 10). Despite the inclusion of de Lauretis in Armstrong and Tennenhouse's volume, however, this statement on the doubleness of the feminist subject clashes with the editors' sense of the limitations of the " 'female' position": "From such a position," they argue, "one may presume to speak both as one of those excluded from the dominant discourse and for those so excluded. But doing so . . . is no more legitimate than Jane Eyre's claim to victim status" (Armstrong and Tennenhouse, 1989, 10).

Insight into modern disciplinary power tends to be blind to the premodernity of the power of battering. Delia, in Hurston's story "Sweat," is situated within a world of power that, according to a Foucauldian taxonomy, is actually premodern, regressive, a world in which battles are fought by parties (husbands and wives) whose access to power is far from equal, in which the sovereign in the form of a husband still wields spectacular power over the (female) body. Bodies in the world of battering are flagrantly marked to signal the sovereign's power; rather than being ubiquitous, such power depends on untainted forms of powerlessness. Hurston depicts a regime in which everything is not complicit, in which some things are simply weak and silenced, in an effort to deploy her writing for the sake of a woman who is merely abused. Monarchical power survives in the family, allowing us to distinguish between despotic and insurrectionary uses of power.

An analysis of contemporary battering, again, does well to draw on Foucault's concepts of *both* modern and classical power. Considered from a cultural standpoint, as *Defending Our Lives* well illustrates, the battered woman is produced by institutions such as those alluded to by de Lauretis, the police, the judiciary, and the medical profession; by our sources of entertainment and pleasure (including the arts); and certainly by the ideology of gender. Batterers themselves have picked up on the effectiveness of modern disciplinary methods. Like Ike, in *I, Tina*, they typically install a system of surveillance of their victim's every move, designed to mold her into a voluntarily obedient individual. Battered women are pressured to internalize their batterer's projected negative image of them—which, in the case of the melancholic woman, as I have emphasized earlier, displaces unclaimed matricidal violence—so that a system of apparent self-governance emerges. They blame themselves for the rocky relationship with their batterer and blame their bodies for the injuries they receive and sustain (just as the melancholic woman blames herself for the "sins" of her mother). (In *The Psychic Life of Power,* Judith Butler discusses the various implications of her related central concern that "the formation of primary passion in dependency renders the child vulnerable to subordination and exploitation. . . . [T]his situation of primary dependency conditions the political formation and regulation of subjects and becomes the means of their subjection" [Butler, 1997, 7].) In offering her an identity—that is, insofar as she begins to conceive of herself as nothing more than "a battered woman" and of pain as her essence—the batterer may come close to shaping her "soul."[4]

Yet, in the old-fashioned or classical arena of violence and torture that the battered woman eventually enters (as is vividly apparent in the case of Tina Turner), punishment erupts into spectacle, pain is inflicted, and the body is revealed to be the batterer's primary target. Reversing Foucault's historical trajectory, the batterer marks the victim, brands her with infamy, so that her tortured body reflects the "truth of the crime" (Foucault, 1979, 35). Like the public execution in Foucault's analysis of pre-nineteenth-century forms of punishment, the acute stage of battering restores "sovereignty by manifesting it" through "invincible force," bringing into play the dissymmetry between the subject who dared to violate the law and the "all-powerful sovereign" who flaunts his strength (Foucault, 1979, 48, 49). Rather than the equal implication of all involved parties, here we have "imbalance and excess," the superior "physical strength of the sovereign beating down upon the body of his adversary and mastering it" (Foucault, 1979, 49). Power, also hidden and disseminated, in the domestic space is recentered. Declining the medical profession's usual participation in the construction of the battered woman, a medical staff worker in Sandra Cisneros's "Woman Hollering Creek" exclaims, "I was going to do this sonogram on her—she's pregnant, right?—and she just starts crying on me. *Híjole*, Felice! This poor lady's got black-and-blue marks all over. I'm not kidding. From her husband. Who else?" (Cisneros, 1992, 54).

"Panopticonism," Foucault writes, "is the general principle of a new 'political anatomy' whose object and end are not the relations of sovereignty but the relations of discipline" (Foucault, 1979, 208). Nonetheless, Foucault's premodern power persists in the era of the panopticon—as do victims (and their advocates) unimplicated in the forces that victimize them. Yet it is not merely a matter of the coexistence of two forms of power: while there may no longer be a supreme sovereign publicly marking bodies, thereby sanctioning such punishment, faceless systemic "battering" encourages and protects physical brutality on the part of "sovereigns" whose castles are their private homes. Premodern punishment does not grind to a halt as modern discipline spreads; rather it descends to the microlevel of society, to the level inhabited by women's bodies, where it is supported by, and in turn supports, all the subtleties of modern discipline that operate on souls.

My sense of the shortcomings of Armstrong and Tennenhouse's theory of representation is not meant to ignore or minimize the difficulty of developing strategies for speaking on behalf of the inexpressive subject without re-disempowering her, or of using literacy against those who have themselves used it for the sake of their empowerment without vouching for the exclusivity of that power. Foucault's monarch, like Scarry's torturer, like contemporary batterers—all capitalize on pain's inclination to remain prelinguistic (whatever its complex cause). We are thus led to the central problem of women's pain, to the muteness that cowers before the language of power that, in Armstrong and Tennenhouse as well as Foucault, is so widespread.

Despite the liabilities of such expression, however, several literary texts may be invoked that, italicizing differences rather than suppressing them, share Wini Breines and Linda Gordon's notion that battering is a socially constructed phenomenon, and in turn illustrate specific Foucauldian disciplinary measures taken by institutions of modern power that produce "the battered woman," even as they publicize the misery of women brutally beaten, savagely tortured, in some cases eventually killed—texts that, in bell hooks's terms, "talk back," and in Lacanian terms, gaze back. That is, such texts jeopardize the power structure that depends on the exclusion of such women's pain by forcing it to acknowledge the very base of stony silence that constitutes it, or to put this more positively, by enabling it to traverse its own (sadistic) fundamental fantasy.

Providing our focus here, Drabble's *The Needle's Eye*, Cisneros's "Woman Hollering Creek," Naylor's *Linden Hills*, and Walker's *The Third Life of Grange Copeland* expose subtle, modern disciplinary power (in the form of noncorporeal systemic battering) as well as the grosser premodern spectacular power (in the form of literal encryptment and physical torture of the female body), to which the former mode of power inevitably relapses. In representing such abuse, these writers resist the batterer's as well as the system's thrusting of battered women into asymbolia. As opposed to Armstrong and Tennenhouse, for whom the relationship of inexpressiveness to expressiveness is merely that of powerlessness to undifferentiated power, I want to argue that, in this particular world of power differentials, it is equal to the relationship of asymbolia and mourning.

II. JUDICIAL BATTERING

In *Violence Against Wives: A Case Against Patriarchy*, Dobash and Dobash report that "In 1971, almost no one had heard of battered women, except, of course, the legions of women who were being battered and the relatives, friends, [etc.] . . . in whom some of them confided" (Dobash and Dobash, 1979, 2). Yet in 1972, Margaret Drabble was at work rectifying this obliviousness, publishing *The Needle's Eye*, in which she castigates the legal system for its nonchalance toward the case of Rose Vassiliou, a viciously battered wife—for its complicity with battering.

Beginning with the nineteenth century, writes Foucault, "the sentence that condemns or acquits is not simply a judgement of guilt, a legal decision that lays down punishment; it bears within it an assessment of normality and a technical prescription for a possible normalization. Today the judge—magistrate or juror—certainly does more than 'judge'" (Foucault, 1979, 20–21). When Rose Vassiliou, in *The Needle's Eye*, seeks a divorce from her batterer, the judge, who labels Rose "highly eccentric," is not at all subtle in exemplifying Foucault's point (Drabble, 1972, 43). It is only due to a legal hitch that the judge rules in Rose's favor, granting her the divorce and custody of her three children: for "a passionate desire to rid oneself of one's money is *technically* not as grave a matrimonial offence as the inflicting of black-eyes, split lips, cuts and manifold bruises" (Drabble, 1972, 52, my emphasis). Even as the law happens to favor Rose, the judge passes along his assessment of abnormality, which is echoed so pervasively (for giving away a substantial portion of her fortune, Rose is considered mad by her parents, her husband, her solicitors, even by a few friends) that Rose—like a typical Foucauldian subject produced by subjection—begins to define herself as "hopelessly impulsive," "simply incapable . . . of behaving in a rational and considered manner" (Drabble, 1972, 45).

Rose's virtues—e.g., her altruistic desire to help African children by building them a school—are transvalued as the defects of her irredeemably irrational character, situating Rose on the verge of a nervous breakdown. Because Rose, prompted by a photograph of a naked African child plopped down next to its dead mother's corpse, "its face lost, its eyes sagging blank with nothingness, its mouth drooping slightly open" (Drabble, 1972, 97), donates her money to African children, she is (needless to say, ironically) made to doubt her capacity to nurture her own children. Her husband, Christopher, turns her charity against her: "don't you expect me to sympathise with all the subnormal races of Africa, there's enough subnormality on the very doorstep here, . . . you histrionic bitch" (Drabble, 1972, 77). And Rose caves in: "*I* believe it, that's the point, he's right, he's right. I'm a hopeless mother, I know I am, I'm mean and mad and selfish, he's *right* about me, how can I defend myself when he's right?" (Drabble, 1972, 246). Rose starts to feel that she should have endured her husband's abuse, "ought to have gone on taking it" (Drabble, 1972, 270). When Christopher rapes her a week after the divorce, Rose (adopting Christopher's attitude) "felt she had deserved it" (Drabble, 1972, 279). And it is upon reading Christopher's affidavit describing her incompetence as a mother, a document that ratifies the collusion of the legal system with the batterer, that Rose turns temporarily into a madwoman: "she moaned, and started to toss her head about, and her hands flew to her hair, and started to tug at it. . . . [H]er arms were as stiff as sticks, her hair where she had pulled it stood in clumps, she was not there in the flesh" (Drabble, 1972, 248). If a man pulls out a woman's hair enough times, pretty soon she pulls it out for him.

The later Vassiliou court case on Rose's competence to *retain* custody of her children swings in her favor again only on a technicality. The judge, who "had once given custody to a father ["a most unsuitable parent, a religious maniac, a vindictive and violent man"], because his wife was living with her lover" (Drabble, 1972, 338), had been inclined to put the Vassiliou children in the care of Christopher (an undisputed wife beater), except that Christopher, to give Rose a fright, had threatened by telegram to remove the children illegally from the country. Both the judicial system and Rose's husband, who physically batters her for her "subnormality," do their best to collaborate in an art of punishment aimed at normalization, an art thorough and exquisite enough to elicit Rose's participation. Half the time Rose believes, "I must be mad. . . . I should see a psychiatrist" (Drabble, 1972, 252). (Of course it is difficult, if not impossible, to know how much of Rose's self-destructiveness comes exclusively from this collaboration betweeen the judicial system and Rose's husband. My point above is that they at least play a potent role in it. In fact, *The Needle's Eye* is also quite readable as a text of Kristevan melancholia. Rose's mother, "a woman so compellingly negative" [Drabble, 1972, 298], neglects her. Signs of Green's dead mother complex also surface, since Rose's mother is herself depressed: Mrs. Bryanston's "lack of interest in life had afflicted them all: it was a disease, a mildew, which oppressed even strangers" [Drabble, 1972, 298]. But psychic vulnerability to abuse—which indeed Rose possessed, for she sought the intimacy as well as an antidote to boredom lacking in her childhood in Christopher—does not produce a battered woman; and Drabble seems dedicated to highlighting the insidious social/cultural steps of that production.)

The other half of the time Rose is sufficiently clear-sighted to grasp that "Christopher and God" have constructed her martyrdom for her (Drabble, 1972, 253), although the emphasis of the novel would have us replace God with the British legal system. Batterers and the law are more than once paralleled, underscoring the hopelessness of turning to the law to clear up the quagmire of battering, since the law is essentially the batterer writ large. Rose gradually learns that the legal system is as much a "self-perpetuating" morass as her marriage, and equally in labyrinthine league with violence: "far from drawing ends and lines and boundaries," the processes of the law "answered nothing, they solved none of the confusions of the heart and the demands of the spirit, but instead generated their own course of new offences, new afflictions, new perversions" (Drabble, 1972, 173).

Like Breines and Gordon, in "The New Scholarship on Family Violence," Drabble focuses on "collective cultural meaning and community control of marital violence" (Breines and Gordon, 1983, 515). Drabble's narrative adumbrates the message of Breines and Gordon that battered women are (at least) doubly victimized: by batterers as well as agents of social control who automatically put the blame on women. Male domination is seen, in both texts, as part of a complex system of social power relations rather than as merely the result of sexist attitudes or reprehensible behavior of individual men (although individual men are still held accountable). When Christopher complains about the inexorability of the processes of law, which proceed "unruffled" and "unperturbed" (despite "what happens after the case is set in motion") "until they've ground up the last little bit," Rose, making Breines and Gordon's point boldly to the most conspicuous agent of her pain and distress, retorts: "'in that, they rather strikingly resemble you'" (Drabble, 1972, 294). The partnership between batterers and the law is alluded to again when, pondering another woman's court case, Rose is "perplexed by the nonchalance with which abuse and blows had been disregarded" by a judge "who would consider it an act of violence, in his own domestic situation, if a guest were to put down a glass on a polished wooden surface, or drop ash upon a parquet floor" (Drabble, 1972, 79). When Rose seeks an injunction against Christopher for threatening to kidnap the children, the legal authorities more than hint that they are inconvenienced. Although judicial authorities behave as if wife beating is outside their professional domain (a private matter between a man and his "property"), their behavior only means that wife beating is so much *like* their authority that to call batterers in would be redundant.

For of course when police or legal action is *not* taken against a batterer, that inaction indirectly sanctions the abuse. Dobash and Dobash point out that the indifference of many policemen, some of whom identify with batterers, is in general shared by judges who tend not to regard wife beating as "truly criminal behavior," and may even consider the perpetrator's attacks to be "somewhat justified by his wife's provocations" (Dobash and Dobash, 1979, 219). In *The Needle's Eye*, a judge presiding over a case in which the husband made "a regular habit of flinging things at [his wife], slapping her, punching her and so on," is inspired to speak of "things that any man might do under provocation." The judge assumes, too, "that a few blows one way or the other [are] the normal fare of married life" (Drabble, 1972, 79). The disparity between the law's obsession with nonfamily violence and its apathy toward "family violence" is surely part of the legacy of the specific common law that honored the right of men to beat their wives. Husbands and wives were viewed as a single entity: since an individual cannot "offend against himself," it was considered illogical that a woman might take her husband to court for abusing her (Dobash and Dobash, 1979, 208). The concept of the sacrosanct home and the ideal of the family counter efforts to ensure the rights of married women especially, as well as efforts to protect them. "Until the 1950s, in Texas, Utah, and New Mexico," husbands who found their spouses committing adultery and in turn committed homicide were "granted special immunity" (Dobash and Dobash, 1979, 209).

As *The Needle's Eye* testifies, such laws, though defunct, still infect the atmosphere. The novel demonstrates the irresistible force of the idea that the family ought to be saved no matter how extravagant and excruciating the cost in violence to the woman's body, mind, and soul. In graphically presenting Christopher's cruelty, Drabble underscores that price. The grounds of Rose's divorce are "physical violence (medical evidence produced, neighbour's evidence, and a permanent scar on Rose's wrist), abusive language, violent and unreasonable demands, incessant and unmotivated jealousy" (Drabble, 1972, 64)—an appalling enough technical description necessarily cloaking details that the novel turns into vivid spectacles. "Christopher had thrown the tomato ketchup bottle at her and it had broken and gone all over, . . . and Rose had gone on yelling these demented Biblical tags until Christopher, understandably beside himself with rage, had kicked over the table and grabbed at her and said (frightening her into silence), Don't you quote the fucking Bible at me . . ." (Drabble, 1972, 76–77). Christopher locks Rose up in her bedroom, locks her out of the house in her nightdress, beats her black and blue, and yanks her hair out in large patches. Rose feels sure that unless they part they will "kill each other, perhaps even literally" (Drabble, 1972, 78); yet society wants this couple to remain intact.

What is more astonishing is that the novel appears, after all, to want that outcome too. In a politically and philosophically tricky ending, Christopher moves back into the house on Middle Road. Yet this apparent rapprochement is not what it may seem: for, while *The Needle's Eye* concludes with Rose and Christopher's reunion, it does so out of a deep sense of the pathetic inadequacy of the law. On her own with the children, in a gratifyingly shabby neighborhood, Rose achieves "some inexplicable grace" (Drabble, 1972, 141). She takes genuine pleasure in simple acts such as drawing curtains and shopping—" 'I do them all with love' " (Drabble, 1972, 95). She can rest in peace in bed at night, without fear of being disturbed by blows. Nevertheless, Rose takes back her husband—because her personal situation, a marriage that has spawned three children mutually loved by their parents, refuses to reduce to any of the reconfigurations into which the law could set it. Rose submits herself to her husband by the same logic of charity that tore them apart in the first place: "no ulterior weakness of her own, no sexual craving, had prompted her to [take him], she had done it in the dry light of arid generosity, she had done it for others" (Drabble, 1972, 350).

Rose comes to realize the difficulty of building upon her victory in court: "She had resorted to the law, as her father had done before [against her], and now she was a victim of its processes. . . . a court's settlements could not end the confusion" (Drabble, 1972, 172). An abundance of unclassifiable evidence constitutes the case, overflowing legal bounds: "the divorce court had been a game played by others, custody cases were nothing but a sketch, a diagram of woe, and the full confrontation would take place on other territory. The decisions of judges, even when in her favour, were irrelevant" (Drabble, 1972, 174). Legal systems can think only in terms of the desirability of winning, can never understand the necessity of loss. The novel is quite forthcoming as to why for Rose "there was no exemption, no cancelling of bonds, no forgetting" (Drabble, 1972, 174), and why therefore the law is finally so inadequate: "How dreadful it is . . . that children are born of two parents, that they are the property of two parents with equal claim, that they do not spring fully grown from the brain, as Athene sprang from Zeus" (Drabble, 1972, 249).

In *The Needle's Eye,* Rose's batterer exerts a fierce effort to contain her through physical force. His effort is backed up, and covered over, by disciplinary social/legal attempts to quell Rose's desires for autonomy and custody of her children. But finally the power of love exceeds these two modes of Foucauldian power—the former premodern, indulging in spectacular physical abuse; the latter systemic—attempting to close in on Rose. Rose's head splits ("If someone had taken a hatchet and split my skull," she thinks, "I could not suffer more"); she feels blood running in her brain from an "internal wound"; her brain is "wet with blood" ("I bleed, I bleed, I bleed") (Drabble, 1972, 250)—neither as a result of punitive acts of brute force (although Christopher certainly imprints the marks of his strength on Rose's tender flesh) nor because of the disciplinary measures of the judicial system (although it certainly tries to control and mold Rose), but because her children will cry if she leaves them and suffer if she divides them from their father.

Rose Vassiliou eventually assesses her situation's vast complexity, its irreducibility; and so she is able finally to realize what in her demands expression. Rose imagines love "as some huge white deformed and not very lovely god, lying there beneath the questions and the formality, caught in a net of which points alone touched and confined him—points, blows, matrimonial offences, desertions, legalities, all binding love down though he shapelessly overflowed and struggled" (Drabble, 1972, 80). Rose's final decision testifies to her flexibility, in contrast to the fixity of the law, that keeps her uncontainable by that system. Yet, *The Needle's Eye* suggests that, far from opening up a new front of power, expressiveness available to women—in particular mothers—can be rather weak with respect to the traps into which women are typically lured.

Thus Drabble responds to the dilemma posed by Armstrong and Tennenhouse of the writer's difficulty in avoiding violence against others. Drabble lends all her sensibility to her heroine (who therefore is not re-disempowered) but without in turn finding that her heroine becomes the new oppressor. Rose is in fact sufficiently vulnerable at the end to tempt readers to regard her reunion with her husband as part of a martyrdom generated by the disciplinary systems of Foucauldian modern power, if not in addition a function of a melancholia resulting from disappointing, troubled relations with her own meek, silent, depressed mother. It may very well seem that Rose makes a conventional, socially controlled sacrifice, typically demanded especially of women by family discipline as well as psychically advantageous in the case of melancholic women (" 'I'm just depressed,' she said, 'that's all' " [Drabble, 1972, 151]), as we have witnessed in earlier chapters. But the difference is that the novel has been *dedicated* to showing that Rose constructs her self best of all by paying high prices for the sake of children, be they African, her own, anyone's.

I *can* imagine other readings, stressing the sly social control behind Rose's final decision, and perhaps even using Kristeva's model of melancholia to argue that Rose punishes herself all the way to the very end through sacrifice for others in order to retain an encrypted maternal object/Thing. But I think Drabble means to offer a twist, in holding out here for the possibility that a woman can make a sacrifice and not be masochistic, for the possibility that female care may have a source other than the dominant power structure that, some might argue, manipulates that care into being (it is neither dupe nor ally). To perceive Rose's sacrifice for children as weak or foolish, as naive, is in this novel to perceive it with the profit-hungry eyes of Rose's violent husband, or in the commonplace terms of a bourgeois judge. In *doubling* Rose's act of generosity to children, Drabble has arranged her plot to show that female recalcitrance may take place within, but is not of, male hegemony, and thus does not lead to normal empowerment. The outcome of *The Needle's Eye* is neither subjection, whether external or internal, nor cooperation with the dominant power structure, but charitable agency.

While it seems more than likely that during most of the novel Rose is enthralled by a detrimental love object in the form of her husband Christopher, obstructing her passage beyond an imaginary register ("she had loved him, certainly— . . . she had been ill with love, ill with longing" [Drabble, 1972, 318]), in the end, despite the apparent self-destructiveness of Rose's decision to live again with her batterer, Drabble seems to want to align her character's behavior with the symbolic power of Drabble's own text. It is as if, through the representation of Rose's pain and torture, her destructive fantasy is traversed. Through Drabble's entry into signification, which takes on the hefty task of critiquing the legal system, Rose's final decision (even such a risky and suspect one) becomes her own. Rose becomes free, in other words, to act on her desire. Or, put in terms of a Jamesian paradox, she is no longer barred from choosing any position. And perhaps to be able to act on one's desire is the most effective form of gazing back.

III. HOLLERING PAIN

In "Woman Hollering Creek," Sandra Cisneros focuses on simple, private life, apparently uninvaded by complex, power-laden institutions such as Drabble's byzantine judicial system. Cisneros's main character, Cleófilas, however, cannot escape public institutions, because a force probably more efficacious than the judicial system, police, or medical profession in constructing the battered woman worms its way into the Mexican woman's world in "Woman Hollering Creek." Cisneros looks at a particularly beguiling mode of Foucauldian modern power—the *telenovela*—which teaches that "to suffer for love is good. The pain all sweet somehow. In the end" (Cisneros, 1992, 45), and *thus* confronts the violence of representation. "Woman Hollering Creek," moreover, links Foucauldian disciplinary power operating through soap operas to the success of Foucauldian spectacular power, such as that wielded by Juan Pedro Martínez Sánchez over Cleófilas. The story provides a narrative not only unimplicated in these forms of power but one that shrewdly assesses their daunting collaboration. Cisneros's challenge was to produce a nonsentimental, nonviolent narrative about a battered woman who is made vulnerable by soap operas to her husband's physical abuse. The women's narrative conveyed by the telenovela naturalizes the sweetness of pain; Cisneros writes to denaturalize that oxymoron. Aware of the danger of colonization in this process, Cisneros collapses the distance between the silent (and, I might add, motherless) Cleófilas and herself in part by collapsing the distance between Cleófilas and the narrator, who is capable of excitement over the mother's dress in last night's episode of *The Rich Also Cry*, because that is what the dress the narrator plans on wearing to Cleófilas's wedding will look like once it is "altered a teensy bit" (Cisneros, 1992, 46). Cleófilas herself seems only to slip from being like the unbattered narrator (at least as she is presented in the story) to being a battered woman. "The first time she had been so surprised she didn't cry out or try to defend herself. . . . [H]e slapped her once, and then again, and again; until the lip split and bled an orchid of blood, she didn't fight back, she didn't break into tears, she didn't run away as she imagined she might when she saw such things in the *telenovelas*" (Cisneros, 1992, 47). Cleófilas's second surprise is that she reacts no better than soap opera heroines who endure everything for love. (The very unnaturalness of her suffering pain all the more powerfully inserts the act into an artificial discourse.) Thrust into the asymbolic, Cleófilas is left "speechless, motionless, numb" (Cisneros, 1992, 48), thus illustrating Scarry's point that "[i]ntense pain is . . . language-destroying" (Scarry, 1985, 35), and as a result needs someone to speak for her who can avoid the temptation of turning her voicelessness (powerlessness) into that speaking subject's power. Cisneros's narrator, steeped in narratives of battering yet endowed by Cisneros with the cultural sophistication to produce a counternarrative, is in a prime position to provide yet another alternative to what Hartsock identifies as the two "alternatives imposed by Enlightenment thought and postmodernism: Either one must adopt the perspective of the transcendental and disembodied voice of 'reason' or one must abandon the goal of accurate and systematic knowledge of the world. Other possibilities exist and must be (perhaps can only be) developed by hitherto marginalized voices" (Hartsock, 1990, 171).

Cleófilas "sits mute beside [the men's] conversation," waiting, nodding in agreement, politely grinning and laughing at the appropriate moments (Cisneros, 1992, 48). Muteness is now the stuff of the narrator's narrative, which has become, for the purpose, omniscient. The narrator conveys the widening gap that Cleófilas gradually apprehends between Cleófilas's fantasy lover and her husband Juan Pedro, who "kicks the refrigerator and says he hates this shitty house and is going out where he won't be bothered with the baby's howling and her suspicious questions, and her requests to fix this and this . . ." (Cisneros, 1992, 49). The narrator astutely picks up too on Juan Pedro's typical insistence on certain domestic patterns and typical disproportionate irritation, or even fury, when these patterns are broken: "each course of dinner [must] be served on a separate plate, like at his mother's, as soon as he gets home, on time or late" (Cisneros, 1992, 49). (The batterer's pique is often focused on dinner; so it has been said that microwave ovens have helped to cut down on battering.)

If Cleófilas exemplifies the voiceless victim, the narrator, at first not obviously distinct from Cleófilas, eventually aspires to the role of expert on battering. She seems to be aware, for example, of what Lenore Walker in *The Battered Woman* calls the "loving stage" (phase three), in which batterers endearingly seek forgiveness (Walker, 1979, 65–70): Cleófilas "stroked the dark curls of the man who wept and would weep like a child, his tears of repentence and shame, this time and each" (Cisneros, 1992, 48). The narrator feels the special vulnerability of the body of the pregnant woman, who in this case knows that she must walk a tightrope between protecting her batterer, by deceiving her doctor about her wounds, and protecting her unborn baby, by making sure that she gets her batterer's permission to be examined. The text even raises its analysis of woman abuse to the level of Breines and Gordon by placing Juan Pedro's violence in a broader social context, by referring to Maximiliano (one of Juan Pedro's buddies) "who was said to have killed his wife in an ice-house brawl when she came at him with a mop" (Cisneros, 1992, 51) and alluding to newspapers "full of such stories. This woman found on the side of the interstate. This one pushed from a moving car. This one's cadaver, this one unconscious, this one beaten blue. Her ex-husband, her husband, her lover, her father, her brother, her uncle, her friend, her co-worker. Always" (Cisneros, 1992, 52). Woman abuse, this story implies, is a pervasive phenomenon; Juan Pedro (like all other individual batterers) is one cog in a vast piece of heavy social machinery.[5]

"Woman Hollering Creek" pulsates on many borders—between the individual and the social, Mexico and Texas, Spanish and English, the nonbattered and battered woman, narrative and a holler, the discursive and nondiscursive. As the story builds, it produces more and more discourse until discourse (reverse discourse?) bursts into a shout (another form of reverse discourse?) that manages to be both tortured and triumphant, which in turn produces a gurgling that manages to be both infantilized (like a giggling) and knowing (like Cixous's Medusa's laughter). By the time the reader has grasped the import of the holler, the story itself—another "Woman Hollering Creek"—assumes the status of the nondiscursive. It is as if the *narrative* eventually releases itself in a holler, a pure expression of female "anger or pain" (Cisneros, 1992, 46), so that the usual power imbalance between narrative and the nondiscursive is corrected. We realize that the purpose of the narrative is to transport us to the holler, and then to implode into one.

Pain is not appropriated here by agents of power—Cisneros reverses the usual pattern that Scarry highlights. Instead of moving from prediscursive pain—through pain—to discursive power, Cisneros works through the discursive to reach the painful muteness it is founded on, ironically symbolizing asymbolic pain at the moment of contact, in an attempt to reconfigure the structure predicated on the lack of such symbolization. "The evil eye, which seeks to outstare linear, continuist history and turn its progressive dream into nightmarish chaos, is exemplary once more" (Bhabha, 1994, 55).[6]

IV. "DREAMS OF DARK KINGS"

Foucault theorizes that with the advent of the nineteenth century "the great spectacle of physical punishment disappeared; the tortured body was avoided; the theatrical representation of pain was excluded from punishment. The age of sobriety in punishment had begun" (Foucault, 1979, 14). If battering conformed to the history of power that Foucault traces, physically brutal battering would have declined and faded away, its imitation of despotic brutality to the tortured body a transcended anachronism, as noncorporeal systemic battering became more and more pervasive. Drabble and Cisneros (as well as current statistics) suggest otherwise: if Drabble shows that male abuse of a woman's body is endorsed by assumptions almost too self-evident to require legal articulation, and if Cisneros shows that that abuse is the currency of narratives too widespread (literally in the very air) to be challenged within language, both writers demonstrate that the fine-tuning, disseminating, and internalizing of the ideology of abuse, rather than outmoding corporeal battering merely endorse it, duplicate it in a larger arena, stealthily or invisibly.

In her novel about an unmistakably abused wife, *Linden Hills*, Gloria Naylor restores Foucault's prepanopticon dungeon. Naylor lays out the double entrapment of the abused wife and thus offers an impressively full, culturally based answer to the undying question (raised relentlessly by the prosecution during the Lorena Bobbitt trial) of why the battered woman fails to leave. *Linden Hills* illustrates how the domestic carceral (which points to women's incarceration in the home and away from a teleology that views home and marriage as sweet alternatives to an external gothic world of ghosts, robbers, and rapists) and the literal carceral reinforce each other's grip. The battered woman is caught in a vicious circle: the subtle punishment of her mind and soul primes her for the gross punishment of her body; the cessation of physical torture only releases her to a comparatively pleasant world in which her mind and soul are subtly punished.

Naylor therefore, in *Linden Hills*, takes on both centered and decentered power: her heroine is the product of "multiple mechanisms of 'incarceration"" (Foucault, 1979, 308). Willa is tortured by a devilish man, who behaves quite like, and conceives of himself as, a king—in a line of "dark kings with dark counselors leading dark armies against the white god" (Naylor, 1985, 10). Surrounded by a moat with a drawbridge, Nedeed's home is his castle; he uses his morgue-basement as a dungeon to contain his disobedient wife-prisoner. He puts her down there, without food, with their young son—who predictably gets sick, shrinks, and dies—during the coldest week of the year. Invisibility too is a trap.

Yet the domestic carceral is by no means underplayed. The efflorescence of Willa's will at the end of *Linden Hills* occurs in part through her realization that she has been, "from the second she was born" (Naylor, 1985, 280), the victim of disciplinary coercion in the service of femininity. Willa answers her self-posed question—"How did she get down in that basement?" (Naylor, 1985, 278)—by rehearsing her cultural training in becoming a "good girl" (Naylor, 1985, 277), "a good mother," and "a good wife" (Naylor, 1985, 279). Tracing her own trajectory from domestic to literal incarceration, Willa recalls wanting to marry Luther Nedeed, take his name, bear his child, clean his home, cook his meals, and then (apparently) to walk down twelve steps into a cold, damp basement to be his prisoner. Willa testifies to the process by which she gradually assumed "the constraints of power," inscribed within herself a power relation in which she played the role of master and slave, and became "the principle of [her] own subjection" (Foucault, 1979, 202–203). The kitchen carceral, then, facilitates Willa's descent into the basement; the physically torturous basement carceral produces Willa's craving for the kitchen. Once freed from her literal imprisonment, Willa is obsessed with the desire to do housework.

Naylor had hoped that Willa would discover the desirability of completely walking out by reading the former Mrs. Nedeeds' various texts—diaries, cookbooks, and photographs—collecting dust in the basement. For they comment loudly on the carceral nature of Nedeed domestic life. But what they seem to teach instead is the fine art of self-abasement, featuring self-mutilation. Once caught in the double jaws of the domestic/literal carceral (however she arrived there in the first place), a woman is not only more likely to end up being physically attacked by her husband (rather than by a stranger), but she seems equally apt to attack herself. Luwana Packerville (who literally belongs to her husband since he purchases her as a slave) marks (at least 665, possibly 666) lines on her skin with a pin and her own blood to record the number of times her husband and son speak to her after a year of excruciating *silence*. Priscilla McGuire wipes out her photographed face, labeling the blank space "me." Evelyn Creton exhausts herself cooking vast quantities of food; she gains twenty-nine postnuptial pounds, takes up binge-purging, and commits suicide with prussic acid (Naylor,

1985, 249). Silence, the wiping out of identity, the death of subjectivity—all are here culturally induced.

Disciplinary processes within a system of surveillance deeply ensconced in culture and heavily played upon by the Nedeed husband (no matter which avatar) are adopted by the Nedeed wife herself, so that she keeps herself in line, meting out self-punishment when she crosses over. Victimization thus begins to resemble, to *become*, female masochism; in this way too, Naylor intimates, the female masochist/melancholic may be made. Insofar as the Nedeed wife generates her jouissance out of her incarceration (as in *Story of O* and its sequel), her only means of self-production, of self-reclamation, is extravagance within her training, excessive self-discipline. But insofar as her incarceration provides the limit of her agency and subjectivity, as it eventually does, she goes uninscribed, her desire, agency, and subjectivity unformed and unexpressed. She achieves the asymbolic condition of depression, as it is culturally produced here in all its masochistic excess.

Perhaps this is why Naylor has Willie (a young man) express, through the poetry in his head (he is averse to writing it down), the battered woman's pain. Created when he was five years old, Willie's first poem was a response to his question of "how can my mother love my father when he makes her cry?" (Naylor, 1985, 275). Willie's last poem (number 666, aligning him with Luwana) is likewise inspired by a batterer and a battered woman's pain: " 'There is a man in a house at the bottom of a hill. And his wife has no name' " (Naylor, 1985, 277). Since Willie is not a woman, there can be no implication that a woman's pain is her subjectivity, all that she has to express; since he is not a writer (not Naylor), there can be no implication that he has founded a subjectivity on superiority to women's inexpressive pain. Hence he is free to disclose its horror, which again we observe from the poignant point of view of the child: " 'My mom got beat up every night after payday by a man who couldn't bear the thought of bringing home a paycheck only large enough for three people and making it stretch over eight people, so he drank up half of it. And she stayed . . . because a bruised face and half a paycheck was better than welfare, and that's the only place she had left to go with no education and six kids' " (Naylor, 1985, 58).[7]

Comparing Mahler with Bessie Smith, Billie Holliday, and Muddy Waters, all of whom try "to say something with music that you can't say with plain talk," Laurel's grandmother, Roberta, proceeds to comment that "There ain't really no words for love or pain" (Naylor, 1985, 235)—which is why Willa (like the women in "Woman Hollering Creek") wails, cries, screams, and howls hers. Italicizing the ineffableness of Willa's pain (and love), Naylor uses myriad signifiers of semiotic sounds. Willie alone hears. Everyone else seems to be absorbed in living out the suburban dream of Linden Hills, occupied by the classiest, most sophisticated, best educated African-Americans—where the literal carceral is unthinkable. Like certain

"Foucauldian" critics, citizens of Linden Hills are attuned solely to the expressive. While women (such as Laurel) actively battle against the domestic carceral, the literal carceral is assumed to be too primitive (pre-nineteenth century) to exist. Testifying to the underside of the domestic carceral, Nedeed nonetheless wields enough premodern power to kill his son and destroy, if not kill, his spouse.

At the end everyone in Linden Hills merely watches Mrs. Nedeed go up in smoke: "[T]ell me I'm dreaming—they're watching it burn," Willie, astonished, announces to Lester (Naylor, 1985, 302). That theory can be as deaf to the victims of premodern power as the residents of Linden Hills is perhaps not to theory's total discredit, since the victims of modern power are all expression, and the victims of premodern power tend to be silent. Feminism itself is still evolving from a prehistorical stage, during which, to quote bell hooks, "women who are daily beaten down, mentally, physically, and spiritually—women who are powerless to change their condition in life" were "a silent majority" (hooks, 1984, 1). Even Naylor cannot quite get them to speak. For Naylor is writing about the task of expressing something—something akin to the condition of melancholia—that falls short of expression and therefore is in need of mourning. All the subtlety of literary talent must be committed to ensure that female nondiscursiveness (e.g., intermittent madness and maternal love in Drabble; triumphant dehumanized howling in Cisneros; extravagant masochistic acts in Naylor) will be expressed so that its energy can be harnessed in the production of a counterhegemony (a talking/gazing back) as well as put to work in a public ritual of mourning the myriad losses entailed in such ongoing brutality (a verbal cure). For only as the (masochistic) jouissance of these women is spun into linguistic desire can subjectivity emerge.

V. THE SPECTACLE EFFECT

A novel that offers a full-fledged portrait of the vicious batterer as well as of the material and psychic devastation that he wreaks is Alice Walker's *The Third Life of Grange Copeland*. Walker contributes to the debate on the cultural production of battering also by invoking throughout her novel the intertwined question of the social construction of the black batterer, and thus raises a key question that complicates the gender argument we have followed to this point. Noting the asymmetry of power relations between men and women is surely insufficient for comprehending relative positions of power in all situations of heterosexual violence. How does gender inextricably interact with other social categories that (over)determine discrepancies of power? (The O.J. Simpson case specifically poses relevant complications: how ought his stronger gender positioning be weighed against his weaker racial positioning?) Future analyses of domestic woman abuse will no doubt gain their sophistication by examining in detail the interplay of multiple sociocultural determinants of power rather than by means of a concept of oceanic complicity based on the premise that all discourse is necessarily acculturated and therefore tainted with power.

The Third Life of Grange Copeland is a meditation on the linkage of two points presented obliquely in the opening pages: Grange, Brownfield's father, works "for a cracker" and "the cracker own[s] him" (Walker, 1970, 4); Margaret, Brownfield's mother, seems like "their dog in some ways. She didn't have a thing to say that did not in some way show her submission to his father" (Walker, 1970, 5). White men beat down black men; black men, in turn, beat down black women, and black sons; black sons later beat down black women. At least in his first life, Grange plays the role of the batterer with panache: "Their life followed a kind of cycle that depended almost totally on Grange's moods" (Walker, 1970, 11); like clockwork, Grange returns home drunk each Saturday night, threatens to kill his wife and Brownfield, and then rolls out the door into the yard, "crying like a child" (Walker, 1970, 12). Each week the same dreary pattern unfolds, and then it unfolds again in the life of Grange's son, for Brownfield inherits the sins of his father.

Caught in the generational cycle, he too batters upon being battered. Resembling torturers in *The Body in Pain*, Brownfield breaks down his wife, Mem, by attacking her speech, sarcastically urging her to "talk like the *rest* of us poor niggers" (Walker, 1970, 56). Also conforming with Scarry's paradigm, he targets the home, domestic pleasure, and peace. Brownfield is especially apt to fly into a rage when supper is not on the table the minute he walks in the door. Although Mem comes close to killing herself to set up the family in a decent house, Brownfield transforms that reality back into a dream: Mem and her daughters are forced to live in a virtual pig sty. The family ideal upholds sexist law, which itself upholds the privilege of batterers, yet the home is exactly what batterers ironically are compelled to tear down: the first right of ownership is the right to destroy.

Brownfield also typically accuses Mem of infidelity (with white men), a figment of his imagination; drunk, he beats Mem regularly on Saturday nights; holidays, especially Christmas Eve, are tough times for Mem (as they are for most battered women). One such night Brownfield beats Mem "senseless," knocks out a tooth, and loosens more. In what seems like an unstoppable cycle, Brownfield (again typically) stoops to venting his anger on helpless animals and children as well, by pouring oil in streams to kill fish, drowning cats, beating his young daughters, and (prefiguring Nedeed) freezing to death his too-light-skinned, infant son.

Walker's method of conveying the horror of Brownfield's treatment of Mem, her method of indicting him through representation, of gazing back, is to present his various acts of violence as literary spectacle. In a sense she imitates the batterer whose violence against his wife, children, and home she depicts. Walker puts the gory details on display: unnuanced violence apparently deserves unnuanced representation. Literary representations of violence at times must rely on, as Laura Tanner describes it, "a highly visual mode of narration . . . to direct the reader's [feminist] gaze upon a scene in a manner similar to the enforced perspective of [a] camera's frame" (Tanner, 1994, 12), which is what we have also seen, for example, in *I, Tina* and what no doubt lent itself in *I, Tina* to the production of a splashy film, *What's Love Got To Do With It*, out of the book. During one incident, "Brownfield's big elephant-hide fist hit [Mem] square in the mouth." He shakes her "until blood dribbled from her stinging lips. . . . [S]he just hung there from his hands until he finished giving her half-a-dozen slaps, then she just fell down limp like she always did." With his foot Brownfield gives Mem a kick in the side; he threatens to cut her throat; he finishes her off with a "resounding kick in the side of the head" (Walker, 1970, 90–91). And like so many of the domestic battles in *The Third Life of Grange Copeland* (paralleling those in Donna Ferrato's photographs), this one is witnessed by the children (Naylor's Willie too might be invoked here): we watch Brownfield fire his gun into Mem's face through her two youngest daughters' terrified eyes. By building specularity into the text in this way, Walker offers a double dose of the pain.

To convey the ghastliness of Brownfield's spectacular punishment, Walker breathes into it a second spectacular life; to achieve the effect she wants, she mimics Brownfield's actions in graphic words. Like the realist writer whose "reality effect" Barthes explains, she sets up a "*direct* collusion of a referent and a signifier," expelling the signified from the sign. Brownfield's violence is given no denotative significance—it does not mean anything beyond or different from itself—and so again Barthes's words apply: "a signified of denotation" is eliminated, and what slips into its place is "spectacle" as a "signified of connotation" (Barthes, 1982, 16). Just as Brownfield's violence marks Mem's body in an act of premodern power (the *mark*, in Foucault, that elides the signified is distinct from the later *sign* of punishment where the punishment fits the crime, so that Foucault's monarchical effect entails Barthes's reality effect), Walker stamps the page with the "truth of the crime," making homeopathic use of a reiteration of violence.

The technical issue, in short, is how to acknowledge violence without transmitting it, which is the *thematic* issue of *The Third Life of Grange Copeland* as well. For it appears that it is in the nature of violence to reproduce itself (like Grange Copeland himself, it has multiple lives). Gender ideology—the concept of manhood—is one reproductive form: Mem complains, " 'just think of how many times I done got my head beat by you just so you could feel a little bit like a man, Brownfield Copeland' " (Walker,

1970, 94). Other social etiologies are identified, although impaired masculinity/social castration still might seem to be the underlying sore spot: Brownfield's rage at "his life and his world . . . made him beat her," "blame everything . . . on her" (Walker, 1970, 55). For he "could not stand to be belittled at home after coming from a job that required him to respond to all orders from a stooped position" (Walker, 1970, 56). Walker wants to stress that racist socioeconomic conditions are responsible for the transmission of violence, that black men displace their quite justified anger against white men (and women) onto black women. (So does Toni Morrison: after "big, white, armed men," in *The Bluest Eye*, interrupt Cholly and Darlene and then sadistically force them to continue having, what can only at this point be simulated, intercourse, Cholly cultivates "his hatred of Darlene." Hating the more powerful hunters would have "consumed him, burned him up like a piece of soft coal," so he hates the "one whom he had not been able to protect, to spare, to cover from the round moon glow of the flashlight" [Morrison, 1994, 150–51].)

But Walker is equally compelled to qualify this point about displacement. Racial oppression is at the same time considered to be an excuse for black male violence against black women. In blinding the violent black male to his own responsibility, in providing a barrier to recognition of black agency, this line of argument only serves as another form of white corruption. "You gits just as weak as water, no feeling of doing *nothing* yourself," Grange pleads to Brownfield. "Then you begins to think up evil and begins to destroy everybody around you, and you blames it on the crackers. . . . Nobody's as powerful as we make them out to be. We got our own *souls*, don't we?" (Walker, 1970, 207). Walker presents, and in turn critiques, a constructivist explanation of the black batterer, since it attributes excessive force to the white, dominant power structure. Walker urges black men to claim their violence against women in an initial effort to reclaim their souls. In a chapter titled "Reconstructing Black Masculinity," bell hooks argues similarly that "black male agency," "salvation," and "growth" will become reachable goals once black men relinquish "phallocentrism" (inherited from white patriarchy) and "envision new ways of thinking about black masculinity" (hooks, 1992, 106).

The reproduction of battering occurs then, in Walker, in two fields: whites batter black men who then batter black women, all of which is literarily recreated as counterspectacle. Walker replaces the transitivity of battering with self-conscious literary theatricality, in a sense turning the batterer's spectacular punishment against him (and thereby transforming the subtitle of this essay, "Spectacular Domestic Punishment," into a pun). This is not to say, or perhaps I should say it is not only to say, that just as whites beat blacks and black men beat black women, the black woman (novelist) verbally beats black men. For Walker's exhortation to black men that they retrieve their souls by taking responsibility for their lives implies the possibility of being something other than a link in a chain of abuse, of not being merely a fascinated transmitter of the spectacle. If battering, in other words, is no longer seen as a mechanical social inevitability but as a fascinating spectacle, then other (more imaginative, less violent) spectacle effects become possible. The trauma can become unmoored. Without letting the white, dominant power structure off the hook, Walker's writing performs black male violence to unhinge it from the social forces that seem to generate it; and in thus loosening it, her writing enacts the possibility of conversion. Her homeopathic strategy is double: in reproducing the spectacle of power, Walker leaves women's pain in a state of opacity (refusing to usurp it for the sake of her own literate power), as she injects through writing self-consciousness into theatrical male violence to enable its reinscription.

As if addressing Armstrong and Tennenhouse's theory, *The Third Life of Grange Copeland* invests its hope finally in Ruth, Grange's literate and educated granddaughter, oddly mentioning that if Ruth were to be shipwrecked on a deserted island, the novel she would most like to have in her possession is *Jane Eyre*! Walker, along with Hurston, Drabble, Cisneros, and Naylor, attempts what Homi Bhabha considers to be our political obligation: both to "realize, and take responsibility for, the unspoken, unrepresented pasts that haunt the historical present" (Bhabha, 1994, 12). These women writers work toward producing the therapeutic, political effects of the *publication* of woman abuse: the talking back of the talking/writing cure, the gazing back of the abused, in a determined effort to raze the structure predicated on the abused, to render indeterminate the edifice of male power that domestic woman abuse renders determinate. This is the symbolic direction we must collectively move in, bridging the gap as best we can between academic feminism and women in pain, without fretting too much over our possible complicity with representational offenses. For without signification, there can be no counter to the muteness/asymbolia that domestic violence reinstates and in turn thrives upon.

A gaze surprises him . . . , disturbs him, overwhelms him and reduces him to a feeling of shame (Lacan, 1973, 84).

NOTES

This chapter is a reprint of Frances L. Restuccia, "Literary Representations of Battered Women: Spectacular Domestic Punishment," *Genders*, vol. 23 (Spring 1996), pp. 42–71.

1. It may seem to my readers, as it did to one of the editors of *Genders*, that I might also take up here Susanne Kappeler's *The Pornography of Representation*. While it is true that Kappeler ends her book with a plea for "communication, not

representation" and basically sees representation(s) as "a crucial strategy in the supreme subject's endeavour to maintain his position of power and privilege and the social, political and economic organization that supports it," she repeatedly calls for a transformation of representation away from a pornographic, subject-object, or master-slave model and toward an intersubjective model in which women would actively participate. To Kappeler, representation has been "the means by which the subject objectifies the world," but it isn't intrinsically doomed to enact such cruelty forever. Kappeler acknowledges, in fact, that the feminist critique of the pornography of representation must operate within the realm of representation (Kappeler, 1986, 222, 165, 198).

2. In *Allegories of Empire*, Jenny Sharpe offers a more nuanced and compelling postcolonialist critique of *Jane Eyre* that (in the spirit of Mae Henderson) underscores racial difference within gender identity. *Jane Eyre* may very well rely "on the figuration of various colonial 'others,' " as Sharpe asserts (she takes Spivak's point that the "native female" is "excluded from a discourse of feminist individualism" further in arguing that "the silent passivity of the Hindu woman is the grounds for the speaking subject of feminist individualism"), but it does not do so necessarily as a function of representation (Sharpe, 1993, 33, 55).

3. In *Intimate Violence,* after noting that "Armstrong and Tennenhouse risk obliterating any distinction between semiotic violence and its empirical counterpart," Laura Tanner suspends the reader of "a representation of violence . . . between the semiotic and the real, between a representation and the material dynamics of violence which it evokes, reflects, or transforms" (Tanner, 1994, 6).

4. Because cases of female batterers and male battered victims are relatively rare, male pronouns will be used to refer to batterers and female pronouns to refer to battered victims.

5. This level of the analysis of woman abuse that I attribute here to "the text" seems to be the complicated product of Cleófilas's indirectly expressed consciousness as well as the narrator's concern, an intermingling that once again collapses writer/narrator/character boundaries.

6. Jean Wyatt has written an essay that takes up related issues, "On Not Being La Malinche: Border Negotiations of Gender in Sandra Cisneros's 'Never Marry a Mexican' and 'Woman Hollering Creek.' " See: *Tulsa Studies in Women's Literature* 14.2 (Fall 1995): 243–71.

7. Willie's family history allows him, at a funeral, to detect Willa's absence through the store-bought cake that Nedeed brings—said by Nedeed to have been made by Willa (" 'It was no trouble, my wife baked it' " [Naylor, 1985, 146])—implying that Willa's "identity" is the product of her domestic subjugation: home-baked cake defines her presence. Having grown up observing his mother being battered, Willie can imagine uncannily Willa's victimization to the point that he frees her at the moment she obtains the will to free herself. (Readers tend to interpret Willie's sliding of the metal bolt on the basement door as an accident sufficiently contrived to strain narrative credibility. This is the trend in the essays on *Linden Hills* in *Gloria Naylor: Critical Perspectives Past and Present*.) But Naylor's carefully worded description—"Since his arms were full, he braced the crate against the two doors. Reaching under it, he felt the metal bolt slide toward the left . . ." (Naylor, 1985, 297)—suggests an intentional act, since Willie has not cause to brace the crate otherwise.

Afterword

At various points in *Melancholics in Love*, I have underscored the need for both psychoanalytic and social explanations of domestic woman abuse. Despite Foucault's conception of psychoanalysis as itself a regulating component of the power structure, his condemnation of its "normalizing functions" and its allegiance to "the family system"—that is, its attachment of sexuality to "the system of alliance," its assumption of "an adversary position with respect to the theory of degenerescence," and its functioning "as a differentiating factor in the general technology of sex"—(Foucault, 1978, 5, 112, 130), I have found it necessary to draw from both Kristeva and Foucault to expose the insidious collaboration of psychic and cultural forces operating in domestic abuse. I have tried to emphasize a psychic/social coconstruction not only of the battered woman but also, more broadly, of the melancholic woman.

In fact, the relation of this study's psychoanalytic to its social/cultural approach to melancholic and battered women is tricky, if not a bit confusing, as it is the case that Foucault himself also congratulates psychoanalysts for linking power and desire "in a more complex and primary way than through the interplay of a primitive, natural, and living energy welling up from below, and a higher order seeking to stand in its way," for realizing, instead, that "Where there is desire, the power relation is already present." (Foucault even attributes to psychoanalysts the insight "that sex is not 'repressed' " [Foucault, 1978, 81].) In other words, whether the (Kristevan) psychic and the (Foucauldian) social considerations of *Melancholics in Love* are antagonistic is a tough question, since Foucault himself both attacks and embraces psychoanalysis.

Continuing his embrace: Foucault writes that it is "to the political credit of psychoanalysis . . . that it regarded with suspicion . . . the irrevocably

129

proliferating aspects which might be contained in . . . power mechanisms aimed at controlling and administering the everyday life of sexuality." (Foucault, 1978) Yet he not only critiques psychoanalysis for conceiving the category of the sexual in terms of the law, death, blood, and sovereignty—whereas it ought to be conceived as a "deployment of sexuality" based on "techniques of power that are contemporary with it" (Foucault, 1978, 150)—but he also regards psychoanalysis itself as an active part of that deployment, as what subjected "us to that austere monarchy of sex, so that we became dedicated to the endless task of forcing its secret, of exacting the truest of confessions from a shadow" (Foucault, 1978, 159), or as what dupes us into thinking we are repressed so that naively we can hope for liberation. Psychoanalysis appears to be shrewdly capable of seeing through the very power mechanisms in which it participates.

Another contemporary critic who has attempted a conjoining of psychoanalysis and Foucault to analyze social ills is of course Judith Butler. In *The Psychic Life of Power,* Butler correctly points out that Foucault has failed to explain the psychic form that power takes. What he has missed, she proceeds to elaborate, is that it is passionate attachment to one's early caretakers that accounts for power's ability to constitute the subject. Primary dependency becomes the means of the subjection of subjects. The "formulation of primary passion in dependency renders the child vulnerable to subordination and exploitation" (Butler, 1997, 7). "Subjection exploits the desire for existence, where existence is always conferred from elsewhere; it marks a primary vulnerability to the Other in order to be" (Butler, 1997, 21). One's relation of subjection to one's original others, to Butler, results in a susceptibility to Foucault's Power.

These premises of Butler's latest work chime well with my own; nonetheless, I believe that her alignment of Foucauldian power with psychoanalytic law misses the point of distinction between the two, a distinction that Foucault himself insists upon, as he sees the very theory of repression he detests as originating from the psychoanalytic postulate that "all sexuality must be subject to the law" (Foucault, 1978, 128). Again we do find some ambivalence in Foucault: psychoanalysts wisely coordinate power and desire in a way outside the workings of repression; at the same time, repression, the hypothesis central to psychoanalysis, is grounded in the faulty psychoanalytic notion of sexuality's subjection to the law. Is sexuality *subjected* to power, or not? If so, how does that power subject sexuality in a way different from how psychoanalytic law does so?

Foucault writes that "a power whose model is essentially juridical, centered on nothing more than the statement of the law and the operation of taboos" (Foucault, 1978, 85) is blind to the "productive effectiveness," "strategic resourcefulness," and "positivity" of power (Foucault, 1978, 86). He in turn challenges the principle that "power always had to be exercised in the form of law" (Foucault, 1978, 88). For him, it is a question of the crucial difference between the repression of sex, as it is constituted by law, and the proliferation of sexuality, as it is produced by power. One (such as Butler) might claim that the psychoanalytic law's constitution of desire parallels Foucauldian power's production of sexuality, or subjectivity, but Foucault says the opposite: he puts such a law and modern power in opposition. By power, Foucault writes that he does not mean "a mode of subjugation which, in contrast to violence, has the form of the rule" (Foucault, 1978, 92). Still, my approach has been to make use of both forms of power—one the negative variety based on law, the other the positive, productive variety—in reflection of the coexistence of premodern and modern power operating in domestic woman abuse. *Must* one whose model of power is primarily juridical be blind to the productive effectiveness, strategic resourcefulness, and positivity of power? I worry, as I have explained, about the reverse, the blindness on the part of those who adopt the model of modern power to premodern power. And psychoanalysis seems to me the best method of keeping juridical power in sight.

To return to *The Psychic Life of Power:* Butler even invokes the topic of the sexual abuse of children, proposing in an argument similar to the one I make about domestically abused women that such abuse exploits the love necessary for the child's existence; advantage is taken of passionate attachment. I of course have tried to illustrate specifically that a daughter's passionate attachment to a maternal figure, excessively clung to rather than relinquished, produces a susceptibility to woman abuse. What Butler argues about all subject formation—that passionate attachment produces a vulnerability to power—in my view needs to be argued in relation to abused and battered women in particular. (I do part ways with Butler insofar as she relates melancholia to heterosexual subjectivity in general, as I explain in an essay, "The Subject of Homosexuality: Butler's Elision," in *Clinical Studies: International Journal of Psychoanalysis,* vol. 5, no. 1, Dec. 1999.)

To some readers my analysis of melancholia as well as of the relation of melancholia and domestic woman abuse may seem like "mother bashing." My proleptic response to this objection is that politics or in particular feminism only loses in the end if it keeps us on principle from perceiving what leaves a woman open to abuse: whether it be the death of a mother (and surely to point to effects of her death is not to blame her?) or her active neglect or mistreatment of her daughter. Psychoanalysis, of course, is not in the business of judgment, which certainly facilitates its effectiveness. In other words, the psychoanalysis of melancholics has no stake in *blaming* the mother; rather it seeks to locate, to treat, sources of misery.

On the other hand, as I have more than intimated, it *is* often the case that the social antecedents of the mother's role in the daughter's melancholia are quite visible. (In other words, if the mother is "at fault," it is not *all* the mother's "fault.") Several of the texts analyzed in *Melancholics in Love* make it clear that the "matricide" necessary for a daughter to commit in order to become a desiring subject is apt to be committed for her by a social system that deadens the mother in a variety of possible ways, precluding daughterly "matricide" by precluding the mother's own ability to desire. As Jacques Hassoun points out in *The Cruelty of Depression,* the melancholic's mother tends to be unable to transmit the experience of loss, tends to have found no instrument of desire. "The object of her lack runs up against insignificance. It is this that the melancholic will inherit" (Hassoun, 1997, 55). Although I have not generally found it necessary to illustrate the by now banal point of the privileged social role of man's desire in creating this insignificance, I allude to it every time I read the woman's melancholic text (publicizing domestic violence) as a site of what might be called re-significance.

I have periodically referred to the melancholic text's resignification of the domestically abused woman's plight, which term again aligns me with Butler. But I want to clarify that my stress has been on something more than resignification; it has been on transference, from which resignification results. In myriad contexts, we have observed transference of the maternal object onto authoritative, neglectful, and abusive partners. In turn, we have examined the expression of that transference in writing (or film) that transfers both object cathexes onto the text itself. What initially looks like a mere reflection, or continuation, of melancholia—because it has been translated into language propelled by desire, language that serves as a bridge to the symbolic order—after all functions to loosen the melancholic passionate attachments. Texts produced out of melancholia lead the way (via a "reverse discourse") to a writing cure, through incorporating and thereby confronting the lost/nonlost maternal figure as well as that maternal figure's reincarnation in an abusive partner in the production of a new, proper object, an object of the melancholic's own. The missing signifier that would have enabled detachment from the original passionate attachment emerges. The signifier of matricide that was unable to receive a first inscription is now inscribed. Hence a gap is formed between the newly produced symbolic and the maternal Thing peeled away from it—now represented within that symbolic order and as a result let go—so that a lack is constituted, and the melancholic may move from her stuck position to desiring subjectivity. Significance has been brought to the symptom, which has been written through a series of displacements.

Melancholics are apt to fall in love, then, with abusive partners; and abusive partners, with whom women fall in love, transform women into melancholics (or reinforce the melancholia, which is why such lovers are attractive in the first place, if there is a preexisting depression). I have written in part about the social construction of battered women and have pointed out the consequent *social* production of melancholics, of nondesiring inertness, the undoing of subjectivity. But whatever the cause—psychic, social, or some combination of the two, which is usually the case—of the battered woman's immersion in melancholic jouissance, she must withdraw from it. As a result, the process of mourning through representation (as just described), producing or renewing desire, is essential. The battered woman must regain subjectivity through linguistic expression, and as she does, through a cultural articulation of reenactments of her pain, the fantasy that positioned her there—I am mainly referring to hers, but perhaps also his, culture's, or again some combination—is traversed. A political act of reconfiguring the symbolic order is simultaneously committed, an act meant to alter, to improve the arena that reduces the maternal figure's desiring ability and facilitates the batterer's capacity to enact violence, thus condemning the abused woman to asymbolia.

Although my psychoanalytic lens is thicker than any other I peer through, my analysis is in accord with Wendy Brown's in her essay "Wounded Attachments." The desire that emerges must not be a "wounded desire"—an oxymoron if not a contradiction itself in my view. Stilling the pain of the wound must not reinfect the wound, although such a paradoxical soothing would be the melancholic's exquisite temptation. Brown explores the avenue of "Nietzsche's counsel on the virtues of 'forgetting,' " for, as she writes, "if identity structured in part by *ressentiment* resubjugates itself through its investment in its own pain, through its refusal to make itself in the present, memory is the house of this activity and this refusal" (Brown, 1995, 74).

I invoke Brown here, at the end of my study, because she warns against something I hope *Melancholics in Love* is not perceived as doing: "abetting the steady slide of political into therapeutic discourse." Still, we must note that Brown herself qualifies that warning with an injunction to "acknowledge the elements of suffering and healing we might be negotiating" (Brown, 1995, 75). Brown and I are in sync, then, in assuming that remembering must precede forgetting (as we are in harmony with Anita Brookner who writes that to "remember is to face the [beloved] enemy"), in order to light the lamp of desire, "to rehabilitate," as Brown puts it, "the memory of desire . . . , the moment of desire . . . prior to its wounding" (Brown, 1995, 75). My aim has by no means been to cast blame on mothers (through Kristeva, in fact, I have theorized the value of forgiveness) but to locate the pathway back to the site of the shutting down of desire, since it is only by such a return that the fundamental fantasy extinguishing desire might be traversed, so that analysis itself may be lost.

Bibliography

Acker, Kathy. 1978. *Blood and Guts in High School*. New York: Grove Press.

Armstrong, Nancy. 1987. *Desire and Domestic Fiction: A Political History of the Novel*. New York: Oxford University Press.

Armstrong, Nancy and Leonard Tennenhouse. 1989. "Introduction: Representing violence, or 'how the west was won.' " In *The Violence of Representation: Literature and the History of Violence*. Ed. Nancy Armstrong and Leonard Tennenhouse. London: Routledge.

Atwood, Margaret. 1976. *Lady Oracle*. New York: Ballantine Books.

Austen, Jane. 1972 [1816]. *Emma*. New York: W.W. Norton.

———. 1995 [1817]. *Persuasion*. New York: W.W. Norton.

Barthes, Roland. 1982. "The Reality Effect." In *French Literary Theory Today*. Ed. Tzvetan Todorov. New York: Cambridge University Press.

Benjamin, Jessica. 1988. *The Bonds of Love: Psychoanalysis, Feminism, and the Problem of Domination*. New York: Pantheon Books.

Bhabha Homi. 1994. *The Location of Culture*. New York: Routledge.

Bracher, Mark. 1996. "Editor's Introduction." *Journal for the Psychoanalysis of Culture and Society* 1, no. 1 (Spring): 1–13.

Breines, Wini and Linda Gordon. 1983. "The New Scholarship on Family Violence." *Signs: Journal of Women in Culture and Society* 8, no. 3: 490–531.

Brookner, Anita. 1983. *Look at Me*. New York: E. P. Dutton.

Brooks, Peter. 1985. "Freud's Masterplot: A Model for Narrative." In *Reading for the Plot: Design and Intention in Narrative*. New York: Random House.

Brown, Wendy. 1995. *States of Injury: Power and Freedom in Late Modernity*. Princeton: Princeton University Press.

Butler, Judith. 1990. *Gender Trouble: Feminism and the Subversion of Identity*. New York: Routledge.

———. 1993. *Bodies That Matter: On the Discursive Limits of "Sex."* New York: Routledge.

———. 1997. *The Psychic Life of Power: Theories in Subjection*. Stanford: Stanford University Press.

Cisneros, Sandra. 1992. "Woman Hollering Creek." In *Woman Hollering Creek and Other Stories*. New York: Random House.

Coming to Power: Writings and Graphics on Lesbian S/M. 1987. Ed. members of Samois. Boston: Alyson Publications, Inc.

Copjec, Joan. 1994. *Read My Desire: Lacan against the Historicists*. Boston: MIT Press.

Defending Our Lives. 1993. Cambridge: Cambridge Documentary Films, Inc.

de Lauretis, Teresa. 1984. *Alice Doesn't: Feminism, Semiotics, Cinema*. Bloomington: Indiana University Press.

———. 1987. *Technologies of Gender: Essays on Theory, Film, and Fiction*. Bloomington: Indiana University Press.

———. 1989. "The violence of rhetoric." In *The Violence of Representation: Literature and the History of Violence*. Ed. Nancy Armstrong and Leonard Tennenhouse. London: Routledge.

Deleuze, Gilles. 1971. *Masochism: An Interpretation of Coldness and Cruelty*. Trans. Jean McNeil. New York: George Brazillier.

Deleuze, Gilles and Felix Guattari. 1977. *Anti-Oedipus: Capitalism and Schizophrenia*. Trans. Robert Hurley, Mark Seem, and Helena R. Lane. New York: Viking Press.

Derrida, Jacques. 1994. *Specters of Marx: The State of the Debt, the Work of Mourning, & the New International*. Trans. Peggy Kamuf. New York: Routledge.

de St. Jorre, J. 1994. "The Unmasking of O." *New Yorker* (August 1st): 42–49.

Dobash, Emerson R. and Russell Dobash. 1979. *Violence against Wives: A Case against Patriarchy*. New York: The Free Press/Macmillan.

Drabble, Margaret. 1967. *Jerusalem the Golden*. New York: Penguin.

———. 1969. *The Waterfall*. New York: Penguin.

———. 1972. *The Needle's Eye*. New York: Ballantine.

Ferrato, Donna. 1991. *Living with the Enemy*. New York: Aperture.

Fink, Bruce. 1995. *The Lacanian Subject: Between Language and Jouissance*. Princeton: Princeton University Press.

Foucault, Michel. 1978. *The History of Sexuality: An Introduction*, Vol. I. Trans. Robert Hurley. New York: Random House.

———. 1979. *Discipline and Punish: The Birth of the Prison*. Trans. Alan Sheridan. New York: Random House.

———. 1980. *Power/knowledge: Selected interviews and other writings*. Ed. Colin Gordon. New York: Pantheon.

Freud, Sigmund. 1917. "Mourning and Melancholia." In *The Standard Edition of the Complete Psychological Works of Sigmund Freud*, vol. 14. Ed. and trans. James Strachey. London: Hogarth.

———. 1923. "The Ego and the Id." In *The Standard Edition of the Complete Psychological Works of Sigmund Freud*, vol. 19. Ed. and trans. James Strachey. London: Hogarth.

Fuss, Diana. 1995. *Identification Papers*. New York: Routledge.

Gillespie, Cynthia K. 1989. *Justifiable Homicide: Battered Women, Self-Defense, and the Law*. Columbus: Ohio State University Press.

Gloria Naylor: Critical Perspectives Past and Present. 1993. Ed. Henry Louis Gates and K. A. Appiah. New York: Amistad.

Green, André. 1986 [1980]. "The Dead Mother." In *On Private Madness*. Trans. Katherine Aubertin. Madison, Connecticut: International Universities Press.

Gurewich, Judith Feher. 1996. "Who's Afraid of Jacques Lacan?" In *The Subject and the Self: Lacan and American Psychoanalysis*. Ed. Judith Feher Gurewich and Michel Tort. Northvale, New Jersey: Jason Aronson, Inc.

Halperin, David M. 1995. *Saint Foucault: Towards a Gay Hagiography*. Oxford: Oxford University Press.

Hartsock, Nancy. 1990. "Foucault on Power: A Theory for Women?" In *Feminism/ Postmodernism*. Ed. Linda J. Nicholson. New York: Routledge.

Hassoun, Jacques. 1997. *The Cruelty of Depression: On Melancholy*. Trans. David Jacobson. Reading, Massachusetts: Addison-Wesley.

Henderson, Mae Gwendolyn. 1990. "Speaking in Tongues: Dialogics, Dialectics, and the Black Woman Writer's Literary Tradition." In *Reading Black, Reading Feminist: A Critical Anthology*. Ed. Henry Louis Gates, Jr. New York: Meridian Press/Penguin.

hooks, bell. 1984. *Feminist Theory: from margin to center*. Boston: South End Press.

———. 1989. *Talking Back: thinking feminist, thinking black*. Boston: South End Press.

———. 1992. *Black Looks: race and representation*. Boston: South End Press.

Hurston, Zora Neale. 1985. "Sweat." In *Spunk: The Selected Stories of Zora Neale Hurston*. Berkeley: Turtle Island Foundation.

Irigaray, Luce. 1981. "And the One Doesn't Stir without the Other." Trans. Helene Vivienne Wenzel. *Signs: Journal of Women in Society and Culture* 7, no. 1: 66–67.

Kappeler, Susanne. 1986. *The Pornography of Representation*. Minneapolis: University of Minnesota Press.

Khan, M. Masud R. 1979. *Alienation in Perversions*. London: Hogarth.

Kristeva, Julia. 1982. *Powers of Horror: An Essay on Abjection*. Trans. Leon S. Roudiez. New York: Columbia University Press.

———. 1986. "Stabat Mater." In *The Kristeva Reader*. Ed. Toril Moi. Trans. Leon S. Roudiez. New York: Columbia University Press.

———. 1989. *Black Sun: Depression and Melancholia*. Trans. Leon S. Roudiez. New York: Columbia University Press.

———. 1995. *New Maladies of the Soul*. Trans. Ross Guberman. New York: Columbia University Press.

Lacan, Jacques. 1977 [1966]. *Écrits: A Selection*. Trans. Alan Sheridan. New York: W.W. Norton.

———. 1981 [1973]. *The Four Fundamental Concepts of Psycho-Analysis*. Ed. Jacques-Alain Miller. Trans. Alan Sheridan. New York: W.W. Norton.

Miller, D. A. 1981. *Narrative and Its Discontents*. Princeton: Princeton University Press.

———. 1990. "The Late Jane Austen." *Raritan* 10, no. 1 (Summer): 55–79.

Morrison, Toni. 1994 [1970]. *The Bluest Eye*. New York: Penguin.

Naylor, Gloria. 1985. *Linden Hills*. New York: Penguin.

Oliver, Kelly. 1998. *Subjectivity without Subjects: From Abject Fathers to Desiring Mothers*. Lanham, Maryland: Rowman & Littlefield.

Réage, Pauline. 1965. *Story of O*. Trans. Sabine d'Estrée. New York: Grove Press.

————. 1971. *Return to the Château: Story of O, Part II.* Trans. Sabine d'Estrée. New York: Grove Press.

Rose, Jacqueline. 1986. *Sexuality in the Field of Vision.* London: Verso.

Scarry, Elaine. 1985. *The Body in Pain: The Making and Unmaking of the World.* New York: Oxford University Press.

Schiesari, Juliana. 1992. *The Gendering of Melancholia: Feminism, Psychoanalysis, and the Symbolics of Loss in Renaissance Literature.* Ithaca: Cornell University Press.

Sedgwick, Eve Kosofsky. 1991. "Jane Austen and the Masturbating Girl." *Critical Inquiry* 17, no. 4 (Summer): 818–37.

Sharpe, Jenny. 1993. *Allegories of Empire: The Figure of Woman in the Colonial Text.* Minneapolis: University of Minnesota Press.

Silverman, Kaja. 1985. "*Histoire d'O*: The Construction of a Female Subject." In *Pleasure and Danger: Exploring Female Sexuality.* Ed. Carole S. Vance. New York: Routledge & Kegan Paul.

————. 1988. "Masochism and Male Subjectivity." *Camera Obscura* 17: 31–67.

Sokolsky, Anita. 1994. "The Melancholy Persuasion." In *Psychoanalystic Literary Criticism.* Ed. Maud Ellmann. London: Longman.

Sprengnether, Madelon. 1990. *The Spectral Mother: Freud, Feminism, and Psychoanalysis.* Ithaca: Cornell University Press.

Tanner, Laura. 1994. *Intimate Violence: Reading Rape and Torture in Twentieth-Century Fiction.* Indianapolis: Indiana University Press.

Torok, Maria and Nicolas Abraham. 1994. *The Shell and the Kernel: Renewals of Psychoanalysis.* Trans. Nicholas T. Rand. Chicago: University of Chicago Press.

Turner, Tina and Kurt Loder. 1986. *I, Tina.* New York: Avon Books.

Walker, Alice. 1970. *The Third Life of Grange Copeland.* New York: Quality Paperback Book Club.

Walker, Lenore E. 1979. *The Battered Woman.* New York: Harper & Row.

Willis, Susan. 1987. *Specifying: Black Women Writing the American Experience.* Madison: University of Wisconsin Press.

Wyatt, Jean. 1995. "On Not Being La Malinche: Border Negotiations of Gender in Sandra Cisneros's 'Never Marry a Mexican' and 'Woman Hollering Creek.' " *Tulsa Studies in Women's Literature* 14, no. 2 (Fall): 243–71.

Zizek, Slavoj. 1989. *The Sublime Object of Ideology.* London: Verso.

————. 1991. *Looking Awry: An Introduction to Jacques Lacan through Popular Culture.* Cambridge: MIT Press.

Index

139

About the Author

Frances L. Restuccia is the author of *James Joyce and the Law of the Father* (Yale, 1989). She has also written numerous articles in journals such as *Raritan, American Imago, Gender and Psychoanalysis, Genders, JPCS,* and *Clinical Studies.* Her next study will focus on Lacanian Love, in its many guises and as it is manifested in both literature and film. In addition to being the editor of the Contemporary Theory Series at The Other Press, she teaches contemporary literary and cultural theory in the English department at Boston College.